Steck-Vaughn

THE COMPLETE EDITION

WORLD HISTORY
and YOU

Vivian Bernstein

Consultant
Karen Tindel Wiggins
Director of Social Studies
Richardson Independent School District
Richardson, Texas

STECK-VAUGHN®
C O M P A N Y
ELEMENTARY • SECONDARY • ADULT • LIBRARY

ABOUT THE AUTHOR

Vivian Bernstein is the author of *America's Story, America's History: Land of Liberty*, *World Geography and You*, *American Government*, and *Decisions for Health*. She received her Master of Arts degree from New York University. Bernstein is active with professional organizations in social studies, education, and reading. She gives presentations to school faculties and professional groups about content area reading. Bernstein was a teacher in the New York City Public School System for a number of years.

ACKNOWLEDGMENTS

Executive Editor: Diane Sharpe
Senior Editor: Martin S. Saiewitz
Project Editor: Meredith Edgley

Design Manager: Rusty Kaim
Photo Editor: Margie Foster
Electronic Production: JoAnn Estrada, Jill Klinger

CREDITS

Cover Photography: (Sphinx) © Index Stock, (ship) © Marco Corsetti/FPG, (Berlin Wall) © D. Aubert/Sygma, (map) © Superstock

p.3 © Giraudon/Art Resource; p.4 © Tom Bean/Tony Stone Images; p.6 (top) © J. Kostich/Leo de Wys, (bottom) © John Reader/Photo Researchers; p.10 © David Sutherland/Tony Stone Images; p.11 (top) © Fridmar Damm/Leo de Wys, (bottom) The Granger Collection; p.12 (top) The Bettmann Archive, (left) The Granger Collection; p.13 (top) North Wind Picture Archive, (left) The Granger Collection; p.14 (top) © Eric J. Lessing/Art Resource, (bottom) The Granger Collection; p.17 © Ronald Sheridan Photo Library/Ancient Art & Architecture Collection; p.18 The Granger Collection; p.19 (top, middle) The Granger Collection, (bottom) © Giraudon/Art Resource; p.22 North Wind Picture Archive; p.23 © Lance Nelson/The Stock Market; p.24 (top) North Wind Picture Archive, (left) The Granger Collection; p.25 (top) © Mark Harris/Tony Stone Images, (bottom) The Granger Collection; p.29 © Dilip Mehta/Contact Press Images/The Stock Market; p.30 © Scala/Art Resource; p.31 (top) © Superstock, (bottom) © Victoria & Albert Museum, London/Art Resource; p.32 (top) © Ric Ergenbright Photography, (left) The Bettmann Archive; p.35 © Superstock; p.36 © China Stock/Yang Xiuyun; p.37 (top) © Giraudon/Art Resource, (middle) © Ronald Sheridan Photo Library/Ancient Art & Architecture Collection, (bottom) The Granger Collection; p.38 (top) © Giraudon/Art Resource, (middle) © Superstock, (bottom) The Granger Collection; p.39 The Granger Collection; p.43 © Superstock; p.44 © J. Messerschmidt/Leo de Wys; p.45 The Granger Collection; p.46 (top) The Granger Collection, (left) © Ronald Sheridan Photo Library/Ancient Art & Architecture Collection; p.47 (top, bottom) North Wind Picture Archive, (middle) Archive Photos; p.48 (top) North Wind Picture Archive, (middle) The Granger Collection, (bottom) © Michele Burgess/The Stock Market; p.49 (both) The Granger Collection; p.52 © Superstock; p.53 (top) © Eric J. Lessing/Art Resource, (left) © Scala/Art Resource; p.54 (top) North Wind Picture Archive, (middle) © Scala/Art Resource, (bottom) The Granger Collection; p.55 The Granger Collection; p.56 (top) © Larry Mulvehill/Photo Researchers, (middle) © Scala/Art Resource, (bottom) The Granger Collection; p.60 The Granger Collection; p.61 (top) The Bettmann Archive, (middle) © Oudna/Ronald Sheridan Photo Library/Ancient Art & Architecture Collection, (bottom) The Granger Collection; p.63 (top) The Granger Collection, (bottom) © Scala/Art Resource; p.64 The Granger Collection; p.67 © Scala Art Resource; p.68 (top, bottom) The Granger Collection, (middle) © Eric J. Lessing/Art Resource; p.71 The Granger Collection; p.72 (top) The Bettmann Archive, (bottom) The Granger Collection; p.73 © Steve Vidler/Leo de Wys; p.76 © Fridmar Damm/Leo de Wys; p.77 The Granger Collection; p.78 © J. Cassio/Leo de Wys, (middle, bottom) The Granger Collection; p.79 (top) © Mehmet Biber/Photo Researchers, (left) The Granger Collection; p.82 Stock Montage; p.83 (top, bottom) The Granger Collection, (middle) North Wind Picture Archive; p.84 © China Stock; p.85 (top) North Wind Picture Archive, (middle) © David Lawrence/The Stock Market, (bottom) The Granger Collection; p.86 (top) © Fridmar Damm/Leo de Wys, (bottom) The Bettmann Archive; p.91 © Scala/Art Resource; p.92 © The Pierpont Morgan Library/Art Resource; p.93 (middle) North Wind Picture Archive, (bottom) © Giraudon/Art Resource; p.94 (both) The Granger Collection; p.95 (top) The Bettmann Archive, (middle) The Granger Collection, (bottom) © Superstock; p.98 The Bettmann Archive; p.99 (top) The Bettmann Archive, (middle) North Wind Picture Archive, (bottom) The Granger Collection; p.100 (both) North Wind Picture Archive; p.101 (top) © Superstock, (bottom) North Wind Picture Archive; p.104 © Art Resource; p.105 (top) © Superstock, (middle, bottom) The Granger Collection; p.106 (top) The Granger Collection, (middle, bottom) © Scala/Art Resource; p.107 (top) The Granger Collection, (middle) © Superstock, (bottom) Stock Montage; p.108 © Superstock; p.111 The Granger Collection; p.112 (top) The Granger Collection, (bottom) © Scala/Art Resource; p.113 (left, right) The Granger Collection, (middle) The Bettmann Archive; p.114 (top, middle) North Wind Picture Archive, (bottom) The Granger Collection; p.117 © Superstock; p.118 The Granger Collection; p.119 (top, middle) The Granger Collection, (bottom) © Eric J. Lessing/Art Resource; p.120 (top, middle) The Granger Collection, (bottom) North Wind Picture Archive; p.124 © Superstock; p.125 © Brian Seed/Tony Stone Images; p.126 © Lee Boltin Picture Library; p.127 (top) © George Holton/Photo Researchers, (bottom) North Wind Picture Archive; p.128 (top) © Cynthia Ellis, (middle) The Granger Collection, (bottom) © Harvey Lloyd/Gamma Liaison; p.129 The Granger Collection; p.132 Stock Montage; p.133 (both) The Granger Collection; p.134 (top) Archive Photos, (bottom) The Granger Collection; p.135 (top) North Wind Picture Archive, (left) The Bettmann Archive; pp.139, 140, 141 The Granger Collection; p.142 (top) The Granger Collection, (bottom) National Portrait Gallery/Smithsonian Institution; p.143 (top) The Granger Collection; p.144 (top, bottom) The Granger Collection; pp.146, 148 The Granger Collection; p.149 (top) North Wind Picture Archive, (bottom) The Granger Collection; p.150 (top) The Granger Collection, (bottom) The Bettmann Archive; p.151 (top) North Wind Picture Archive, (left) The Granger Collection; p.152 (top) The Bettmann Archive, (bottom) © Superstock; p.155 North Wind Picture Archive; p.157 (top) The Bettmann Archive, (left) Archive Photos; p.158 Hulton Deutsch; p.159 (top) The Bettmann Archive, (left) North Wind Picture Archive; pp.162, 163, 164 The Granger Collection; p.167 © Schalkwijk/Art Resource; p.168 (top) The Bettmann Archive, (middle, bottom) The Granger Collection; p.169 (top, bottom) The Bettmann Archive, (middle) The Granger Collection; p.170 The Granger Collection; p.171 The Bettmann Archive. Continued on page 374.

ISBN 0-8172-6328-4

Printed in the United States of America.   8 9 VH 02 01

Contents

1950

1945 World War II

1945–1991 Cold War

People in History

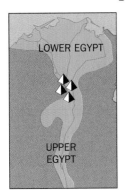

List of Maps

List of Skill Builders

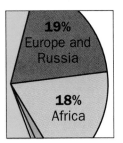

Charts, Graphs, and Diagrams

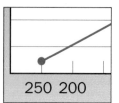

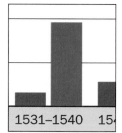

250 200

1531–1540 154

To the Reader

You are about to read an exciting story about the world. As you read *World History and You*, you will learn how people started the first cities and why many early civilizations disappeared. You will learn how wars and inventions have changed the world forever.

Your study of world history will begin by traveling back in time for thousands of years. The earliest people spent most of their time just finding enough food to eat. Later, after people learned how to grow food, they began to live in villages and cities. As one civilization conquered another, empires were formed. Great religions began. Important ideas developed and spread. People formed strong nations. Today nations trade goods, share technology, and solve problems together.

World History and You will help you become a better social studies student. Start by learning the vocabulary words for each chapter. Review vocabulary words from earlier chapters. Study each map and think about the ways geography can change the history of a place. Then read the text of each chapter carefully. By reading the chapter a second time, you will improve your understanding of history. Complete the chapter activities carefully, and your skills in writing and social studies will improve.

As you study world history, you will learn about men and women who changed the world they lived in. You will discover how past events have created the world we have today. You will learn about mistakes people made in the past. By learning from past mistakes, you can work for a better tomorrow. As you begin your journey into world history, remember that you, too, are part of the story.

Vivian Bernstein

Unit 1   The Ancient World

It is easy for us to know what happened ten years ago. People wrote in books, newspapers, and magazines about what was happening then. But 10,000 years ago, people did not yet know how to write. It is very difficult for us to know about people's lives 10,000 years ago.

We can learn about people of long ago from bones, tools, and other items we have found in the earth. Bones help us know what the first people looked like. We can tell how old the bones are and when these people lived. Tools from long ago tell us how people hunted or farmed. About 5,000 years ago, some people began to write their language on pieces of wet clay. We can learn more about people who wrote on clay than about earlier people who did not write.

Bones, stones, and clay have helped us learn about the problems people had long ago. One big problem was finding enough food and water. Many of the bones of people of long ago have been found near rivers. We believe that people lived near rivers because there was more food there than in places without water.

What was life like for people of long ago? Who built the first villages? What other items did people leave behind that help us learn

about their history? As you read Unit 1, think about the ways the people of long ago solved their problems. Think about why rivers were important to these early people. Read about the ideas the ancient world gave to us.

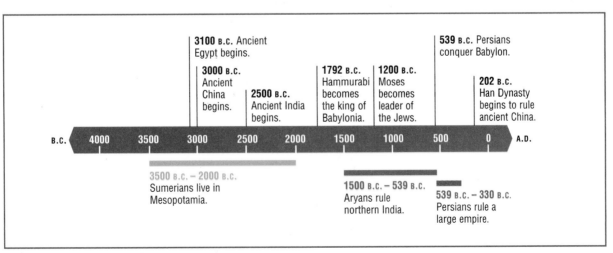

3100 B.C. Ancient Egypt begins.

3000 B.C. Ancient China begins.

2500 B.C. Ancient India begins.

1792 B.C. Hammurabi becomes the king of Babylonia.

1200 B.C. Moses becomes leader of the Jews.

539 B.C. Persians conquer Babylon.

202 B.C. Han Dynasty begins to rule ancient China.

B.C. 4000 3500 3000 2500 2000 1500 1000 500 0 A.D.

3500 B.C. – 2000 B.C. Sumerians live in Mesopotamia.

1500 B.C. – 539 B.C. Aryans rule northern India.

539 B.C. – 330 B.C. Persians rule a large empire.

CHAPTER 1

The First People

The first people did not live the way we live today. They did not grow food or live in houses. They did not read or write. In this chapter we will learn how the first people lived.

Archaeologists help us learn about people of long ago. Archaeologists are men and women who dig into the **earth**. They find and study the bones of people who lived thousands of years ago. The bones tell how people of long ago looked and how they lived. Archaeologists have also found animal bones from long ago. Some of these bones were used as **tools** for hunting.

Archaeologists have found tools used by people who lived during the **Stone Age**. It is called the Stone Age because most of the tools were made of stone. Stone tools lasted longer and were stronger than tools made of bone or wood. The Stone Age began more than 2,000,000 years ago. It ended about

THINK ABOUT AS YOU READ

1. **How did the first people live?**
2. **What started the agricultural revolution?**
3. **Why did Stone Age farmers live near rivers?**

NEW WORDS

♦ **archaeologists**
♦ **earth**
♦ **tools**
♦ **Stone Age**
♦ **agricultural revolution**
♦ **tame**

PEOPLE & PLACES

♦ **Stone Age people**

An archaeologist works slowly and carefully to remove old bones and tools from the earth.

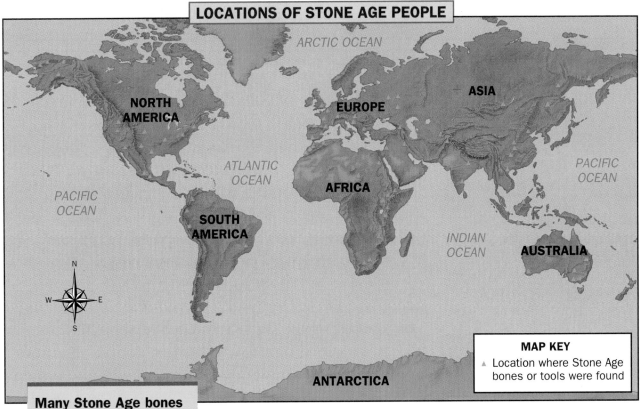

LOCATIONS OF STONE AGE PEOPLE

MAP KEY

▲ Location where Stone Age bones or tools were found

Many Stone Age bones and tools have been found near rivers. Where are some of these rivers located?

5,000 years ago. The people who lived then are called Stone Age people.

For thousands of years, Stone Age people spent most of their time looking for food. They did not know how to grow food. They found wild berries and nuts to eat. Most people were hunters. They killed animals for food. They made clothes from animal skins. Sometimes they made tools from animal bones.

People of the Stone Age learned to use fire. Fire gave heat and light. Stone Age people used fire to help them cook food and keep warm. Fire also kept people safe. Dangerous animals stayed away from fire at night.

For thousands of years, Stone Age people moved from place to place looking for food. They stayed in one place as long as there was food. When they could no longer find food, they moved to another place. They usually stayed near rivers. There were more animals and plants near rivers. Most Stone Age people moved many times. They did not build houses.

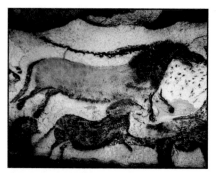
Cave painting from the Stone Age

Stone Age tool

Stone Age people sometimes lived in caves. They built fires in their caves to keep warm. Some people knew how to paint pictures. They made pictures on the walls of their caves. We can learn more about Stone Age people from the pictures they painted.

After thousands and thousands of years, Stone Age people learned how to grow their own food. This was the start of the **agricultural revolution**. The agricultural revolution was a change in the way people got their food. People learned to plant seeds to grow fruits and vegetables for food.

People became farmers. As time passed, they grew more and more food. Sometimes they grew enough food to feed wild animals. People began to **tame** dogs, goats, sheep, and cows. Some of these animals helped families with their work. Sometimes people killed the animals for food.

The agricultural revolution changed the lives of Stone Age people. Stone Age farmers did not have to move from place to place to hunt animals. They could live in one place. They lived on small farms. Some people built small mud houses on their farms. Sometimes people built their homes close together in small villages. Then they could work together and learn from each other.

Stone Age farmers needed water to grow food. Many times there was not enough rain. Farmers began to build their farms near rivers. They used river water to grow food.

As time passed, Stone Age people learned better ways to grow food. They made better stone tools. Stone Age people did not know how to make metal tools. They did not know how to read or write. After many years people in some parts of the world began to do these things. You will read about some of these people in the next chapters.

Using Vocabulary

Finish Up   Number your paper from 1 to 6. Choose the word or words in dark print to best complete each sentence. Write on your paper the word or words you choose.

Stone Age	**tamed**	**archaeologists**
earth	**tools**	**agricultural**

1. Men and women who study old bones to learn about people of long ago are called _____ .

2. Soil and rocks are part of the _____ .

3. Stone Age _____ were items that were used for hunting or farming.

4. The _____ was a period of millions of years in which most people used stones or animal bones to make tools.

5. The _____ revolution was a change in the way Stone Age people got their food.

6. Stone Age farmers _____ wild animals by giving them food to make them less afraid.

Read and Remember

Write the Answer   Number your paper from 1 to 6. Write one or more sentences on your paper to answer each question.

1. When was the Stone Age?

2. Why is the Stone Age called by this name?

3. How did Stone Age people use the animals they killed?

4. How did fire help Stone Age people?

5. Why did Stone Age people tame wild animals?

6. Why did Stone Age people start their farms near rivers?

Skill Builder

Understanding Continents and Oceans   We live on the planet **Earth**. Earth has large bodies of land called **continents**. There are seven continents. Earth also has four large bodies of water called **oceans**. The four oceans separate some of the

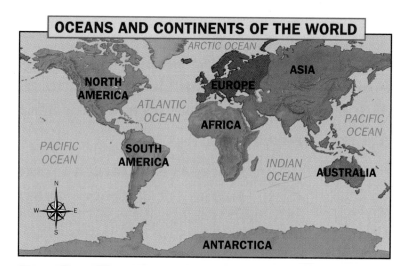

continents. Look at the map. Number your paper from 1 to 7. Then write on your paper the answer to each question below.

1. What are the seven continents?

2. What are the four oceans?

3. Which two continents do not touch any other continents?

4. Which ocean separates Africa and Australia?

5. Which five continents have coasts along the Atlantic Ocean?

6. Which two continents are closest to Europe?

7. Which ocean touches both North America and Asia?

Using Map Directions   The four main directions are **north, south, east,** and **west**. On maps these directions are shown by a **compass rose**. The compass rose shortens the directions to **N, S, E,** and **W**. Study the map above. Find the compass rose. Number your paper from 1 to 4. Then finish each sentence with **north, south, east,** or **west**. Write the correct answers on your paper.

1. South America is _____ of Antarctica.

2. Africa is _____ of Europe.

3. The Pacific Ocean is _____ of Asia.

4. North America is _____ of the Atlantic Ocean.

Journal Writing

Write a short paragraph that tells how the agricultural revolution changed the lives of Stone Age people.

Riddle Puzzle

Number your paper from 1 to 8. Choose a word in dark print to best complete each sentence. Write the correct answers on your paper.

caves	**planted**	**rivers**	**eat**
tamed	**stronger**	**used**	**improved**

1. Stone Age farmers _____ seeds to grow fruits and vegetables.

2. The lives of Stone Age people _____ after the agricultural revolution.

3. Stone Age people sometimes lived in _____ .

4. Stone Age people _____ wild animals.

5. Stone Age people _____ fire to help them keep warm.

6. During the Stone Age, people built their farms near _____ .

7. Before they built farms, Stone Age people found wild berries and nuts to _____ .

8. Stone Age tools were _____ than tools made of bone or wood.

Now look at your answers. Circle the first letter of each answer you wrote on your paper. The first answer should look like this:

    ⓟlanted

The letters you circle should spell a word. The word answers the riddle below.

RIDDLE: What did Stone Age people have on their cave walls that you might find on your own walls today?

Write on your paper the answer to the riddle.

CHAPTER 2

People of Ancient Egypt

THINK ABOUT AS YOU READ

1. **Why was ancient Egypt called "the gift of the Nile"?**
2. **How was ancient Egypt ruled?**
3. **Why did ancient Egyptians build pyramids and tombs?**

NEW WORDS

- civilization
- fertile soil
- irrigate
- pharaohs
- god
- pyramids
- tombs
- slaves
- weapons
- temple

PEOPLE & PLACES

- ancient Egypt
- Nile River
- Egyptian
- Hatshepsut
- King Tutankhamen

Imagine how difficult it is to grow food in a land that is always hot and dry. The people of ancient Egypt faced that problem long ago. Egypt is a hot, dry land in Africa. It gets little rain. The Nile River flows through Egypt. More than 7,000 years ago, people in Africa learned to use water from the Nile River to grow food. As more people began to farm together along the Nile, they developed the **civilization** of ancient Egypt.

Egypt has been called "the gift of the Nile." This is because the Nile River prevented Egypt from being a huge desert. Without the Nile, people in ancient Egypt would not have been able to grow crops. The Nile made it possible for the civilization of ancient Egypt to last thousands of years.

The Nile is the longest river in the world. It is more than 4,150 miles long. Every summer in ancient Egypt, the Nile flooded the land around it.

Today, many people visit Egypt to see the great pyramids.

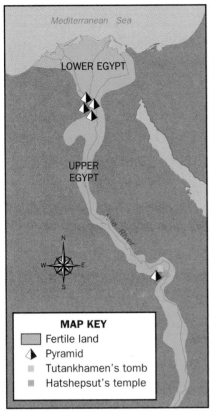
Ancient Egypt

Without the Nile River, all of the land in Egypt would be desert.

Egyptian pharaoh

The floods left **fertile soil** on the land near the river. This soil was good for growing food. The farmers planted after the floods. If there was a lot of water in a flood, they could plant many crops. If there was not very much water, they planted fewer crops.

About 5,000 years ago, farmers found a way to use the Nile River to **irrigate** their land. They brought water from the river to use on dry land in order to grow plants and food. The farms were better and larger when people irrigated. Farmers did not have to wait until after the floods to plant their seeds. The farmers learned to work together to bring water from the Nile to their farms. People made rules as they worked together. They began to live in villages.

Soon there were many villages. Around 3100 B.C., one king began to rule all the villages in Egypt. Later, Egyptian rulers were called **pharaohs**. The pharaohs made laws for all the people of Egypt. People believed a pharaoh was both a **god** and a ruler. The pharaohs were very powerful. All farmers had to give some of their food to the pharaohs.

Most of the pharaohs were men, but one of the greatest pharaohs was a woman. Her name was Hatshepsut. Hatshepsut helped Egypt become a very rich country. She sent ships to trade items with other

We have learned much about ancient Egypt from items found in Tutankhamen's tomb. This item shows the pharaoh and his wife.

King Tutankhamen

countries. Many large buildings were built when Hatshepsut was pharaoh.

Since Egypt has little rain, there are few trees. The ancient Egyptians did not have much wood for building. Instead, they often used mud bricks. The Egyptians also cut stone blocks to make buildings. Strong metal tools helped the Egyptians cut stone.

The people of ancient Egypt built large stone buildings called **pyramids** in the desert. These pyramids were built for pharaohs. Inside the pyramids were **tombs** for the dead. One of the most famous tombs was built for the young King Tutankhamen. His tomb was not in a pyramid. It was cut deep into rock.

Why did the Egyptians work so hard at building these tombs and pyramids? They built them because they believed that people lived again after they died. They believed that the dead needed a good place to spend their next lives. Egyptians put the bodies of the dead inside tombs. They left food, water, and clothing in the tomb for the dead person to use in the next life. They painted pictures of people on the walls of the tombs. The Egyptians believed that the people in these pictures would be friends with the dead person in the next life.

This drawing is about the death of an Egyptian queen. The many symbols in the drawing are Egyptian writing.

Cup from King Tutankhamen's tomb

Archaeologists have learned about life in ancient Egypt from the paintings, foods, and other items found inside tombs and pyramids. Today there are 35 major pyramids still standing in Egypt. The oldest pyramids are almost 5,000 years old.

Many people in Egypt were **slaves**. Slaves were not free men and women. They were not paid for their work. Slaves were forced to build pyramids for the pharaohs. Thousands of slaves built the pyramids. They built many other buildings, too.

The Egyptians were some of the first people to write their words. At first they used tiny pictures to show the words. They needed many small pictures. Then they wrote small signs to show different sounds and ideas. Egyptian writing had more than 800 signs. Archaeologists have found papers and stones with Egyptian writing. We have learned much about the ancient Egyptians by reading their writing.

Ancient Egypt was a great country for more than 2,800 years. As time passed, the pharaohs had less power. Other people gained control of the land, and the pharaohs lost their power. Egypt became weak. Then other countries ruled Egypt.

In the next chapter, you will read about other great people of long ago.

Hatshepsut

Hatshepsut was one of the few women to rule ancient Egypt. Many people believe she was one of the greatest pharaohs. Hatshepsut ruled Egypt for 21 years from about 1503 B.C. to about 1482 B.C.

Although it was a custom that pharaohs be male, Hatshepsut declared herself pharaoh. She sometimes even wore clothing that was like the clothing that male pharaohs had worn. Sometimes she also wore a false beard that was like the beards that male pharaohs had worn.

Hatshepsut brought peace to Egypt. She was one of the few pharaohs who was not interested in war. She is best known for her interests in trading and building.

During Hatshepsut's rule, Egyptian traders went on ships to other lands in eastern Africa. The Egyptian traders took their beads, metal tools, and **weapons** to trade. In exchange the traders received such things as ivory, gold, live animals, and trees. Egypt became very rich because of this trade.

Many buildings were made during Hatshepsut's rule. One huge **temple** was built for Hatshepsut. This famous temple was built into the sides of hills. Hatshepsut planned that this temple would be her tomb when she died. She had the walls of the temple decorated with pictures. The pictures tell the story of the important events during Hatshepsut's rule. One story tells about the Egyptian trade in eastern Africa.

Hatshepsut's temple is still standing. It is considered one of the greatest buildings in Egypt. Each year many people visit the temple. There they learn about the history of ancient Egypt during this great pharaoh's rule.

Queen Hatshepsut

Hatshepsut's temple

Questions about People in History are shown with this star on the Using What You Learned pages.

Using Vocabulary

Match Up Number your paper from 1 to 4. Finish the sentences in Group A with words from Group B. Write on your paper the letter of each correct answer.

Group A

1. The _____ from the Nile floods was good for growing crops.

2. To _____ their land, farmers brought water from the Nile River.

3. Hatshepsut had people build a _____ as a place for the gods.

4. Some tombs were inside large, stone buildings called _____.

Group B

a. pyramids

b. temple

c. irrigate

d. fertile soil

Skill Builder

Understanding A.D. and B.C. on a Time Line Dates tell us when events in history happened. We say that events happened before or after the birth of a man called Jesus. A **time line** helps us show which events happened first. Look at the time line below. Events that happened before Jesus' birth are marked **B.C.** Events that happened after Jesus' birth are marked **A.D.** When counting B.C. years, the highest number tells the oldest event. When counting A.D. years, the lowest number tells the oldest event.

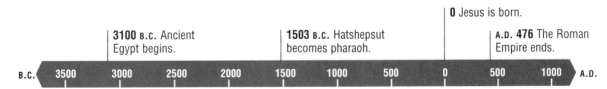

Number your paper from 1 to 4. Then write on your paper the older date in each pair.

1. 1503 B.C.   3100 B.C.

2. 3100 B.C.   A.D. 476

3. A.D. 1503   1503 B.C.

4. A.D. 476   0

15

Read and Remember

Finish Up   Choose a word in dark print to best complete each sentence. Write on your paper the word you choose.

Hatshepsut   **civilization**   **Nile**   **Egyptians**   **slaves**

1. Ancient Egypt has been called the "gift of the _____."

2. The pharaoh was the ruler of all _____ .

3. _____ was known for her interests in building and trading.

4. The _____ of ancient Egypt lasted for more than 2,800 years.

5. Egyptian _____ were forced to work hard without pay.

Think and Apply

Cause and Effect   A **cause** is something that makes something else happen. What happens is called the **effect**.

> **Cause**   Stone Age people learned to farm.
> **Effect**   People did not need to move from place to place to find food.

Number your paper from 1 to 4. Write sentences on your paper by matching each cause on the left with an effect on the right.

Cause

1. Ancient Egyptians believed in life after death, so _____

2. Farmers in ancient Egypt found a way to irrigate dry land, so _____

3. Ancient Egypt had few trees, so _____

4. Archaeologists have learned to read stones with Egyptian writing, so _____

Effect

a. they have learned a lot about the ancient Egyptians.

b. they did not have to wait until after the floods to plant their seeds.

c. many buildings were made from stone blocks.

d. they left food and clothing in tombs.

People of the Fertile Crescent

THINK ABOUT AS YOU READ

1. **Why did many people want to live near the Fertile Crescent?**

2. **Why were Sumerian priests such a powerful group?**

3. **Why was Hammurabi a great king for Babylonia?**

NEW WORDS

♦ crescent
♦ scarce
♦ city-states
♦ priests
♦ classes
♦ conquered

PEOPLE & PLACES

♦ Middle East
♦ Tigris River
♦ Euphrates River
♦ Fertile Crescent
♦ Mesopotamia
♦ Sumerians
♦ Babylonians
♦ Hammurabi
♦ Babylonian Empire

Egypt and the Nile River are in an area that today we call the Middle East. Two other long rivers in the Middle East are the Tigris River and the Euphrates River. Like the Nile River, the two rivers sometimes flooded the land around them. The floods brought fertile soil to the land. The land around the rivers and to the west forms a **crescent** shape. This area is called the Fertile Crescent. The land between the two rivers was once called Mesopotamia. Thousands of years ago, civilizations developed in Mesopotamia and the Fertile Crescent.

Most of the Middle East is hot, dry land with little rain. Water is **scarce** in most of the Middle East. Many people in this area wanted to live near the rivers and the good soil of the Fertile Crescent.

The Sumerians were the first people we know of who lived in Mesopotamia. They lived there from about 3500 B.C. to about 2000 B.C. They became good

The Sumerians were some of the first people to use wheels.

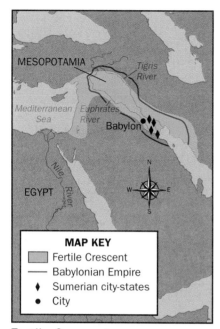
Fertile Crescent

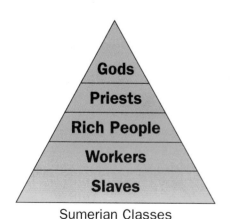
Sumerian temple

Sumerian Classes

farmers at about the same time as the Egyptians. The Sumerians worked together to irrigate their farms. Sometimes floods would destroy good crops. The Sumerians learned to control the floods. They built strong walls near the rivers. The walls stopped the river water from covering the land.

The Sumerians created a system to write their words and numbers. Their writing was made of many small signs. They wrote on pieces of wet clay. They dried the clay in the sun.

The Sumerians built many **city-states** where people lived and worked together. Each city-state had its own ruler. The city-states fought with each other to win control of all of Mesopotamia.

The Sumerians believed that many gods ruled the earth. The gods let people grow food. In return the people had to work for their gods. They gave the gods food and clothing. **Priests** worked in temples for the gods. The Sumerians believed that only priests knew what the gods wanted. The people had to obey the priests in order to please the gods. This made the priests very powerful.

The Sumerians divided people into different groups called **classes**. Every Sumerian belonged to a class. Priests were the most powerful class. Rich people were also a powerful class. Workers were in another class. Slaves were in the lowest class. Many people were slaves.

Around 1800 B.C. people from another part of Mesopotamia **conquered** the Sumerians. These people were the Babylonians. The Babylonians learned much from the Sumerians. They learned to write on wet clay. They learned to be good farmers.

The Babylonians had a great king. His name was Hammurabi. He ruled from about 1792 B.C. to 1750 B.C. During that time he conquered most of the Fertile Crescent. The land he conquered became part of the Babylonian Empire, or Babylonia. The people

One Babylonian king had people build the Hanging Gardens of Babylon for his wife.

Sumerian clay tablet with writing

Hammurabi talking to a god

of Babylonia traded with people in Egypt and with people in other far-off lands.

Hammurabi became famous because he put all of the laws of his empire together. He put together almost 300 laws. These laws were written on a very large stone. The stone was placed where all the people could read it. The laws were called the Code of Hammurabi.

What kind of laws were on the stone? Some laws said that strong people should not hurt weak people. One law said that if a man destroyed the eye of another person, that man's own eye must be destroyed. Many laws had to do with land, money, and family life. Some laws were fair to women. Women could own land. The Code of Hammurabi was written for all Babylonians.

The Babylonian Empire grew weaker after Hammurabi died. Many people wanted to rule the fertile land around the rivers. There were many wars. The Fertile Crescent was conquered again and again.

In the next chapter, you will read about other people who lived in the Middle East long ago.

Using Vocabulary

Finish Up   Choose a word in dark print to best complete each sentence. Write on your paper the word you choose.

classes   **crescent**   **priests**

conquered   **scarce**   **city-states**

1. There was little rain in the Middle East, so water was _____.

2. The fertile area around the Tigris and Euphrates rivers has a long, curved _____ shape.

3. The Sumerians built many _____ where people lived and worked together.

4. Groups of people are sometimes called _____.

5. The _____ were the most powerful Sumerian class because they worked for the gods.

6. The Babylonians became the rulers of the Sumerians when they fought and _____ the Sumerians.

Read and Remember

Find the Answer   Find the sentences that tell something true about the Fertile Crescent and its peoples. Write on your paper the sentences you find. You should find four sentences.

1. The Fertile Crescent is the land around the Nile River.

2. Many people wanted to control the land of the Fertile Crescent.

3. The Sumerians built only one city-state.

4. The Sumerians believed that many gods ruled the earth.

5. The Sumerians were divided into classes.

6. Hammurabi put together laws for his empire.

7. The Babylonians wrote on paper instead of clay or stone.

Think and Apply

Compare and Contrast Number your paper from 1 to 8. Then read each sentence below. Decide whether it tells about Sumerians, Babylonians, or both groups of people. Write **S** on your paper for each sentence that tells about Sumerians. Write **B** on your paper for each sentence that tells about Babylonians. Write **SB** on your paper for each sentence that tells about both Sumerians and Babylonians.

1. The people lived in the Fertile Crescent.

2. The people lived in city-states.

3. The people were the first people we know of in Mesopotamia.

4. The people were part of an empire.

5. The people had to follow Hammurabi's laws.

6. The people could write their own words.

7. Around 1800 B.C. these people were conquered by people from another part of Mesopotamia.

8. The people were good farmers.

Skill Builder

Using Map Keys Sometimes a map uses a color or a symbol to show something on the map. A **map key** tells what the color or the symbol means. Look at the map of the Fertile Crescent on page 18. Study the map and the map key. Number your paper from 1 to 5. Then write the answers on your paper.

1. What is the symbol for a Sumerian city-state?

2. What is the symbol for a city?

3. What color is used to show the Fertile Crescent?

4. Was Babylon a city or a city-state?

5. Was the Nile River part of the Babylonian Empire?

Other People of the Ancient Middle East

THINK ABOUT
AS YOU READ

1. How did the Phoenicians make writing simpler?
2. How was Judaism different from other religions in the Middle East?
3. In what ways were the Persians good rulers?

NEW WORDS

♦ alphabet
♦ religion
♦ Judaism
♦ Ten Commandments
♦ honest
♦ Christianity
♦ Bible
♦ Old Testament

PEOPLE & PLACES

♦ Phoenicians
♦ Jews
♦ Mediterranean Sea
♦ Persians
♦ Palestine
♦ Israel
♦ Jerusalem
♦ Moses

In this chapter you will read about other people who lived in the Middle East. Two of these groups, the Phoenicians and the Jews, lived near the Mediterranean Sea. Another group, the Persians, conquered most of the Middle East.

Early Phoenicians lived near the Mediterranean Sea at about the same time that the Sumerians lived in the Fertile Crescent. The Phoenicians, however, became a great sea power by the year 1000 B.C. The map on page 23 shows where the Phoenicians lived. The Phoenicians built good ships. They sailed in their ships to many far-off places. They traded in other lands. They brought back many items from their trips.

The Phoenicians were the first people to use an **alphabet** for writing. They made an alphabet with 22 letters. The Phoenician alphabet was simpler than Egyptian signs or Sumerian signs. The ancient

The Phoenicians sailed to many far-off places.

Jerusalem is a city with many ancient buildings and modern buildings.

Phoenician Alphabet About 1000 B.C.	English Alphabet
⅄	A
⅄	B
⅂	C
⊿	D
Y	F,U,V,W,Y
⅊	H
⅃	L
⅏	M
O	O
⅌	Q
+	T

Some letters of the Phoenician alphabet

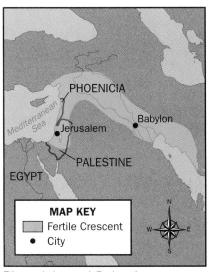
Phoenicia and Palestine

Egyptians and other people of the Middle East had to know hundreds of signs in order to write. The Phoenicians only had to know 22 letters! The alphabet we use today comes from the Phoenician alphabet of long ago.

The Jews were another group of people who lived near the Mediterranean Sea. The Jews lived in a land that became known as Palestine. Today part of the land of Palestine is called Israel. The capital city is Jerusalem.

The Jews had their own **religion**. It was called **Judaism**. People who believe in Judaism believe in only one god. The Jews were the first people that we know of to believe in one god. Other people of the Middle East believed in many gods.

For a long time, there was not very much food to eat in Palestine. There was a lot of food in Egypt. The Egyptians had food in difficult times because they had saved food in large buildings. They saved this food for the times when farmers would not be able to grow enough food. So the Jews left Palestine and went to live in Egypt. As time passed, there were many Jews in Egypt.

Moses led the Jews out of Egypt.

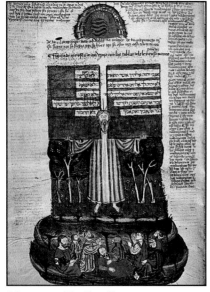
Moses with the Ten Commandments

The Egyptian pharaoh made the Jews work as slaves. The Jews were forced to build tombs and pyramids. Jews who did not want to work as slaves were beaten or killed.

Around 1200 B.C., a man named Moses became the leader of the Jews in Egypt. Moses and the Jews left Egypt. They went into the desert between Egypt and Palestine. They were in the desert for forty years.

In the desert Moses showed the Jews two large stones. Ten laws were written on the stones. These laws were called the **Ten Commandments**. Jews believe that God gave these laws to Moses in the desert. The laws teach people to be kind, fair, and **honest**. One law says that people must not steal. Another law says that people must not kill or hurt other people. Today these laws are an important part

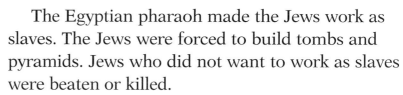

Jews praying in Jerusalem

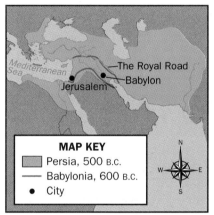

MAP KEY
Persia, 500 B.C.
Babylonia, 600 B.C.
● City

Mediterranean Sea
The Royal Road
Jerusalem
Babylon

N
W E
S

The Persian Empire, 500 B.C.

Persian coin

of Judaism. The laws later became part of another religion called **Christianity**. You will learn more about Christianity in Chapter 10.

The Jews wrote down their history in a book. This book became the first part of the **Bible**. The stories about the Jews of long ago and the laws of Moses are in the **Old Testament** of the Bible. People have been reading the Bible for many years.

After the Jews were in the desert for forty years, they went back to Palestine. The Jews conquered Palestine. Many years later the Jews were also conquered. They were conquered by the new rulers of the Fertile Crescent. Then in 586 B.C., Palestine was conquered again. This time the Jews were conquered by the Babylonians. The Jews were forced to leave Palestine. Many Jews were taken to Babylon to live. They did not want to live in Babylon. But they continued to believe in Judaism while they were in Babylon.

About 539 B.C. the Persians took control of Babylonia. The Persians conquered most of the Middle East. They even conquered part of Europe. No other people of the ancient world conquered as much land as did the Persians.

One Persian king said the Jews could go back to Palestine. Thousands of Jews left Babylon. They made Palestine their home again.

The Persians were good rulers. They were fair to the people they conquered. They built many good roads in the countries they ruled. The Persians had a good way to send letters. People on horses carried letters all over the empire. The Persians also used metal coins as a system of money.

The Persians ruled the Middle East for more than 200 years. Then they, too, were conquered. Who conquered the Persians? You will learn the answer to that question in Chapter 7.

Using Vocabulary

Find the Meaning   Number your paper from 1 to 5. Write on your paper the word or words that best complete each sentence.

1. A **religion** is a belief in _____ .

    a pharaoh   one god or many gods   a ruler

2. An **alphabet** has _____ that people use in their writing.

    pencils   clay   letters

3. **Judaism** and **Christianity** are religions that share _____ .

    money and rulers   laws and ideas   buildings and farms

4. The **Ten Commandments** are laws that Jews believe _____ gave to Moses in the desert.

    God   the Phoenicians   Tutankhamen

5. The **Old Testament** of the Bible tells the history of the _____ of long ago.

    Persians   Phoenicians   Jews

Read and Remember

Choose the Answer   Number your paper from 1 to 4. Write the correct answers on your paper.

1. Where did the Phoenicians and the Jews live?

    near the Mediterranean Sea   near the Tigris River   near the Pacific Ocean

2. Where did the Jews first live?

    Persia   Egypt   Palestine

3. Who conquered Babylonia?

    Egyptians   Persians   Phoenicians

4. What did the Persians build in the countries they ruled?

    good roads   pyramids   tombs

Finish Up Choose a word in dark print to best complete each sentence. Write on your paper the word you choose.

food   **ships**   **Palestine**   **Babylon**   **honest**   **Phoenician**

1. The Phoenicians built many good _____ .

2. The alphabet we use today comes from the _____ alphabet.

3. The Jews went to Egypt because they needed _____ .

4. The Ten Commandments teach people to be kind and _____ .

5. The Jews conquered _____ after living in the desert for forty years.

6. A Persian king said that the Jews could leave _____ .

Journal Writing

Write a short paragraph about the Phoenician alphabet. Tell why it was easier to use than Egyptian or Sumerian writing.

Think and Apply

Categories   Number your paper from 1 to 6. Read the words in each group. Decide how they are alike. Choose the best title for each group from the words in dark print. Write the title on your paper.

Egyptians   **Persians**   **Phoenicians**
Judaism   **Moses**   **Palestine**

1. built ships
good traders
made writing easier

2. led Jews from Egypt
Ten Commandments
1200 B.C.

3. capital city is Jerusalem
part of it is Israel
conquered by Jews

4. one god
Old Testament
Jews

5. conquered Babylonia
good rulers
metal coins

6. forced Jews to work as slaves
had food in difficult times
ruled by the pharaoh

Skill Builder

Reading a Chart   A **chart** lists a group of facts. Charts help you learn facts quickly. Read the chart below about groups of people who lived in the ancient Middle East. Number your paper from 1 to 7. Then write the correct answers on your paper.

PEOPLE IN THE ANCIENT MIDDLE EAST

People	Kinds of Rulers	Types of Work	Interesting Facts
Egyptians	pharaohs	farming, raising animals, trading	Built tombs for dead people. Egypt's doctors were well known for their medical services.
Sumerians	priests and kings	farming, raising animals, trading	Believed all parts of nature, such as wind, rain, and floods, were gods. Created a system of writing.
Babylonians	kings	farming, raising animals, trading	Believed in many gods. Created an important set of laws.
Phoenicians	kings and rich traders	sailing, exploring new lands, trading	Explored the Mediterranean Sea. Made an expensive purple dye that was usually sold to kings and their families.
Jews	judges at first; later ruled by kings	farming, raising animals, trading	Had laws called the Ten Commandments. Believed in one god.
Persians	kings; other leaders for smaller parts of the empire	farming, raising animals, trading	Built a road that was 1,677 miles long. Used coins for money.

1. What kinds of rulers did the Sumerians have?

2. Which group of people was first ruled by judges?

3. Which group of people sailed, explored new lands, and traded?

4. How many of the groups shown on the chart farmed, raised animals, and traded?

5. Based on the chart, what is one interesting fact about Egyptians?

6. Which group of people built a long road?

7. Which group of people was **not** ruled by kings?

CHAPTER 5

Life in Ancient India

THINK ABOUT AS YOU READ

1. **Why was the Indus River important in ancient India?**
2. **How did the Aryans change India?**
3. **What kinds of ideas from the ancient Indians do we still use in the world today?**

NEW WORDS

♦ irrigation
♦ Hinduism
♦ caste system
♦ castes
♦ outcastes
♦ reborn
♦ Buddhism
♦ monks

PEOPLE & PLACES

♦ ancient India
♦ Himalayas
♦ Indus River
♦ Pakistan
♦ Aryans
♦ Hindus
♦ Buddha
♦ Buddhists

We use numbers every day. Numbers are on money and on pages of books. Long ago the people of ancient India began to use numbers. We use the same kind of numbers today that the ancient Indians used. Our numbers are more than 1,500 years old.

India is a large country in southern Asia. India is separated from the rest of Asia by the Himalayas. The Himalayas are very tall mountains.

The Indus River was an important river in ancient India. The land around the river has very fertile soil. Today the land around the Indus River is part of the country called Pakistan. Pakistan was once part of India.

Civilizations in ancient India began near the Indus River. They began around the year 2500 B.C. Do you remember how the Egyptians and the Sumerians used water and fertile soil from their rivers to grow

The ancient city of Mohenjo-Daro was built near the Indus River.

The Aryans made Hinduism an important religion. Here a Hindu god is holding up a mountain.

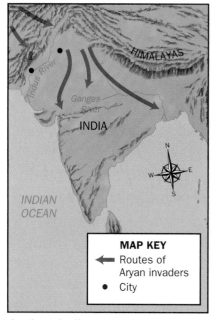
Ancient India

food? The ancient Indian farmers also did this. They used water from the Indus River for **irrigation**.

The ancient Indians built cities near the Indus River. These were large cities with straight streets and brick houses. The ancient Indians made metal tools. They created a writing system. They did not have an alphabet. Their writing was made of many tiny pictures and numbers.

About 1500 B.C. people from a far-off land conquered the land around the Indus River. These people were called Aryans. We are not sure from where the Aryans came. Many people believe that Aryans may have come from the Middle East.

The Aryans were good fighters. They conquered all of the land around the Indus River. They conquered much of India. The Aryans became farmers. They also raised cows and sheep. They made many Indians work as their slaves.

The Aryans changed India in many ways. These changes are an important part of Indian life today. One change was that family life in India became very

Farmers in India were in the third caste.

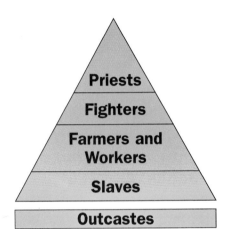

Priests

Fighters

Farmers and Workers

Slaves

Outcastes

Castes in Ancient India

A Hindu god

important. Another change was that a family's wealth was based on the number of cows the family had. A third change was that the Aryans made **Hinduism,** or the Hindu religion, important. Millions of Indians believe in Hinduism today. These people are called Hindus. Hinduism is the main religion in India today. A fourth change was the growth of the **caste system**.

Under the caste system, all people belonged to different groups. These groups became known as **castes**. Castes became part of the Hindu religion. There were four main castes. The priests and their families were in the highest caste. Priests worked in the temples for the gods. Rulers and fighters were in the next caste. Farmers and workers were in the third caste. Servants and slaves were in the lowest caste. A large group of people were not in any caste at all. These people were called **outcastes**. Indians in the four castes tried to stay away from the outcastes. The outcastes were forced to do the worst jobs.

People were born into the caste of their parents. People could not change castes. A farmer could not become a priest. People could only marry those from their own caste.

The Aryans believed that all people were **reborn** after they died. They believed that good people were reborn into a better caste. A good person might be reborn as a priest. A bad person might be reborn as a slave or an outcaste. The Aryans also believed there were many gods. These ideas became part of the Hindu religion.

Buddhism, or the Buddhist religion, also began in ancient India. It began about the year 500 B.C. Buddhism began with a man in India who became known as the Buddha. The Buddha did not believe in the Hindu gods. The Buddha taught that people should not be put into castes. He taught that people must be good and kind to each other. The Buddha said that people would be happy when they did not care about owning money, jewelry, or other items.

These Hindus are praying along the Ganges River in India.

A statue of Buddha

Many Indians liked what the Buddha said. People who believed in what the Buddha said were called Buddhists. This religion was spread from India to most of Asia by Buddhist **monks**. They started Buddhist schools in many parts of Asia. Buddhism became one of the major religions of the world. However, more Indians today follow Hinduism than follow Buddhism.

The Aryans ruled much of northern India for about 1,000 years. Then the Persians from the Middle East conquered the Aryans. The Persians ruled northern India for about 200 years. They, too, were conquered by other people. India was conquered many times during its long history.

The ancient Indians gave the world many important ideas. Hinduism and Buddhism came from India. Our numbers were first made by the people of ancient India. Ancient Indians were also known for their work in science.

Another ancient group of people lived in Asia. Like the ancient Indians, these people also had many important ideas that we still use today. You will read about these people in the next chapter.

Using Vocabulary

Finish the Paragraph   Number your paper from 1 to 5. Use the words in dark print to finish the paragraph below. Write on your paper the words you choose.

outcastes   **Buddhism**   **castes**   **reborn**   **Hinduism**

The Aryans made ___1___ an important religion. This religion divided people into four groups called ___2___. People who did not belong to one of the four groups were ___3___. The Aryans believed that after people died they were ___4___ as another living thing. About 500 B.C. in India, the Buddha started a new religion called ___5___. This religion said that people would be happy when they did not care about owning things.

Read and Remember

Finish the Sentence   Number your paper from 1 to 5. Write on your paper the word or words that best complete each sentence.

1. The ancient Indians used water from the _____ for irrigation.

Mediterranean Sea   Nile River   Indus River

2. The _____ we use today were created by the ancient Indians.

numbers   ships   alphabets

3. The _____ made family life in India important.

Egyptians   Aryans   Persians

4. The _____ did not believe in the Hindu gods.

Aryans   Buddha   Indians

5. _____ believed that people should not be divided into groups.

Aryans   Buddhists   Hindus

Think and Apply

Distinguishing Relevant Information   Information that is **relevant** is information that is important for what you want to say or write. Imagine that you want to tell a friend about life in ancient India. Then read each sentence below. Decide which sentences are relevant to what you will say. Write the relevant sentences on your paper. There are five relevant sentences.

1. Farmers irrigated fertile soil near the river in order to grow crops.

2. People in ancient India built brick houses and large cities.

3. A family's wealth was based on the number of cows the family had.

4. The Himalayas are very tall mountains.

5. Hinduism is the main religion in India today.

6. Many Indians believed in what the Buddha said.

7. Pakistan was once part of India.

8. Ancient Indians used the caste system to put people into groups.

Skill Builder

Reading a Diagram   A **diagram** is a way of showing information. Study the diagram of the Indian caste system on page 31. Number your paper from 1 to 4. Then write on your paper the answer to each question.

1. Who belonged to the highest caste?

2. Who belonged to the lowest caste?

3. Which castes were higher than the caste of farmers and workers?

4. Which group was not in a caste?

Journal Writing

Write a paragraph about the ways the Aryans changed India.

Life in Ancient China

China is a very large country in eastern Asia. The ancient civilization of China began around 3000 B.C. It began near a very long river called the Huang He. *Huang He* means "Yellow River."

Chinese people farmed the fertile soil along the Huang He. They used the Huang He to irrigate their farms. The Huang He often flooded the land. The floods sometimes destroyed farms, houses, and even whole villages. When this happened, the people called the river "China's Sorrow." The Chinese began to work together to stop the floods. They built strong dirt walls near the river. Sometimes these walls stopped the floods from destroying their farms.

China was ruled by **dynasties** for thousands of years. A dynasty is a family of kings. When the ruling king died, his oldest son became the new king. When that king died, his oldest son became the next king.

THINK ABOUT AS YOU READ

1. **How was ancient China ruled?**
2. **What was the Great Wall of China?**
3. **What kinds of things did the ancient Chinese know how to make?**

NEW WORDS

- dynasties
- invaded
- soldiers
- respected
- silk
- china
- civil service system

PEOPLE & PLACES

- China
- Huang He
- Chinese
- Beijing
- Han Dynasty
- Great Wall of China
- Confucius

Many people visit the Great Wall of China each year.

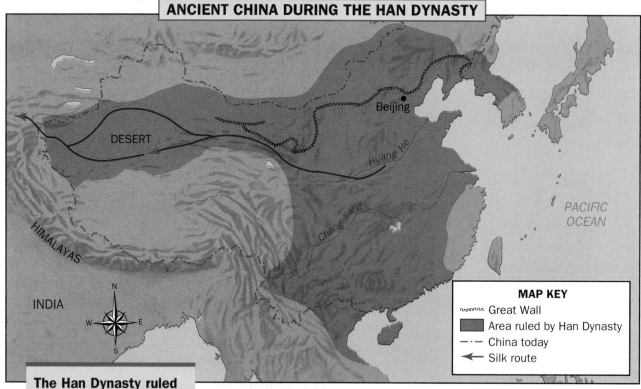

DESERT

Beijing

Huang He

PACIFIC OCEAN

Chang Jiang

HIMALAYAS

INDIA

N
W E
S

MAP KEY
〰 Great Wall
⬛ Area ruled by Han Dynasty
-·- China today
← Silk route

The Han Dynasty ruled much land in ancient China. Is China today larger or smaller than the land that the Han Dynasty ruled?

Huang He

The first dynasty began its rule around 1700 B.C. Some dynasties ruled China for hundreds of years. Many dynasties ruled from the city of Beijing.

The Han Dynasty was one of the greatest dynasties. The Han family became rulers in 202 B.C. They ruled ancient China for more than 400 years. China became strong and rich during the Han Dynasty. The Han Dynasty conquered much of Asia. During this time China began to trade with people to the west. They even traded with people as far away as Europe.

Sometimes people from the north **invaded** China. In 221 B.C. the Chinese began building a tall, strong wall. The Great Wall of China was about 1,500 miles long. It was about 20 feet high and very wide. It took many years to build the wall. The wall helped keep out people who were invading from the north. **Soldiers** stood on top of the Great Wall to watch for invading people. The wall helped keep the Chinese people safe. Many years later the Chinese made the wall much longer. The Great Wall is still standing in China today.

Families in China often worked together.

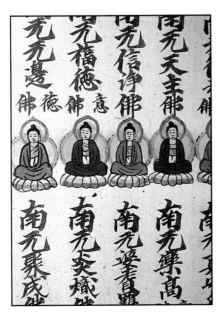
Chinese writing with drawings of Buddha

Confucius teaching his ideas

Many people in ancient China followed the ideas of Buddha. The Chinese also followed the ideas of another great teacher. His name was Confucius. Confucius lived about 2,500 years ago. He taught many important ideas about people, government, and family.

Confucius believed that people should be helpful, kind, and honest. He told people to obey their rulers. He said that rulers must be fair to their people. Confucius also taught that the family was the most important group in Chinese life. He said that family members should take care of one another. He taught that older members of the family should always be **respected**.

Family life was very important in ancient China. Children obeyed their parents. After a man and a women were married, they lived in the house of the husband's parents. As the family grew bigger, they built new rooms onto the house. In some families one hundred people lived in one home. The large families worked together on farms. Family life is still very important in China today.

For hundreds of years, the Chinese would not share their secrets of making silk.

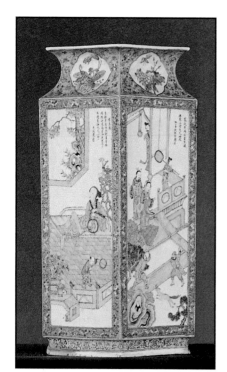

Vase made of china

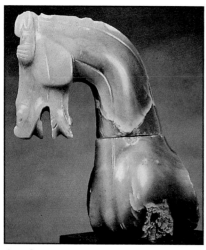

Art from the Han Dynasty

The Chinese created their own system of writing. Their writing had thousands of signs. The Chinese had a sign for every word. A Chinese person had to learn thousands of signs in order to read and write. Chinese writing today still has thousands of signs.

The Chinese knew how to make many things. They could make strong metal tools. They made carts that had wheels. These carts were pulled by horses. Almost 5,000 years ago, Chinese people began to make beautiful soft cloth called **silk**. For hundreds of years, the Chinese would not tell anyone how to make silk cloth. China made a lot of money by selling silk to other countries. Chinese people traveled on a long road to trade their silk in lands west of China. Around A.D. 600 the Chinese began to make thin, delicate dishes out of white clay. Today these fine dishes are called **china**.

The Chinese were the first people to make paper as we know it today. They made paper from rags. Then the Chinese learned how to print paper books. People in Europe did not begin printing paper books until hundreds of years later.

The ancient Chinese found ways to do many things that people in other areas of the world did not yet know how to do. Today we still use many of the ideas we learned from the ancient Chinese.

Confucius (551–479 B.C.)

Confucius was teaching in China at about the same time that people in India were learning from the Buddha. Confucius taught all students who wanted to learn. He gave people rules about how to behave. He taught that people should treat others the same way they would want to be treated. Confucius said, "What you do not want done to you, do not do to others."

Confucius lived during a time of much war in China. Rulers in different parts of China often fought with each other. Confucius believed that there could only be peace if there was a good government. He believed that a ruler should be good and honest to the people. Then the people would obey the ruler.

Confucius wanted an important position in the government. Then he could teach his ideas to kings and to many more people. But he never got the job he wanted. After Confucius died, some of his students continued to teach his sayings to other people. They also wrote his ideas and sayings in books.

More than 300 years after Confucius died, rulers in the Han Dynasty began to study his ideas. Confucius had believed that government workers should earn their jobs by doing good work. This is why the Han Dynasty set up a **civil service system**. Through the civil service system, people could get government jobs. To get a government job, a person first had to pass a civil service test about the ideas of Confucius.

Confucius was a great thinker and a wise teacher. His ideas about government and how to behave are studied all over the world today.

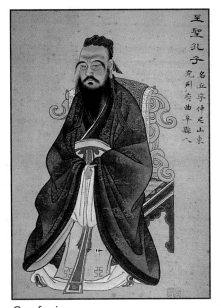

Confucius

Questions about People in History are shown with this star on the Using What You Learned pages.

Using Vocabulary

Match Up   Finish the sentences in Group A with words from Group B. Write on your paper the letter of each correct answer.

Group A

1. Families of kings called _____ ruled China for thousands of years.

2. China was attacked when people from the north _____ the country.

3. One way a person might show _____ for the older members of a family is to listen to their ideas.

4. A test for a government job in China was a _____ test.

5. The Chinese _____ were people whose main job was to protect China.

Group B

a. invaded

b. soldiers

c. civil service

d. respect

e. dynasties

Read and Remember

Finish the Paragraph   Number your paper from 1 to 4. Use the words in dark print to finish the paragraph below. Write on your paper the words you choose.

china   silk   Huang He   Great Wall

The people of ancient China knew how to make many things. They built dirt walls to stop the floods of the __1__ from destroying their farms. To help keep China safe, they built the __2__ . The people of ancient China made beautiful __3__ cloth. They also used white clay to make dishes called __4__ . The Chinese also knew how to make paper and strong metal tools.

Write the Answer   Write one or more sentences on your paper to answer each question.

1. What are two changes that occurred during the Han Dynasty?

2. What was family life like in ancient China?

 3. Why did Confucius want an important position in the government?

 4. Why did the Han Dynasty set up the civil service system?

Journal Writing

Write a few sentences about some of the important ideas of Confucius.

Think and Apply

Fact or Opinion   A **fact** is a true statement. An **opinion** is a statement that tells what a person thinks.

> **Fact** The Han Dynasty ruled ancient China for more than 400 years.
> **Opinion** The Han Dynasty was the greatest dynasty in the history of China.

Number your paper from 1 to 8. Write **F** on your paper for each fact below. Write **O** on your paper for each opinion. You should find four sentences that are opinions.

1. The Great Wall was about 1,500 miles long.

2. People should study the ideas of Confucius.

3. Ancient Chinese writing had thousands of signs.

4. Buddha was a better teacher than Confucius was.

5. Many dynasties ruled from the city of Beijing.

6. People in ancient China should have lived further away from the Huang He.

7. The family is the most important group in a person's life.

 8. Confucius said that a ruler should be good to the people.

Unit 2 Two Thousand Years of Change

From 800 B.C. to A.D. 1500, the world changed in many ways. New empires began. People fought wars about lands, religions, and ideas. People learned new ways to make books and art. Populations increased. Trade also increased. People traded spices and crops. They also traded ideas. New ideas about government would be followed for hundreds of years to come.

Who were some of the people of those times? The ancient Greeks gave the world the first ideas about government run by the people. The ancient Romans gave the world new ideas about laws. People in the Byzantine Empire enjoyed new ideas about art, science, building, and learning. Muslims and Christians spread their religions to many lands. During those years people fought many wars. They killed one another and destroyed towns and farms. Sometimes wars helped people learn about new ideas. Some wars also helped to increase trade. Wars changed the way people lived.

What happened to the people of ancient Greece and Rome? How did two religions change the way many people lived? What changes happened during the long years of the Middle Ages? As you read Unit Two, think

about some of the changes that happened between 800 B.C. and A.D. 1500. Think about how the ideas from that time period affect our lives today.

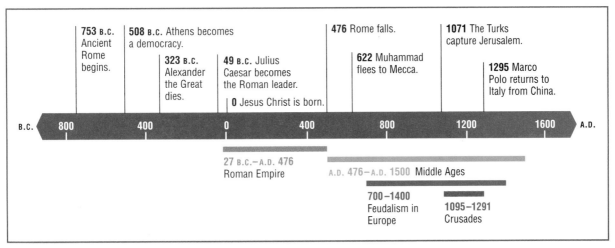

753 B.C. Ancient Rome begins.

508 B.C. Athens becomes a democracy.

323 B.C. Alexander the Great dies.

49 B.C. Julius Caesar becomes the Roman leader.

0 Jesus Christ is born.

476 Rome falls.

622 Muhammad flees to Mecca.

1071 The Turks capture Jerusalem.

1295 Marco Polo returns to Italy from China.

| B.C. | 800 | 400 | 0 | 400 | 800 | 1200 | 1600 | A.D. |

27 B.C.–A.D. 476 Roman Empire

A.D. 476–A.D. 1500 Middle Ages

700–1400 Feudalism in Europe

1095–1291 Crusades

The Story of Ancient Greece

THINK ABOUT AS YOU READ

1. **How were the Greek city-states of Athens and Sparta different?**
2. **How was Athens a democracy?**
3. **What did the people of ancient Greece give the world?**

NEW WORDS

- peninsula
- colonies
- citizens
- democracy
- culture
- Golden Age

PEOPLE & PLACES

- Greece
- Greeks
- Black Sea
- Sparta
- Athens
- Aspasia
- Socrates
- Aristotle
- Philip II
- Alexander the Great
- Pericles
- Parthenon

Greece is a small country in Europe. It is near the Mediterranean Sea. The main part of Greece is on a **peninsula**. A peninsula is a body of land with water on almost all sides. The rest of Greece is made up of islands. The ancient civilization of Greece began around 3000 B.C.

Unlike India and China, ancient Greece did not begin near a river. There are few rivers and little fertile soil in Greece. The Greeks could not grow enough food. They needed to get food from other lands.

The Mediterranean Sea was important to ancient Greece. Long ago the Greeks built ships. They sailed on the Mediterranean Sea and on the Black Sea. They sailed to many far-off places. They built Greek **colonies** in these far-off places. The Greeks brought food from their colonies back to Greece.

Greece has many tall mountains. Around 800 B.C. the Greeks began to build many city-states on the flat

The Greeks built many temples for their gods. This temple is called the Parthenon.

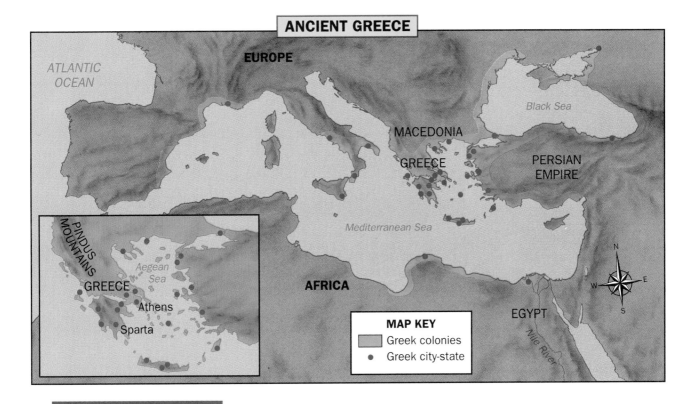

EUROPE

ATLANTIC
OCEAN

Black Sea

MACEDONIA

GREECE

PERSIAN
EMPIRE

Mediterranean Sea

PINDUS
MOUNTAINS

Aegean
Sea

GREECE

Athens

Sparta

AFRICA

EGYPT

Nile River

MAP KEY
Greek colonies
• Greek city-state

The Greeks sailed to and from their colonies. Which two bodies of water did they have to cross to reach their different colonies?

Spartan soldier

land between the mountains. The mountains kept the people of Greece apart. Each city-state had its own laws, rulers, and money.

Sparta was an important city-state in Greece. It was very large and powerful. It had a well-trained army. It conquered other city-states to gain wealth and power. The government of Sparta had two kings.

Sparta had three classes. The first class was **citizens**. Not all people in Sparta were citizens. Only men born in Sparta were citizens. The women of Sparta were not citizens. However, women were allowed to own land and businesses. Women in Sparta had more freedom than women in any other city-state in Greece. The second class in Sparta was people who came from other Greek city-states or from other countries. Many of these people owned businesses. The third class was slaves.

Learning to read and to write was not very important in Sparta. Training to become good soldiers was important. Young boys were taken from their parents. They were trained to be soldiers and to be

Spartan woman

The people of Athens started the first democracy.

Greek Alphabet About 600 B.C.	English Alphabet
A	A
B	B
Γ	C
Δ	D
E	E
⊟	H
I	I, J
K	K
M	M
N	N
O	O
Σ	S
T	T
Υ	U, V, W, Y
X	X
Z	Z

Letters of the Greek alphabet

good in sports such as running. Spartan girls were also trained to be good in sports.

Athens was another important Greek city-state. The people of Athens did not want a king or a queen. They believed people should rule themselves and run the government. Athens became the world's first **democracy** around 508 B.C. Other city-states became democracies. Today many countries use the Greek ideas about democracy.

Athens was a democracy because all citizens were allowed to vote. However, less than half of the people who lived in Athens were citizens. So less than half of the people in Athens could vote. Women and slaves could not vote. People who were born outside of Athens could not vote.

Learning was very important in Athens. There were many schools in Athens. Most boys went to school. Boys learned to read and write. They also learned many sports. Girls did not go to school. But one Greek woman thought girls should learn to read and write. Her name was Aspasia. Aspasia started a school for girls in Athens. Unlike girls in Sparta, girls in Athens were not allowed to play sports.

The Greeks liked the Phoenician alphabet. They changed the Phoenician alphabet a little, and it

Alexander the Great was one of Aristotle's students.

Socrates

Statue of Athena, a Greek goddess

became the Greek alphabet. They used this alphabet for all their writing.

Socrates was a great thinker and teacher in ancient Greece. He taught people to question their ideas. He taught people that there are right ways and wrong ways to behave. Aristotle was another famous Greek teacher and thinker. He started his own school in Athens. He wrote about science, art, and law. People today still study the ideas of Socrates and Aristotle.

The Greeks believed there were many gods. They built fine temples for their gods. They made many tall statues of the gods.

In Chapter 4 you learned that the Persians conquered most of the Middle East. The Persians also tried to conquer Greece. They conquered many Greek city-states. But the Persians could not conquer all of Greece. It took about twenty years for the people of Athens to win the war against Persia. After the war the Greek city-states were free again.

Philip II was a king from a country to the north of Greece. He conquered the Greek city-states in 338 B.C. His son, Alexander the Great, conquered many lands for Greece. Alexander and his soldiers conquered the Persian army. All the Persian lands became Greek lands. Alexander also became the

Alexander the Great conquered Persia and Egypt for Greece.

Alexander the Great

A Greek theater

ruler of Egypt and the Middle East. He conquered northern India. Then he started the long trip back to Greece. He died during the trip in 323 B.C. Alexander the Great was only 33 years old when he died. He had conquered many countries in less than ten years.

Alexander the Great brought Greek **culture** to the lands he ruled. New buildings in Persia were built to look like Greek buildings. People all over the empire began to use Greek money. People in Greece also began to use ideas from other countries. Alexander's empire became a mixture of many cultures.

The ancient Greeks gave the world many things. They started the world's first democracy. They were great builders. The Greeks built strong stone temples. They also built large theaters. Some of these buildings are still standing today. The Greeks also made fine paintings and statues. They wrote many plays. People around the world still enjoy watching the plays of ancient Greece.

Greece was a weak country after Alexander the Great died. The Greeks could not rule all the land that Alexander had conquered. The ancient Greeks were conquered by a stronger country. In the next chapter, you will read about the people who conquered the Greeks.

Pericles (490? B.C.—429 B.C.)

Pericles was a strong leader of democracy in Athens. He was the government leader of Athens from 460 B.C. to 429 B.C. While Pericles ruled Athens, the people of Athens enjoyed peace and good government. Athens became very powerful. This time became known as the **Golden Age** of Greece. It is considered to be the greatest time in the history of ancient Greece.

Pericles was born in Athens about 490 B.C. As a boy, Pericles studied with teachers who made him think and question his own ideas. This helped him become a good leader and a good speaker.

Pericles

Pericles became the leader of Athens in 460 B.C. Much of Athens had been burned by the Persians when they had tried to conquer Greece. Pericles worked to make Athens beautiful. New temples and other buildings were built. The largest Greek temple was the Parthenon. It had beautiful statues and other works of art. Part of the Parthenon is still standing today. People from all over the world come to see it.

Pericles made the Athens navy stronger than it had been. He also made many changes in the government of Athens. He decided that people who worked for the government should be paid for their work. Another change allowed common people to work for the government.

Pericles worked to gain more lands for Athens. The people of Sparta became angry. They did not want Athens to gain too much power. So in 431 B.C., Sparta and other Greek city-states went to war against Athens. Pericles led his soldiers in this war until his death in 429 B.C.

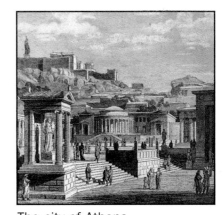
The city of Athens

Using Vocabulary

Finish Up   Choose the word or words in dark print to best complete each sentence. Write on your paper the word or words you choose.

culture   **democracy**   **citizens**
Golden Age   **peninsula**   **colonies**

1. The main part of Greece is on a _____, or land that has water on most sides.

2. The Greek _____ were far-off places that were ruled by Greece.

3. The first class of people in Sparta were the _____.

4. In a _____ the government is run by the people.

5. The people of Athens enjoyed peace, art, and good government during Greece's _____.

6. Money, buildings, beliefs, and ideas are examples of _____.

Read and Remember

Who Am I?   Number your paper from 1 to 6. Read each sentence. Then look at the words in dark print for the name of the person who might have said it. Write on your paper the name of the person you choose.

Pericles   **Socrates**   **Aristotle**
Philip II   **Alexander the Great**   **Aspasia**

1. "I lived in Athens where I wrote about science, art, and law."

2. "I opened a school in Athens so that girls could learn to read and write."

 3. "The Parthenon was built while I was leader of Athens."

4. "My empire became a mixture of many cultures."

5. "I taught people that there are right ways and wrong ways to behave."

6. "When I was king, I conquered the Greek city-states."

Journal Writing

Write a short paragraph that tells why you think Alexander became known as Alexander the Great.

Think and Apply

Understanding Different Points of View   People can look in different ways at something that happens. Look at these two points of view about Pericles.

> Pericles was the greatest leader of Athens.
> Pericles spent too many years fighting in wars.

The people of Sparta and Athens had different points of view about their ways of life. Number your paper from 1 to 6. Read each sentence below. Write **Sparta** on your paper for each sentence that might show the point of view of a person from Sparta. Write **Athens** on your paper for each sentence that might show the point of view of a person from Athens.

1. Women should not own land.

2. Women should be allowed to learn sports and own land.

3. It is better for a city-state to be ruled by kings.

4. The people should run the government.

5. Training to be a soldier is more important than learning to read.

6. Boys should go to school to learn to read and write.

Sequencing Events   Number your paper from 1 to 5. Write the sentences to show the correct order.

Philip II conquered the Greek city-states in 338 B.C.

The Greeks began to build city-states on land between the mountains.

Athens and Sparta went to war in 431 B.C.

Alexander the Great died in 323 B.C. after conquering many lands for Greece.

Athens became a democracy around 508 B.C.

CHAPTER 8

Beginning of the Roman Empire

The Romans were some of the greatest **conquerors** of the ancient world. The Romans built a great empire. They ruled much of the ancient world for over 900 years. The Romans thought their empire would last forever. But their empire grew weaker and weaker until it fell apart. You will read about the beginning of the Roman Empire in this chapter. In the next chapter you will read about the end of the Roman Empire.

The Roman Empire began in the country that is now called Italy. Italy is a country in Europe near the Mediterranean Sea. It is also near Greece. Like Greece, Italy is on a peninsula. Italy also has two large islands. Much of Italy has mountains.

Around 753 B.C. people began to build the city of Rome in Italy. The people of Rome were called Romans. The Romans did not want a king or a queen. Rome became a **republic**. In a republic people vote for their leaders. The Roman republic

THINK ABOUT AS YOU READ

1. **Where did the Roman Empire begin?**
2. **Why was Roman law important?**
3. **How were Julius Caesar and Augustus Caesar good rulers for Rome?**

NEW WORDS

- conquerors
- republic
- Senate
- senators
- veto
- accused
- innocent
- guilty
- trial
- aqueducts

PEOPLE & PLACES

- Romans
- Italy
- Rome
- Carthage
- Julius Caesar
- Augustus Caesar
- Mark Antony

The Romans built aqueducts to carry water into the city.

Roman women were allowed to own land and hold jobs, but they were not allowed to vote.

Roman senators

was led by the **Senate**. People in the Senate were called **senators**.

The Roman republic was not a democracy. Rich people had much more power than poor people. Poor people could not be leaders in Rome. Only some citizens were allowed to vote. Most Romans were not citizens. Most Romans could not vote. After many years some laws were changed. Poor Romans could help make laws. But the rich people of Rome still made most of the laws.

Women had more freedom in Rome than women had in Athens. They could own land and hold jobs. Women in Rome were citizens, but they were not allowed to vote.

Roman law was very important. Many Roman ideas and laws are used by countries today. The Romans used the **veto**. The veto gives government leaders the right to stop a new law from being passed. The Romans also believed that their laws should apply to all people in the empire. They believed that people **accused** of crimes were **innocent** until they were found **guilty**. Romans also believed that an accused person had a right to a fair **trial**.

The Romans borrowed many ideas from Greek culture. They believed in many of the Greek gods.

The center of the Roman Empire was the busy city of Rome.

The Roman god Neptune was also the Greek god Poseidon.

Roman soldiers

They gave these Greek gods Roman names. They made statues and pictures of their gods. They built strong temples. They built many theaters.

The Romans liked the Greek alphabet. They changed some of the Greek letters to make the Roman alphabet. Our alphabet is almost the same as the Roman alphabet.

There were many schools in the Roman Empire. Most boys and some girls went to school. They learned to read, to write, and to do math. Older children learned to read Greek in school.

The Romans built hospitals and good roads. The Romans also built bridges and **aqueducts**. Aqueducts were used to bring water to the city. Some of these roads, bridges, and aqueducts are still in use today.

The Romans had a very strong army. The Roman army conquered all of Italy. There had been Greek colonies in Italy. The Romans conquered these colonies. Later, the Romans conquered all of Greece.

The empire became even greater when the Romans conquered Carthage. Carthage was a great city in North Africa. It was near the Mediterranean Sea. The Phoenicians had built the city of Carthage. Carthage ruled many colonies near the Mediterranean Sea. Find Carthage on the map on page 55.

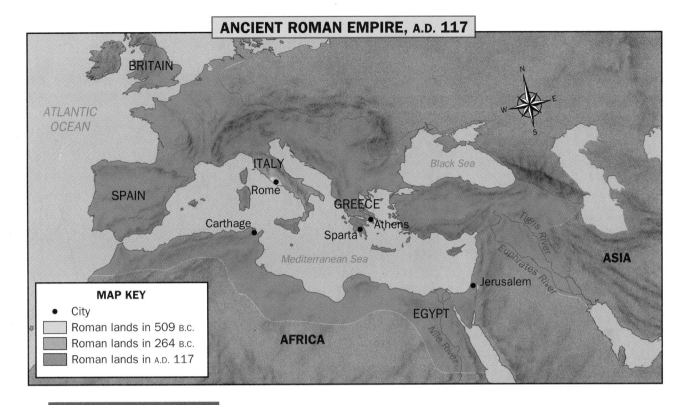

ANCIENT ROMAN EMPIRE, A.D. 117

MAP KEY
• City
Roman lands in 509 B.C.
Roman lands in 264 B.C.
Roman lands in A.D. 117

Rome conquered many civilizations in Europe, Asia, and Africa. Which two civilizations in Africa did the Romans conquer?

Soldiers from Carthage

Both Rome and Carthage wanted to rule the land around the Mediterranean Sea. They fought each other for more than 100 years. In 146 B.C. Rome conquered Carthage. The Romans destroyed the city of Carthage. All the colonies of Carthage became Roman colonies. Then Rome conquered land to the east of the Mediterranean Sea. As the years passed, Rome ruled more and more land.

One of the greatest Romans was Julius Caesar. Julius Caesar became a leader of the Roman army. He conquered a lot of land in Europe for Rome. In 49 B.C. Julius Caesar was named ruler of Rome. He ruled Rome for five years.

Julius Caesar made many changes in Rome. He gave land to poor Romans. Many Romans did not have jobs. Julius Caesar gave these people jobs. People built new roads and temples for Rome. The new roads made it easier to travel through all the land that belonged to Rome. Julius Caesar gave the people in conquered lands the same rights that Romans had. After that, many conquered people wanted to help Rome.

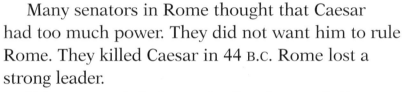
Some roads that were built by the ancient Romans are still being used today.

Julius Caesar in Rome

Augustus Caesar

Many senators in Rome thought that Caesar had too much power. They did not want him to rule Rome. They killed Caesar in 44 B.C. Rome lost a strong leader.

Two men and their armies fought to rule Rome after Julius Caesar died. Augustus Caesar and Mark Antony both wanted to rule Rome. There was a war between them. Mark Antony lost the war. Augustus Caesar became the ruler of Rome.

Augustus Caesar was Rome's first emperor. He became emperor in the year 27 B.C. People do not vote for an emperor. Rome was no longer a republic. Rome was now an empire. Augustus was the one ruler of all the lands in the Roman Empire.

Augustus was a good emperor to his people. He made fair laws for the empire. While he ruled, many new cities were built in the empire. Many roads, bridges, and aqueducts were built all over the Roman Empire. He built a strong army. Augustus ruled for 41 years. Augustus brought peace to every part of the empire. This peace lasted 200 years.

Then the Roman Empire slowly grew weaker and weaker. How did that happen? You will learn the answer in the next chapter.

Using Vocabulary

Analogies   An **analogy** compares two pairs of words. The words in the first pair are alike in the same way as the words in the second pair. For example, **pyramid** is to **Egypt** as **the Great Wall** is to **China**. Number your paper from 1 to 4. Use a word in dark print to best complete each sentence. Write the correct answers on your paper.

aqueducts   innocent   republic   emperor

1. A democracy was to Athens as a _____ was to Rome.

2. Pharaoh was to Egypt as _____ was to Rome.

3. Short is to tall as _____ is to guilty.

4. Roads are to people and goods as _____ are to water.

Read and Remember

Choose the Answer   Write the correct answers on your paper.

1. Where did the Roman Empire begin?

Greece   Persia   Italy

2. When did people begin to build the city of Rome?

753 B.C.   146 B.C.   27 B.C.

3. Who had most of the power in the Roman republic?

kings   rich people   poor people

4. What city fought with Rome for the land around the Mediterranean Sea?

Athens   Sparta   Carthage

5. Which Roman leader ruled for only five years before he was killed?

Julius Caesar   Augustus Caesar   Mark Antony

6. Who became the first Roman emperor?

Julius Caesar   Augustus Caesar   Mark Antony

Think and Apply

Exclusions   Number your paper from 1 to 4. One word or phrase in each group does not belong. Find that word or phrase and write it on your paper. Then write on your paper a sentence that tells how the other words are alike.

1. Greece
   Italy
   Carthage
   China

2. veto
   democracy
   fair trial
   innocent until found guilty

3. bridges
   pyramids
   aqueducts
   hospitals

4. Socrates
   Julius Caesar
   Augustus Caesar
   Mark Antony

Skill Builder

Using Map Directions   Study the map on page 55. Find the compass rose. Then write on your paper the word that best completes each sentence.

1. Spain is _____ of Italy.

   north   west   south

2. Carthage is in the _____ part of Africa.

   northern   eastern   western

3. The Black Sea is north of _____.

   the Atlantic Ocean   Britain   Egypt

4. In order to get from Rome to Jerusalem by boat, the Romans had to sail south and then _____.

   north   west   east

5. The Roman Empire included land as far _____ as Britain.

   north   east   south

6. The _____ was in the southern part of the Roman Empire.

   Tigris River   Black Sea   Nile River

Skill Builder

Reading a Resource Map **Natural resources** are things we get from the earth. Metals such as iron, copper, and gold are natural resources. Foods and animals are also natural resources. A **resource map** uses symbols to show where different natural resources are found. The map key tells you what each symbol means. The resource map below shows where some natural resources were found in the Roman Empire around A.D. 117. Number your paper from 1 to 6. Use the map and the map key to answer the questions. Write the correct answers on your paper.

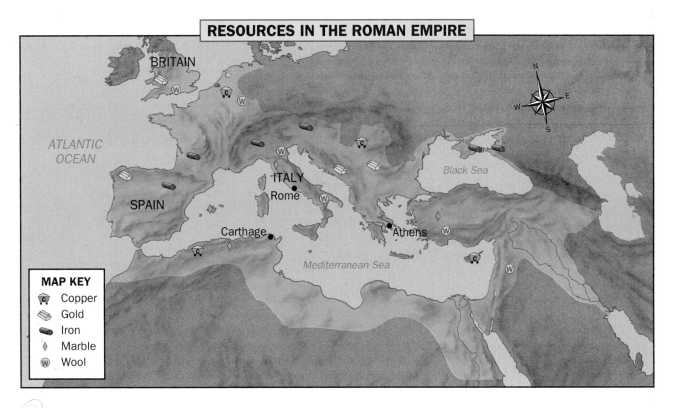

RESOURCES IN THE ROMAN EMPIRE

MAP KEY
- Copper
- Gold
- Iron
- Marble
- Wool

1. What five resources are shown on the map?

2. What symbol is used to show wool?

3. What resource is found near Athens?

4. Did Romans get their wool from Spain or from Italy?

5. What two resources are found in Britain?

6. For which resource might the Romans have crossed the Black Sea?

CHAPTER 9

The Fall of Rome

The Roman people lived in peace for 200 years. This peace began with Augustus Caesar. It ended in the year A.D. 180. Then the Roman Empire slowly grew weaker and weaker. In this chapter you will learn five of the many reasons why the Roman Empire grew weak and fell apart.

One reason the Roman Empire grew weak was that the empire was very large. The people in the conquered lands spoke many different languages. They lived far from the government in Rome. It was hard for the emperor in Rome to rule different people who were so far away.

THINK ABOUT AS YOU READ

1. Why did the Roman Empire grow weak?
2. Why was the Byzantine Empire important?
3. Why was Justinian a great Byzantine emperor?

NEW WORDS

- taxes
- population
- barbarians
- Fall of Rome
- empress
- riots
- plague

PEOPLE & PLACES

- Colosseum
- Byzantine Empire
- Constantinople
- Justinian
- Theodora

The Roman Empire was conquered by people called barbarians.

Romans enjoyed watching fights in the Colosseum in Rome. You can see another picture of the Colosseum on page 43.

Wealthy Romans hunting

Roman coins

A second reason the Roman Empire grew weak was that it did not have good emperors. Many emperors who ruled after Augustus were not good rulers. They knew how to lead an army. But they did not make good laws.

The Roman Empire also grew weak because its army did not have enough good soldiers. Thousands of soldiers were needed for the huge empire. In the days of the Roman republic, the Roman soldiers had been proud to fight for Rome. The soldiers of the Roman Empire were different. Many of the empire's soldiers were from conquered lands. They were paid to fight for Rome. These soldiers did not care about Rome. They did not keep the empire strong.

A fourth reason the Roman Empire grew weak was because too many people were slaves. The rich people of Rome owned many slaves. Slaves were not paid for their work. Poor free people could not get jobs, since slaves were doing most of the work.

A fifth reason the Roman Empire grew weak was that it did not have enough money. It needed money for its huge army. It needed money to build cities and roads. Rome got the money it needed when people paid **taxes** to the emperor. As time passed,

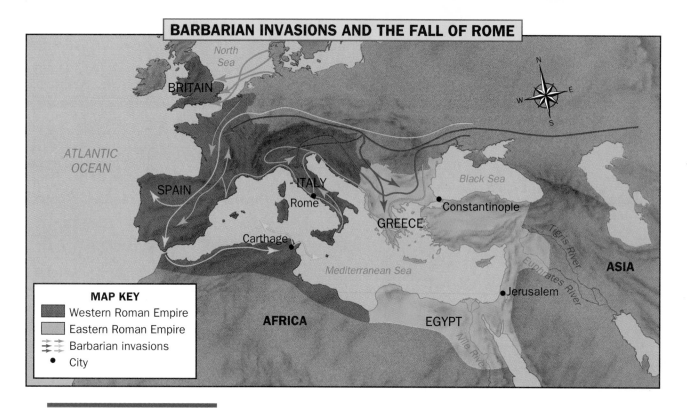

MAP KEY
- Western Roman Empire
- Eastern Roman Empire
- Barbarian invasions
- • City

The Roman Empire became divided. What were two cities in the Eastern Roman Empire?

fewer Romans had jobs. They were poor. They could pay very little taxes. The empire's slaves did not pay taxes at all. Rome did not have the money it needed to rule the empire. Rome grew weaker as the people grew poorer.

As Rome grew weaker, the people of the empire changed. The people of the Roman republic had been proud to be Romans and had worked hard for Rome. But the people of the Roman Empire were different. The rich did not work. They cared mostly about eating good meals and having fun. Most of the poor had lost their jobs. To keep the poor from making trouble, the emperor gave them free food and shows in the Colosseum in Rome. Few people cared about helping Rome. This made it easier for other people to conquer Rome.

Rome grew weaker and weaker during its last 200 years. The **population** of Rome became smaller. There were fewer people to protect the empire. At last, the empire was destroyed by different groups of people who had lived outside the Roman Empire.

Constantinople

Justinian

These groups of people were called **barbarians**. They came from lands to the north, the west, and the east of the Roman Empire. They were farmers, hunters, and good fighters.

The barbarians invaded the Roman Empire again and again. Many of them came to live inside the empire. The weak Roman army could not keep the barbarians out. Then barbarians attacked the city of Rome. They would not let the Roman emperor rule. Barbarians became the rulers of Rome and began to rule different parts of the Roman Empire. The empire fell apart. This was called the **Fall of Rome**. Rome fell in A.D. 476.

Barbarians conquered only the western part of the empire in A.D. 476. The eastern part of the Roman Empire became known as the Byzantine Empire. The Byzantine Empire was strong until its fall in 1453. The main city of this empire was the city of Constantinople. It was located between the Mediterranean Sea and the Black Sea. This location made Constantinople an important trade center. The Byzantine Empire became rich from trade.

People from many cultures lived in the Byzantine Empire. They shared with each other their ideas about arts, science, building, and learning. The Byzantine Empire became a mixture of cultures.

One of the greatest Byzantine emperors was Justinian. He tried to unite the lands of the once strong Roman Empire. He also made many changes in the laws of the Byzantine Empire. Many of these laws are still used in many countries today. Justinian also had great churches built throughout the empire.

The Romans gave the world fair laws, good roads, and fine buildings. After the Fall of Rome, the Byzantine Empire brought almost 1,000 years of learning and culture to the eastern part of Europe. But the Fall of Rome brought many hard years to the people who lived in the western part of the Roman Empire.

Empress Theodora (A.D. 502?–548)

Theodora was an important **empress** of the Byzantine Empire. She was married to Justinian. She had been an actress when she met Justinian. At that time it was against the law for government leaders to marry actresses. Justinian had the law changed so that he could marry Theodora. They married in 522. When Justinian became emperor in 527, Theodora became the empress.

Empress Theodora had many strong ideas about government, women, and religion. As empress she helped Justinian solve many government problems. She decided who would be given government and church jobs. She encouraged Justinian to build hospitals and churches. She also worked to give women more rights. Theodora even started homes to care for poor girls.

In 532 **riots** began between two groups of people. These people destroyed the city of Constantinople and tried to make another person the emperor. Justinian was going to give up his rule. But Theodora encouraged him to stay and fight. He and his soldiers stopped the riots. After the riots Justinian became an even stronger ruler than he had been before. He also worked to make Constantinople beautiful again.

Empress Theodora

In 542 a terrible **plague** made many people in Constantinople sick. Many people died. Justinian became sick. Theodora took his place as ruler of the Byzantine Empire until Justinian became well again. She was a strong and intelligent ruler. Even after Justinian was able to rule again, Theodora continued to make many government decisions. She and Justinian ruled together until her death in 548.

Using Vocabulary

Finish the Paragraph   Number your paper from 1 to 4. Use the words in dark print to finish the paragraph below. Write on your paper the words you choose.

barbarians   **population**   **Fall of Rome**   **taxes**

There were many reasons why the Roman Empire grew weak. Its rulers did not make good laws. Many Romans were poor and could not pay their ___1___ to the emperor. The empire did not have enough money to rule. As Rome became weaker, the ___2___ of the empire became lower. This meant there were fewer people to protect the empire. Many people called ___3___ came from other lands and destroyed the empire. Although the empire had once been great, these reasons led to the ___4___ .

Read and Remember

Find the Answer   Find the sentences below that tell a reason for the Fall of Rome. Write on your paper the sentences you find. You should find five sentences.

1. It was hard for the emperor in Rome to rule people who were far away.

2. Many emperors after Augustus were not good rulers.

3. The Roman army did not have enough good soldiers.

4. Only a few people were slaves.

5. Barbarians invaded Rome from the north, the east, and the west.

6. Constantinople was the main city in the Byzantine Empire.

7. The Byzantine Empire was ruled by Justinian and Theodora.

8. The Roman Empire did not have enough money.

Journal Writing

 Theodora was an important Byzantine empress. Write a few sentences that explain some of the ways that Empress Theodora helped the Byzantine Empire.

Skill Builder

Reading a Line Graph   Graphs are drawings that help you compare facts. The graph below is a **line graph**. A line graph shows how something changes over time. The line graph below shows how the population of the city of Rome grew larger and smaller over the years of the Roman Empire. Study the graph. Number your paper from 1 to 4. Then write the correct answers on your paper.

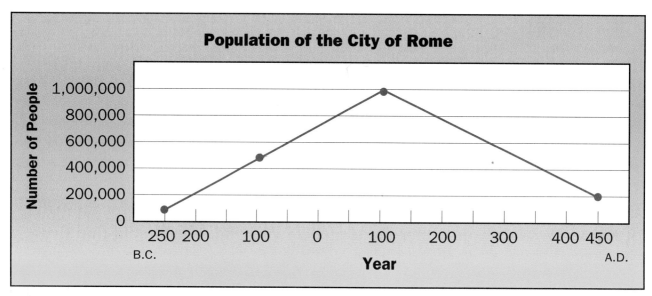

1. In which year did Rome have the largest population?

    100 B.C.   A.D. 100   A.D. 450

2. In which year did Rome have the smallest population?

    100 B.C.   A.D. 450   250 B.C.

3. In which year did Rome have about 500,000 people?

    250 B.C.   100 B.C.   A.D. 450

4. What might have led to the decrease of Rome's population after A.D. 100?

    better foods   barbarian invasions   good hospitals

The Beginning of Christianity

In Chapter 8 you learned that the Romans conquered land around the Mediterranean Sea. The Romans became the rulers

of Palestine. A new religion began in Palestine while Augustus was the emperor of Rome.

The new religion was called Christianity. It began with a Jew named Jesus. He was born in Palestine. Jesus told people to believe in God. Some people did not forget Jesus when he died. These people believed Jesus was a great teacher. They also believed he was the Son of God, and they called him Jesus Christ. The people who believed in Jesus and his teachings became the first Christians.

In Chapter 4 you learned about a book called the Bible. The Old Testament and the **New Testament** are the two parts of the Christian Bible. The laws of

THINK ABOUT AS YOU READ

1. **How did Christianity begin?**
2. **Why did many people want to become Christians?**
3. **How were churches in eastern Europe and in western Europe different?**

NEW WORDS

♦ **New Testament**
♦ **Eastern Orthodox Church**
♦ **patriarch**
♦ **Roman Catholic Church**
♦ **pope**

PEOPLE & PLACES

♦ **Jesus**
♦ **Christians**
♦ **Theodosius**

People who believed in the teachings of Jesus became Christians.

Lions attacking a Christian

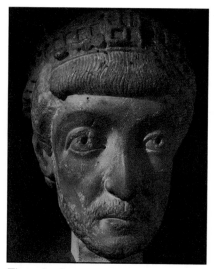
Theodosius

Byzantine art of the baby Jesus

Moses and stories about the Jews of long ago are in the Old Testament. Stories about Jesus and his teachings are in the New Testament.

Many people of the Roman Empire became Christians. The Christians believed in only one god. This made many Roman emperors angry. The Roman emperors had many Christians killed. Some were killed by lions in the Colosseum. But the emperors could not stop people from becoming Christians.

Why did people want to be Christians? Most people in the Roman Empire were poor and lived hard lives. They wanted to believe that one day they would have a good life. Christians believed that they would live a happy life in heaven after they died. They also believed that God loved slaves and poor people as much as God loved rich people.

Theodosius was a Roman emperor who helped Christianity grow. In A.D. 392 he said that Christianity was the religion of the Roman Empire. Most people in the empire became Christians.

When the Roman Empire became divided, two different types of Christian churches developed. The Christians in eastern Europe became part of the **Eastern Orthodox Church**. Their church leaders were in Constantinople. The head of this church is called the **patriarch**. The Christians in western Europe became part of the **Roman Catholic Church**. Their church leaders were in Rome. The head of this church is called the **pope**.

The Fall of Rome in A.D. 476 brought many changes to the people of Europe. There were many hard years. The churches in eastern and western Europe became very powerful. The churches greatly affected every part of life in western Europe and in the Byzantine Empire. In the next chapter, you will learn more about life in Europe during the years after the Fall of Rome.

Using Vocabulary

Match Up   Finish the sentences in Group A with words from Group B. Write on your paper the letter of each correct answer.

Group A

1. The teachings of Jesus are in the _____ of the Bible.

2. The head of the Eastern Orthodox Church is the _____ .

3. Church leaders in Rome were part of the _____ .

4. The head of the Roman Catholic Church is the _____ .

Group B

a. patriarch

b. New Testament

c. pope

d. Roman Catholic Church

Read and Remember

Finish the Sentence   Write on your paper the word or words that best complete each sentence.

1. During the time of Jesus Christ, the _____ were the rulers of Palestine.

   Egyptians   Greeks   Romans

2. Jesus was a _____ .

   Jew   Hindu   Buddhist

3. Many people became Christians because they believed that God loved _____ people.

   only rich   only young   all

4. Emperor _____ said that Christianity was the religion of the Roman Empire.

   Augustus   Julius Caesar   Theodosius

5. The leaders of the Eastern Orthodox Church were in _____ .

   Athens   Rome   Constantinople

Skill Builder

Reading a Time Line   This time line shows some important events that happened before and after the birth of Jesus. Remember that when you count years before Jesus' birth (B.C.), the highest number tells you the oldest event. When you count years after Jesus' birth (A.D.), the lowest number tells you the oldest event. Read the events on the time line.

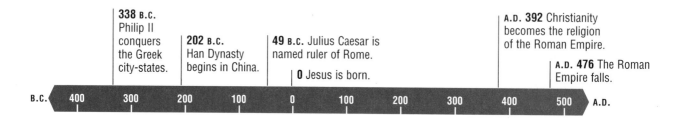

Number your paper from 1 to 9. Then write on your paper the answer to each question.

1. Which happened first: A.D. 200 or 200 B.C.?

2. Which happened last: 0 or 338 B.C.?

3. Which happened last: 100 B.C. or Julius Caesar becoming the ruler of Rome?

4. Which happened first: the birth of Jesus or the beginning of the Han Dynasty in China?

5. What happened in the year A.D. 476?

6. About when did Philip II conquer the Greek city-states?

7. In what year did Christianity become the religion of the Roman Empire?

8. What is the oldest event on the time line?

9. In what year was Jesus born?

Journal Writing

Christianity became a very important religion for many people. Write a few sentences that explain how the Christian religion began and grew.

Europe in the Middle Ages

THINK ABOUT AS YOU READ

1. How did life in Europe change after the Fall of Rome?
2. What kinds of changes did Charlemagne make in Europe?
3. How did the feudal system help people in Europe during the Middle Ages?

NEW WORDS

♦ Middle Ages
♦ feudalism
♦ feudal system
♦ nobles
♦ knights
♦ manor
♦ peasants
♦ castles

PEOPLE & PLACES

♦ Franks
♦ France
♦ Charlemagne

The years after the Fall of Rome were called the **Middle Ages**. The Middle Ages lasted about 1,000 years. They ended about the year 1500.

Life in western Europe was very different after the Fall of Rome. The once strong government of Rome disappeared. Europe was invaded again and again by the barbarians. The barbarians destroyed many cities and killed many people. Because of the barbarians, roads were not safe for traveling.

In the early Middle Ages, there were few schools in Europe. Most people could not read or write. There was little trade because of wars and dangerous roads. Without trade, towns and cities disappeared. People who had lived in towns and cities began farming. Most people tried to make or grow almost everything they needed.

During this time the Roman Catholic Church became very important in western Europe. People

Some manors had farms, a village, a church, and a castle.

Charlemagne

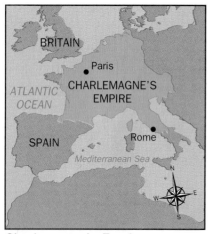
Charlemagne's Empire

Knights

were united by their belief in the Christian religion. The Church tried to encourage learning. The Church also collected taxes and made laws. The Roman Catholic Church grew rich and powerful.

The Franks were one group of barbarians. They conquered the land we now call France. In 768 a man named Charlemagne became the king of the Franks. Charlemagne conquered and ruled most of western Europe. He became the emperor of most of Europe by the year 800.

Charlemagne tried to make life better for the people he ruled. His army kept invaders out of Europe. He started many schools. He made many good laws and encouraged trade. Charlemagne spread Christianity throughout his empire. He also helped to increase the power of the Church.

After Charlemagne died, his sons became the rulers of the empire. They were weak rulers. They began to fight with each other to try to rule more land. Then Charlemagne's empire fell apart. Europe was divided into many kingdoms.

Europe was not safe after Charlemagne died. Barbarians began to invade Europe again. Rulers fought wars with each other. The kings of Europe did not have enough soldiers to protect their lands and people. Once again it was not safe to travel. It was not safe to live in cities. As people moved away from cities during the Middle Ages, a new way of living developed. It was called **feudalism**.

Feudalism was a system that helped the kings keep their lands and people safe. How did the **feudal system** work? A king gave large pieces of land to rich **nobles**. In return for the land, the nobles paid taxes to their king. The nobles also promised to fight for their king. Every noble had many soldiers. These soldiers were called **knights**. The knights worked to keep the land safe.

The nobles ruled the land that the king gave them. The land a noble ruled was called a **manor**.

Nobles built strong castles to protect the people on the manor.

THE FEUDAL SYSTEM

King
protected the people

Nobles
ruled the manors
protected the peasants
gave money to the king

Knights
fought for the nobles
and the kings

Peasants
worked for the nobles
paid taxes
were protected by the nobles

Sometimes a noble ruled many manors. The manor had farms, a church, and a village. Almost everything the people needed was made on the manor. Many people lived their whole lives on one manor. They had no reason to leave the manor. Many people left the cities of Europe and went to live on manors. Feudalism grew. It lasted for about 700 years.

Peasants were the largest part of the feudal system. Peasants were poor people. They lived on manors. They did the farm work. Peasants did all the hard work on the manor. They paid taxes to the noble who owned the manor. In return the noble protected the peasants and gave them small homes.

Nobles lived in large houses on the manor. Some nobles lived in **castles**. To keep safe, nobles built walls around their castles. The walls around the castles kept out invaders. If the manor was attacked, everyone would go into the castle to be safe.

Feudalism helped Europe become safer. There was less fighting. The feudal system gave the kings strong armies to protect their lands and people. The armies kept out the barbarian invaders. Roads were safer for travel. Soon people began moving into towns and cities again. By the 1200s feudalism was starting to become less important. Why did people want to live in towns and cities again? You will find the answer in Chapter 13.

Using Vocabulary

Finish Up   Choose the word or words in dark print that best complete each sentence. Write on your paper the word or words you choose.

noble peasants castles

knights feudalism Middle Ages

1. The years from the Fall of Rome to about 1500 were called the _____.

2. The system in Europe that was made up of the king, nobles, knights, and peasants was known as _____.

3. The _____ were poor people and were the largest group in the feudal system.

4. In the Middle Ages, a _____ was a person who ruled a manor and protected the peasants.

5. Some nobles built walls around large buildings called _____ to keep everyone on the manors safe.

6. Soldiers who fought for the nobles and kings were _____.

Read and Remember

Write the Answer   Write one or more sentences on your paper to answer each question.

1. Why did towns and cities disappear in the early Middle Ages?

2. Why was the Roman Catholic Church important during the early Middle Ages?

3. What are three ways that Charlemagne helped Europe?

4. Why did feudalism develop?

5. Under the feudal system, what did the nobles do for the king in return for land?

6. What did knights do?

7. Which group in the feudal system had the least power?

Journal Writing

During the Middle Ages, many people left the cities and went to live on manors. Write a few sentences to explain why people did this.

Think and Apply

Drawing Conclusions   Read the first two sentences below. Then read the third sentence. Notice how it follows from the first two sentences. The third sentence is called a **conclusion**.

Justinian tried to unite the lands of the Roman Empire.
Justinian had many good laws that are still in use today.

CONCLUSION   Justinian was a strong ruler.

Number your paper from 1 to 5. Read each pair of sentences. Then look in the box for the conclusion you might make. Write on your paper the letter of the conclusion you choose.

1. After the Fall of Rome, the barbarians invaded western Europe often.
   Barbarians destroyed towns and cities all over western Europe.

2. During the Middle Ages, people were united by Christianity.
   During the Middle Ages, the Roman Catholic Church made laws.

3. Charlemagne's army kept invaders out of Europe.
   Charlemagne made many good laws and started schools.

4. Farms and villages were on the manor.
   Many people lived their whole lives on the manor.

5. By the year 1200, Europe was a much safer place to live.
   People began to move into cities again.

a. Charlemagne tried to make life better for the people he ruled.
b. Feudalism became less important.
c. After the Fall of Rome, western Europe was not safe.
d. People had everything they needed on the manor.
e. The Church was very important during the Middle Ages.

CHAPTER 12

Muslims and Their Empire

THINK ABOUT AS YOU READ

1. How did Islam begin?
2. How did Islam spread to other lands?
3. In what ways was the Muslim Empire a center of culture and learning during the Middle Ages?

NEW WORDS

- Islam
- prophet
- Allah
- Five Pillars of Islam
- Ramadan
- pilgrimage
- Koran
- mosques

PEOPLE & PLACES

- Muslims
- Muhammad
- Arabia
- Mecca
- Medina
- Spain
- Great Mosque
- Baghdad

A new religion began in the Middle East during the Middle Ages. This religion is called **Islam**. The people who believe in Islam are called Muslims. The Muslims conquered and ruled a great empire during the Middle Ages.

The story of Islam began with a man called Muhammad. Muhammad lived in Arabia. Arabia is a peninsula in the Middle East. Muhammad was born in the city of Mecca in the year A.D. 570.

Muhammad believed that he was God's **prophet**. A prophet is a person who believes that he or she is spoken to by God. A prophet tells others what God has said. Muhammad believed that Moses and Jesus were also prophets. Muhammad believed that he was the most important prophet.

Muhammad said that the name of God is **Allah**. He said that people must obey Allah by being kind and fair to each other. He also said that all Muslims must perform five duties. These duties are called the

Muslims have built beautiful mosques in which they pray to Allah.

THE SPREAD OF ISLAM

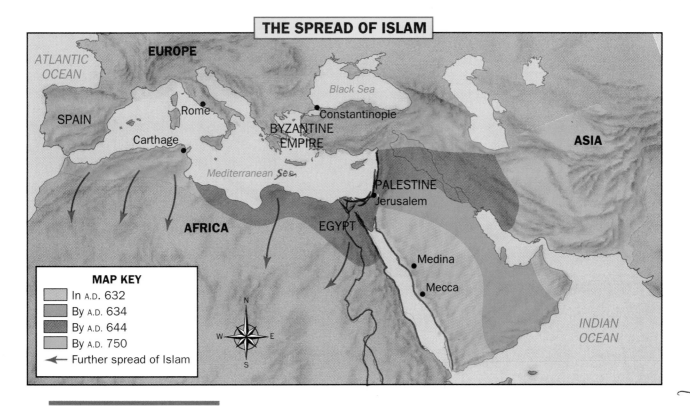

Muhammad taught that Muslims should face Mecca when they pray. In which direction would a Muslim in Egypt face to pray?

Five Pillars of Islam. The first duty is to make a statement about one's belief in Islam. This statement should be "There is no God but Allah, and Muhammad is His prophet." The second duty is to pray five times a day while facing Mecca. The third duty is to give money to help poor people. The fourth duty is to not eat or drink anything during the daylight hours of one month. This month is the Islamic month called **Ramadan**. The fifth duty is to make at least one **pilgrimage**, or journey, to Mecca.

The teachings of Muhammad are in a book called the **Koran**. Muslims in all parts of the world read and study the Koran. The Koran tells a person how to be a good Muslim.

A few people in Mecca believed what Muhammad said. These people became the first Muslims. They believed in Allah. However, at that time most people in Mecca believed in many gods. They wanted to stop Muhammad from teaching his new religion. Some of these people decided to kill him. In 622 Muhammad fled to the city of Medina to be safe.

Muslims read and study Muhammad's teachings in the book called the Koran.

A page from the Koran

Muslims worshipping in Mecca

Muhammad spoke about Allah to the people of Medina. Again and again Muhammad said that he was Allah's prophet. In Medina many people believed what Muhammad said. Soon there were many Muslims in Medina.

Muhammad wanted everyone to believe in Islam. He said that people who fought and died for Islam would go to heaven. Many Muslims wanted to go to heaven when they died. So they became soldiers for Muhammad.

In 630 Muhammad and his soldiers conquered Mecca. Many people in Mecca became Muslims. Muhammad conquered all of Arabia. Islam became the religion of Arabia.

Muhammad died in the year 632. Muslims did not stop fighting for Islam after Muhammad died. Muslim soldiers fought in many lands. They conquered many countries. Many of the conquered people became Muslims.

The Muslims became the rulers of a large empire. The Muslims conquered the Middle East and northern Africa. They conquered the lands that are now Spain and Egypt. They ruled Persia and parts of India.

The Muslim Empire became a mixture of many cultures. Muslims learned much about science,

Millions of people from all over the world have gone to Mecca to pray in the Great Mosque.

math, and art from people in the conquered lands. Muslims also spread new ideas across the empire. The Muslim Empire became a center of culture during the Middle Ages. Many Muslims wrote poems and stories. They made beautiful works of art. The Muslims built great cities with beautiful buildings. Some of these great buildings were **mosques**. A mosque is a place where Muslims worship Allah. One of the most famous mosques is the Great Mosque in the city of Mecca.

A Muslim pilgrimage

The Muslim Empire also became a center of learning. The Muslims started many schools in cities such as Baghdad. They created new medicines and built hospitals. They studied the stars, the sun, and the moon. They used Hindu numbers to create new types of math.

After 200 years the Muslim Empire grew weaker. Muslim leaders began to fight with each other. Different people became rulers of different parts of the empire. The empire fell apart. But Islam continues to be one of the world's great religions.

There are millions of Muslims in the world today. They believe in the religion Muhammad started in Arabia over a thousand years ago. The culture and the history of Islam unite Muslims all over the world.

Using Vocabulary

Find the Meaning   Write on your paper the word or words that best complete each sentence.

1. A **pilgrimage** is a _____ .

   journey   saying   soldier

2. Muslims believe that **Allah** is the name of _____ .

   Muhammad   Islam   God

3. The **Koran** is a book of the teachings of _____ .

   Confucius   Allah   Muhammad

4. **Ramadan** is an Islamic _____ in which Muslims do not eat or drink during the day.

   week   month   year

Read and Remember

Finish the Paragraph   Number your paper from 1 to 7. Use the words in dark print to finish the paragraph below. Write on your paper the words you choose.

religion	**Mecca**	**Five Pillars**	**mosques**
culture	**Muslims**	**Muhammad**	

Islam began with a man called __1__ . He said that people must perform duties called the __2__ of Islam. One of the duties is to pray five times a day facing __3__ . The people who believed Muhammad's teachings became __4__ . These people conquered Mecca and all of Arabia. Islam became the __5__ of Arabia. The Muslim Empire became a center of __6__ during the Middle Ages. Muslims made beautiful works of art and built __7__ for praying to Allah.

Think and Apply

Sequencing Events   Number your paper from 1 to 5. Write the sentences to show the correct order.

Muhammad and his soldiers conquered Mecca in 630.

Muslims became the rulers of a large empire.

Muhammad fled Mecca in 622 and went to Medina.

The Muslim Empire became weak because Muslim leaders began to fight with each other.

Muhammad began to tell his ideas about Allah to people in Mecca.

Skill Builder

Using Intermediate Map Directions
In Chapter 1 you learned about the four main directions—north, south, east, and west. Some compass roses also show four **intermediate,** or in-between, directions. They are **northeast, southeast, southwest,** and **northwest**. For example, southeast is between south and east. Study the map on page 77. Write on your paper the direction that best finishes each sentence.

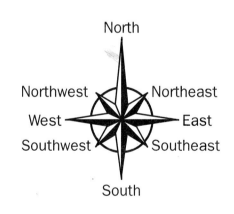

1. Jerusalem is _____ of Constantinople.

   southeast   west   northeast

2. When Muhammad fled from Mecca to Medina, he traveled _____.

   northeast   southwest   northwest

3. According to the map, Islam first spread to the _____.

   northeast   south   northwest

4. The Mediterranean Sea is _____ of the Indian Ocean.

   northeast   southeast   northwest

The Growth of Cities and Trade

THINK ABOUT AS YOU READ

1. **What were the Crusades?**
2. **How did the Crusades change life in Europe?**
3. **Why did people want to move to cities?**

NEW WORDS

- ◆ holy
- ◆ Crusades
- ◆ recaptured
- ◆ goods
- ◆ merchant
- ◆ woodblock printing
- ◆ spices
- ◆ diseases

PEOPLE & PLACES

- ◆ Europeans
- ◆ Turks
- ◆ Pope Urban II
- ◆ Crusaders
- ◆ the East
- ◆ Marco Polo
- ◆ Venice
- ◆ Italian

There were many changes in Europe between the years 1000 and 1500. Europe's population increased. More people began to live in cities. Arts and learning increased. People began to trade more with each other. Europeans could buy things from far-off places like Asia and the Middle East. How did these changes happen?

You have learned that Muslims from Arabia conquered the Middle East. They conquered Palestine in the 600s. For many years the Muslims let Christians go to the city of Jerusalem in Palestine. Christians made pilgrimages to Jerusalem. Jerusalem is a **holy** city for Christians, Jews, and Muslims. However, during the 1000s Muslims called Turks conquered Palestine, the Byzantine Empire, and other parts of Asia. They won control of Jerusalem in 1071. The Turks would not let Christians go to Jerusalem.

As you learned in Chapter 10, the leader of the Roman Catholic Church is called the pope. In 1095

As towns and cities grew, they became centers for buying and selling goods.

Christians fought the Crusades to recapture Palestine from the Turks.

Crusaders fighting Turks

Marco Polo

Pope Urban II told Europeans that they should fight wars to free Palestine from the Turks. Thousands of Christians decided to fight for Palestine.

The Christian wars to capture Palestine were called the **Crusades**. The Crusades were fought in the late Middle Ages. The Christian soldiers who fought in these wars were called Crusaders. Not all Crusaders cared about winning Palestine for the pope. Many Crusaders wanted to win new lands and riches for themselves. Others wanted to open up trade with the Middle East.

The Crusades lasted almost 200 years. The Crusaders captured Jerusalem in the year 1099. Christians ruled Jerusalem for almost ninety years. Then the Turks **recaptured** Jerusalem. By 1291 the Muslims ruled all of Palestine again. The Crusaders were not able to recapture Palestine.

The Crusaders learned about new foods and clothing from the Muslims. The Crusaders brought food, cloth, and new ideas back to Europe. Soon Europeans wanted more **goods** from Asia and the Middle East. Asia and the Middle East were often called the East. Trade increased between Europe and the East.

A man named Marco Polo helped Europeans learn more about the East. Marco Polo was the son of a **merchant**. In 1271 Marco was 17 years old. That year he, his father, and his uncle left Italy and

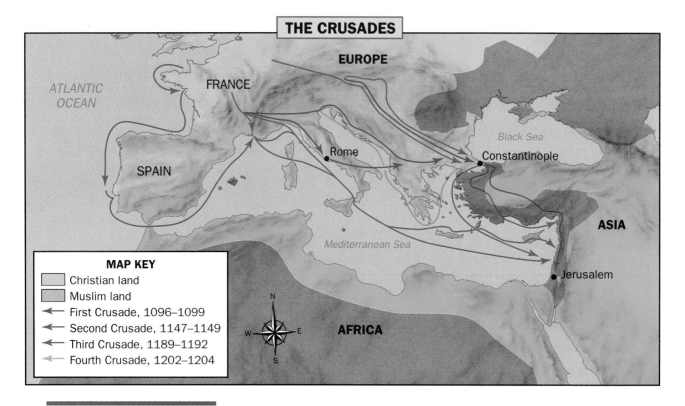

THE CRUSADES

EUROPE

ATLANTIC OCEAN

FRANCE

SPAIN

Rome

Black Sea

Constantinople

ASIA

Mediterranean Sea

Jerusalem

AFRICA

MAP KEY
- Christian land
- Muslim land
- First Crusade, 1096–1099
- Second Crusade, 1147–1149
- Third Crusade, 1189–1192
- Fourth Crusade, 1202–1204

N
W   E
S

Crusaders took many different routes to Jerusalem. Which Crusades crossed the Mediterranean Sea to reach Jerusalem?

Chinese printing block

began their trip across Asia to China. It took almost four years to reach China.

Marco Polo liked what he saw and learned in China. China had an advanced civilization. Many inventions were made in China during the Middle Ages. In the 700s the Chinese invented **woodblock printing**. It was much faster to use woodblock printing to make books than to write books by hand. Europeans would not begin to use woodblock printing until the 1200s.

Marco Polo stayed in China until 1292. During that time he learned to speak the language of China. He traveled all over China. He also worked for the Chinese emperor. When Marco Polo returned to Italy in 1295, he brought many beautiful things with him. He wrote a book about his trip. People read about China. Soon many people wanted to learn more about other far-off lands.

The Crusades and Marco Polo helped trade grow between Europe and the East. Ships carried goods to and from different cities in Europe. Other ships carried goods to the Middle East and Asia.

People bought and sold goods in the Italian city-state of Venice.

Grain and spices

Doctor visiting a man with the plague

Ships brought foods, silk, **spices,** and other goods from the East back to Europe. Venice and other Italian city-states became important trading centers.

Trade brought other changes to Europe. One change was that money became important. People began to use money to buy and sell goods. Another change was that merchants became an important group of people. As time passed, many merchants grew rich and powerful. A third change was that towns and cities became important.

Towns and cities were good places for buying, selling, and storing goods. Many new towns and cities were started. Most cities were built near seas or rivers. Many of these cities became rich trading centers. Cities grew quickly during the Middle Ages. However, people did not carefully plan most cities. City streets were narrow and dirty. Garbage was thrown in the streets. Houses were built close together. There were many fires. Fires moved quickly from one house to another house.

The crowded, dirty cities also made it easier for **diseases** to spread. One terrible disease was the plague. The plague spread quickly through many cities in Europe and Asia during the Middle Ages. The plague became known as the Black Death. It killed millions of people.

During the Middle Ages, people in Europe built many great churches called cathedrals.

Narrow streets in a crowded European city

But even though cities had many problems, many people wanted to live in cities. Cities had churches and schools. There were many kinds of jobs in cities. Many people thought they could have a better life in cities.

Feudalism ended because of the growth of cities. City people had to pay taxes to the king. Now kings had money to pay soldiers to fight for them. The nobles became less important. The kings had more power. Many peasants ran away from manors to go to cities. They had hard lives on the manors. They hoped to find better jobs in cities. As time passed, fewer people lived on manors. More and more people lived in towns and cities. Feudalism slowly ended.

The Middle Ages ended about the year 1500. By then, many people were living and working in towns and cities. Some people were making goods for merchants to buy and sell. Merchants were trading goods in far-off lands. Kings were becoming more powerful. In the years ahead, many more changes would come to Europe.

Using Vocabulary

Finish the Paragraph   Number your paper from 1 to 4. Use the words in dark print to finish the paragraph below. Write on your paper the words you choose.

goods   merchants   spices   Crusades

There were many changes in Europe during the years 1000 to 1500. Christians and Turks fought in the __1__ for the control of the holy city of Jerusalem. These wars helped increase trade with the East. The Crusaders brought back to Europe many __2__, such as foods and cloth. They also brought back __3__ to add to their foods. As trade and money became important, many __4__ who traded with the East became rich and powerful. Cities also became important.

Read and Remember

Finish Up   Choose the word or words in dark print to best complete each sentence. Write on your paper the word or words you choose.

woodblock   Pope Urban II   riches
plague   Marco Polo   Turks

1. The _____ were Muslims who conquered Palestine.

2. Many Crusaders wanted to win new lands and _____ for themselves.

3. In 1095 _____ told Europeans to fight the Muslims in the Crusades.

4. _____ wrote a book about what he saw and learned in China.

5. The Chinese method of _____ printing was faster than writing books by hand.

6. The _____ spread quickly through dirty, crowded cities during the Middle Ages.

Think and Apply

Fact or Opinion Write **F** on your paper for each fact below. Write **O** on your paper for each opinion. You should find two sentences that are opinions.

1. The Turks recaptured Jerusalem from the Christians.

2. The Crusaders learned many new ideas from the Muslims.

3. Marco Polo was very smart.

4. Venice became an important trading center during the Middle Ages.

5. It was easier to live on a manor than to live in a city.

Skill Builder

Reading a Bar Graph A **bar graph** shows facts using bars of different lengths. This bar graph shows how the population in the countryside of England was divided about 1086. England is a country of Europe. Study the graph. Then write the correct answers on your paper.

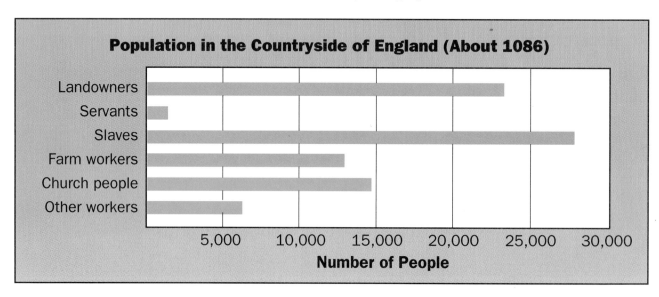

Population in the Countryside of England (About 1086)

Number of People

1. What group of people was the largest?

2. What group was the smallest?

3. Which group had about 13,000 people?

4. About how many church people were there?

Journal Writing

Trade brought many changes to Europe after the Crusades. Write a paragraph that tells three ways that trade changed Europe.

Riddle Puzzle

Number your paper from 1 to 9. Choose a word in dark print to complete each sentence. Write the correct answers on your paper.

holy	Asia	trade	Crusaders	Europe
narrow	seas	money	recaptured	

1. During the Middle Ages, people began to use _____ to buy and sell goods.

2. Millions of people in _____ and Asia died from the Black Death.

3. After almost 90 years, the Turks _____ Jerusalem from the Christians.

4. The _____ were Christian soldiers who wanted to capture Palestine.

5. Jerusalem is a _____ city for Christians, Jews, and Muslims.

6. Marco Polo traveled to _____ in 1271.

7. City streets were _____ and dirty.

8. After the Crusades, Europeans began to _____ with people in Asia.

9. Many cities were built near _____ .

Now look at your answers. Circle the first letter of each answer you wrote on your paper. The letters you circle should spell a word. The word answers the riddle below.

RIDDLE: If Marco Polo were alive today, with what group of people do you think you might find him?

Write on your paper the answer to the riddle.

Unit 3 The Growth of Nations and Ideas

How would a map look that showed the world in the year 1000? The lands and the oceans of today's world would be on the map. But today's nations would not be on the old world map. Before the year 1000, there were no nations in the world. After the year 1000, nations began to form. England, France, Spain, and other nations became strong. Great civilizations in Africa and the Americas also grew during this time.

The years between 1000 and 1800 were years of growth in Europe and other parts of the world. Europe did not grow larger in size. It grew in many other ways. There was a growth of new ideas in Europe. These ideas made learning important again. Art became more important. New ideas about democracy grew in England. The Roman Catholic Church became less powerful, and some people started new kinds of churches.

The number of explorers grew during this time. Many explorers from Europe wanted to find new and better ways to go to Asia. The nations of Europe started colonies in Asia, Africa, and the Americas. The number of colonies increased.

How did nations form after the year 1000? What civilizations were in Africa and in the Americas? Why did learning and democracy

become more important? Why did nations want colonies? As you read Unit 3, think about how nations are different from city-states and from empires. Think about how different our world might have been without explorers or new ideas.

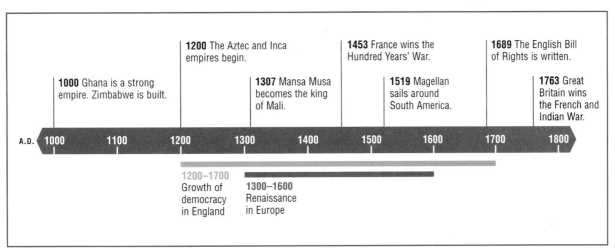

1000 Ghana is a strong empire. Zimbabwe is built.

1200 The Aztec and Inca empires begin.

1307 Mansa Musa becomes the king of Mali.

1453 France wins the Hundred Years' War.

1519 Magellan sails around South America.

1689 The English Bill of Rights is written.

1763 Great Britain wins the French and Indian War.

A.D. 1000 1100 1200 1300 1400 1500 1600 1700 1800

1200–1700 Growth of democracy in England

1300–1600 Renaissance in Europe

CHAPTER 14

New Nations Begin

NEW WORDS

♦ nations
♦ monarchs
♦ isolation
♦ monarchy
♦ Hundred Years' War
♦ battles
♦ executed

PEOPLE & PLACES

♦ United States
♦ Americans
♦ English
♦ English Channel
♦ William the Conqueror
♦ French
♦ Joan of Arc
♦ Orléans
♦ King Ferdinand V
♦ Queen Isabella

As the years of the Middle Ages passed, many changes occurred in Europe. Feudalism was ending. Kings in Europe were becoming more powerful. Kings began to unite the people of their lands. As people in lands united, they formed **nations**.

Nations are made up of people who have the same laws and leaders. Often people of one nation speak the same language. Our nation is the United States. The people of the United States are called Americans. Most Americans speak the English language. They obey American laws.

During the early years of the Middle Ages, there were no nations in Europe. Most people lived on manors. Every manor was ruled by a different noble. The noble made laws for the manor. **Monarchs** had little power. A monarch is a king or a queen.

The growth of cities and trade helped feudalism end. It also helped monarchs become strong rulers.

Barbarians came by sea to invade England.

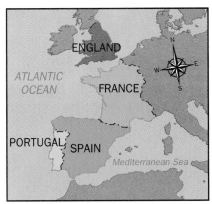
Four Nations in the Middle Ages

William the Conqueror

William and his soldiers conquered England.

There was more money in Europe. People paid taxes to the monarchs. The monarchs had money to build large armies. The armies helped the monarchs become even more powerful. They began to have more control over people in their lands. As time passed, monarchs ruled more and more land. People who lived on this land had to obey the laws of their king or queen.

How did England become a nation? Look at the map on this page. You can see that England is on an island. It is separated from the rest of Europe by the English Channel. This **isolation** helped England become a nation.

In A.D. 43 England was invaded by the Romans. Then in the 400s, barbarians invaded England. They brought new ideas to England. During the Middle Ages, the people of England lived on manors. They were ruled by nobles.

England was invaded again in 1066. A noble from an area of northern France invaded England. His name was William the Conqueror. William and his soldiers were good fighters. They conquered England. William the Conqueror became the king of England.

William was a strong king. He helped England become a **monarchy**. A monarchy is a nation where the monarch has all the power to rule. Everyone in England had to obey William's laws. After William died, different monarchs ruled England for many years. They helped England become one nation.

How did France become a nation? France had also been part of the Roman Empire. Then, as you learned in Chapter 11, barbarians called Franks ruled France. When Charlemagne became king, he gained much power in France. But before and after Charlemagne, kings did not have much power.

During the Middle Ages, France was made up of many states. Some states were ruled by nobles. Other states in France were ruled by England. About the year 1000, French kings began to take land away from

The French freed the city of Orléans from the English during the Hundred Years' War.

Joan of Arc

the nobles. They also wanted the lands in France that were ruled by England. They wanted France to become a strong country.

The English and the French fought in France. They fought for over 100 years. Their fight was called the **Hundred Years' War**. This war helped France become a nation. The war began in 1337.

A young woman named Joan of Arc helped France win the Hundred Years' War. Joan believed that God wanted her to lead the French army against the English. She told the French king. He believed her and gave her a small army.

The English were ruling the French city of Orléans. Joan of Arc led the French army to fight for Orléans. They freed the city of Orléans from the English. But the war had not ended. The English and the French kept on fighting. Joan won other **battles**. Then the English captured Joan of Arc. She was **executed** by the English.

Joan of Arc made the French feel proud to fight for France. The French kept fighting after Joan died. In 1453 the French won the war. England lost most of its land in France.

King Ferdinand V

Queen Isabella

A Muslim building in Spain

France was a powerful monarchy by the end of the Middle Ages. French states were no longer ruled by nobles. Every state was ruled by the king of France. Everyone had to obey the French king and the king's laws.

Spain also became a nation during the Middle Ages. Like England and France, Spain had been ruled by the Romans and then by the barbarians. Then in the 700s, the Muslims conquered and ruled most of Spain. Many people in Spain were Roman Catholics. They did not want to be ruled by Muslims. Roman Catholics fought against the Muslims for about 500 years. Slowly the Catholics recaptured parts of Spain from the Muslims.

At that time Spain was made up of four states. In 1469 King Ferdinand V ruled one state. Queen Isabella ruled another state. Their states were joined when the king and queen married. Later the king and queen became the rulers of the other two states. King Ferdinand V and Queen Isabella led the fight against the Muslims. In 1492 the Catholics won the war against the Muslims. Then Catholics ruled all of Spain.

Spain became a monarchy. King Ferdinand V and Queen Isabella ruled the nation. They made laws for all the people of Spain. One law said that everyone in Spain had to be Catholic. Muslims and Jews had to either leave Spain or become Catholics. People who were not Catholics were punished or killed. King Ferdinand V and Queen Isabella took power away from nobles and church leaders. They became powerful rulers. Spain was becoming an important nation.

England, France, and Spain became nations during the Middle Ages. Each nation had its own language, laws, and monarchs. Many other nations were also beginning. You will read about some of these nations in later chapters.

Using Vocabulary

Analogies   Use the words in dark print to best complete the sentences. Write the correct answers on your paper.

monarchy   isolation   Hundred Years' War   monarchs

1. The English Channel was to _____ in England as the Great Wall was to protection in China.

2. Pharaohs were to ancient Egypt as _____ were to England, France, and Spain during the Middle Ages.

3. A _____ was to England, France, and Spain as a dynasty was to ancient China.

4. Christian soldiers were to the Crusades as Joan of Arc was to the _____.

Read and Remember

Choose the Answer   Write the correct answers on your paper.

1. What separated England from France and the rest of Europe?

   Indian Ocean   Mediterranean Sea   English Channel

2. From where did William the Conqueror come?

   northern France   Spain   Italy

3. For which nation did Joan of Arc and her soldiers win an important battle in the Hundred Years' War?

   England   France   Spain

4. Which nation did King Ferdinand V and Queen Isabella rule after they won the war against the Muslims?

   England   France   Spain

5. Which people in Spain were punished or killed because of their religion?

   Christians   Catholics   Muslims

Think and Apply

Compare and Contrast Read each sentence below. Decide whether it tells about England, France, or Spain. Write **E** on your paper for each sentence that tells about England. Write **F** on your paper for each sentence that tells about France. Write **S** on your paper for each sentence that tells about Spain.

1. The Muslims conquered this land in the Middle Ages.

2. This nation was conquered by a French noble who then became the king.

3. This nation won the battle at the city of Orléans.

4. A law in this nation said that all people had to be Catholic.

5. This nation is separated by water from the rest of Europe.

Skill Builder

Reading a Chart Read the chart below about three new nations. Then write on your paper the answer to each question.

THREE NEW NATIONS

Nation	Date	Events
England	1066	William the Conqueror invaded England and became king. England became one nation.
France	1453	France won the Hundred Years' War. England lost most of its land in France.
Spain	1492	Catholics won the war against Muslims. The states of Spain became one nation under King Ferdinand V and Queen Isabella.

1. When did William the Conqueror invade England?

2. What states became one nation in 1492?

3. What happened when France won the Hundred Years' War?

4. Which was the first to become a nation: Spain, England, or France?

5. In what year did the Catholics win a war against the Muslims?

CHAPTER 15

The Growth of Democracy

The monarchs of Europe were powerful leaders. They believed that God gave them the right to be rulers. The monarchs believed they should make all the laws. Everyone had to obey the monarchs. England was one of the first countries in Europe where monarchs became less powerful. In this chapter you will learn how England slowly became a democracy.

Democracy means rule by the people. Democracy was a powerful idea. It changed the way monarchs ruled their nations. In a democracy people have a voice in their government. In a democracy people

Nobles in England wanted King John to have less power, so they forced him to sign the Magna Carta.

Magna Carta

King John

People paying taxes

vote for their leaders. People vote for men and women who will make their laws. It took hundreds of years for England to become a democracy. It took even longer for democracy to begin in other nations.

In Chapter 7 you read about the world's first democracy. It began in Athens. When Athens was conquered, that democracy ended. During the Middle Ages, people did not rule themselves. They were ruled by powerful nobles and monarchs.

In Chapter 14 you read that William the Conqueror became king of England in 1066. He was a powerful king. But William did not make the laws by himself. He asked a group of nobles and church leaders to help him. Groups of nobles and church leaders also helped the kings who ruled after William. By the year 1300, less powerful people also helped the kings make laws. This was a small step toward democracy.

Another step toward democracy was the **Magna Carta**. The Magna Carta was a paper that said the king must obey the laws. It said a king could not make all the tax laws by himself. It also said that the king could not send people to **prison** just because he did not like them. The king no longer had full power. The Magna Carta was signed by King John, who ruled England from 1199 to 1216. A group of nobles forced King John to sign the Magna Carta in 1215.

Why did King John have to sign the Magna Carta? The nobles in England did not like King John or his taxes. King John often did not obey the laws of England. The nobles wanted King John to have less power. So they wrote the Magna Carta. The nobles said they would not pay any more taxes unless King John signed the Magna Carta. At first King John would not sign. The nobles put together a big army. King John knew he could not **defeat** the nobles' army. He also needed tax money. So he signed the Magna Carta.

How did the Magna Carta change England? Before the Magna Carta, the king could send anyone

Parliament building

King Edward I

to prison. After the Magna Carta, an accused person could not be sent to prison without a trial by **jury**. A jury is a group of people who hear information about an accused person and the crime. Then the jury decides if the accused person has **broken the law**. Today in a democracy, every accused person has the right to a jury trial.

After the Magna Carta was signed, the king could no longer make tax laws by himself. The king worked with a group of people to make laws. This group became known as **Parliament**. When the king wanted people to pay more taxes, he had to ask members of Parliament. They decided whether the people should pay more taxes.

Parliament became important in England. The king no longer had full power. The king had to obey the laws of Parliament. The king could not get tax money without Parliament's help. Parliament brought England closer to democracy.

At first only nobles worked in Parliament. In 1295 people from the **middle class** began to work in Parliament also. In that year King Edward I divided Parliament into two parts. The nobles in Parliament worked in the part called the **House of Lords**. The other part of Parliament was called the **House of Commons**. Middle-class people worked in the House of Commons. Most people in England were not nobles. England moved closer to democracy as the House of Commons became more powerful. After hundreds of years, the House of Commons was more powerful than the House of Lords.

The English **Bill of Rights** of 1689 brought England closer to democracy. It made Parliament more powerful than the English monarch. The Bill of Rights gave Parliament more power to make laws. All tax laws would be written by Parliament. The Bill of Rights gave **freedom of speech** in Parliament to the English people. This means people were allowed to speak in Parliament against the government. The

In 1295 King Edward I divided Parliament into two parts. He is shown here with the House of Lords.

John Locke

Bill of Rights also said that people have a right to a fair and speedy trial. Kings and queens in England ruled together with Parliament.

A man named John Locke helped spread the ideas of democracy. John Locke lived most of his life in England. In 1690 he wrote about his ideas. He wrote that people should choose their rulers. He wrote that people have the right to make laws for themselves. Governments must help and protect people. Locke wrote that kings should not be powerful rulers. Many people liked John Locke's ideas. His ideas helped England's Parliament become stronger. Other nations used Locke's ideas to become democracies.

While England was becoming a democracy, many other changes were taking place in Europe. How were other parts of Europe changing? The answers are in Chapter 16.

Using Vocabulary

Finish Up   Choose words in dark print to best complete the sentences. Write on your paper the words you choose.

**freedom of speech   middle class   jury
House of Lords   Bill of Rights**

1. People in the _____ were not as rich as nobles or as poor as peasants.

2. The English _____ of 1689 was a paper that gave more power to Parliament and more rights to the English people.

3. The right of _____ gave people the right to speak out against the government.

4. Nobles worked in a part of Parliament called the _____ .

5. The Magna Carta said that an accused person could not be sent to prison without a trial by a group of people called a _____ .

Read and Remember

Who Am I?   Read each sentence. Then look at the words in dark print for the name of the person who might have said it. Write on your paper the name of the person you choose.

King John   William the Conqueror   John Locke   King Edward I

1. "I ruled England from 1066 and asked nobles and church leaders to help write the laws."

2. "The nobles would not pay more taxes until I gave up some of my power."

3. "I divided Parliament into two parts so that both the nobles and the middle class could make laws."

4. "I wrote that people should be able to choose their rulers and make laws for themselves."

Think and Apply

Categories   Read the words in each group. Decide how they are alike. Choose the best title for each group from the words in dark print. Write the title on your paper.

Democracy   Parliament   King John   Magna Carta

1. made high taxes
had too much power
signed the Magna Carta

2. trial by jury
written by nobles
king lost power

3. citizens vote
first began in Athens
Parliament made laws

4. writes England's laws
House of Commons
House of Lords

Skill Builder

Reading a Population Map
A **population map** shows
the number of people living in
different places. The map key
of a population map gives colors
or patterns for different numbers
of people. This map shows how
many people per square mile were
living in Europe in 1300. Study the
map. Number your paper from
1 to 4. Then write on your paper
the answer to each question below.

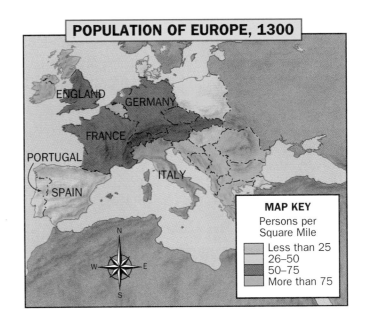

POPULATION OF EUROPE, 1300

MAP KEY
Persons per
Square Mile

Less than 25
26–50
50–75
More than 75

1. What color shows less than 25 people per square mile?

2. How many people per square mile lived in England in 1300?

3. Did France, Spain, or Italy have more people per square mile in 1300?

4. Which two nations had about the same number of people per square mile as Germany had?

CHAPTER 16

The Renaissance

In 1508 the pope gave the artist Michelangelo an important job. The artist was asked to paint the ceiling of a large church in Rome. For four long years, Michelangelo painted the ceiling of the famous Sistine Chapel. He lay flat on his back on top of a high platform as he painted the ceiling. Michelangelo painted pictures that told stories from the Bible. You can see part of this famous work on page 91. Michelangelo was one of the great artists of the **Renaissance**.

The word *Renaissance* means "to be born again," or "**rebirth**." During the Renaissance there was a rebirth of learning in Europe. There was a rebirth of art. People began learning more about science and math. They created new kinds of music. They wrote new **literature**. People asked many questions about the world during the Renaissance. New ideas were born.

The Renaissance began about the year 1300 in Italy. It spread to other countries in Europe in the

Lorenzo de Medici was a wealthy man who spent much of his money on Renaissance art and buildings.

THINK ABOUT AS YOU READ

1. **What was the Renaissance?**
2. **How did the Renaissance change Europe?**
3. **Who were some of the important people in the Renaissance?**

NEW WORDS

- ♦ **Renaissance**
- ♦ **rebirth**
- ♦ **literature**
- ♦ **religious**
- ♦ **Scientific Revolution**
- ♦ **movable type**

PEOPLE & PLACES

- ♦ **Michelangelo**
- ♦ **Sistine Chapel**
- ♦ **Leonardo da Vinci**
- ♦ **Tarquinia Molza**
- ♦ **Johannes Gutenberg**
- ♦ **William Shakespeare**
- ♦ **Elizabeth I**
- ♦ **Henry VIII**
- ♦ **Anne Boleyn**
- ♦ **Spanish**

Renaissance artists sometimes painted pictures about daily life. Here peasants enjoy a wedding feast.

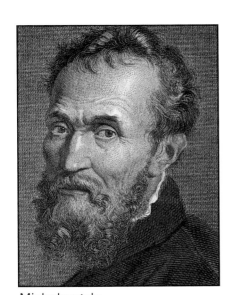
Michelangelo

Michelangelo's statue *David*

late 1400s. The Renaissance lasted about 300 years. It brought important changes to Europe.

What was Europe like before the Renaissance? Before the Renaissance, religion was very important in Europe. People were concerned about going to heaven after they died. Most artists painted only **religious** pictures. Schools in Europe were usually part of churches. Most people did not go to school and could not read or write.

The Renaissance changed Europe. Although religion was still important, people stopped waiting for a good life in heaven. People wanted to enjoy life on earth before they died. Artists painted religious pictures as well as many other kinds of pictures. They tried to find new and better ways to make paintings and statues. Learning became important. Many schools were started. More people went to school.

During the Renaissance, people studied works of art from ancient Greece and Rome. They used ideas from long ago to make new works of art. They also wrote new kinds of literature.

The Renaissance first began in Italy. There are many reasons why it began there. Italy was the center of world trade at that time. Ships from Italy went to

Leonardo da Vinci

Da Vinci's painting *Mona Lisa*

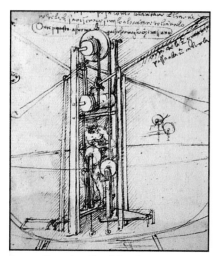
Invention by Da Vinci

Africa and Asia. People brought back to Italy ideas from Asia and Africa. Artists and writers used these ideas to create new kinds of work. The Roman Catholic Church also encouraged arts and learning.

Rich people in Italy gave artists money so that the artists could work. The pope and the Roman Catholic Church also gave artists money to do their work. This helped the growth of art in Italy.

Italy was a center of learning. People from other parts of Europe came to Italy to study with great artists. These people brought ideas from Italy back to other parts of Europe. The Renaissance slowly spread to England, France, Spain, and many other parts of Europe.

Leonardo da Vinci was one of the greatest people of the Renaissance. He lived in Italy. He became one of the world's great artists. His painting *Mona Lisa* became very famous. Da Vinci did more than paint well. He also knew a lot about math and science. He drew pictures for new inventions. He also drew plans for new buildings. Da Vinci was called a "Renaissance Man" because he did so many different things well.

There were also famous women in the Renaissance. Some rich women gave money to artists and writers. Some women were artists. Their paintings are still enjoyed today. One woman, Tarquinia Molza, was a "Renaissance Woman." She spoke many languages and studied math and science.

The **Scientific Revolution** began during the Renaissance. This was a time of many inventions and discoveries. Scientists showed that it was important to experiment and to watch things closely. Important facts were learned about the sun, the earth, and the planets. People learned more about medicine and how the human body works.

Books were important during the Renaissance. In China, people had been printing books for hundreds of years. In Europe before the Renaissance, books were still being written by hand. There were few

Johannes Gutenberg was able to print books very quickly with his movable type invention.

William Shakespeare

Many of Shakespeare's plays were performed in this theater.

books in Europe. People in Europe then learned to print books using woodblock printing.

A man named Johannes Gutenberg changed the way books were made in Europe. About the year 1450, Gutenberg began to use **movable type** to print books. Movable type was a faster, easier way to make books. People no longer had to carve out each letter. By 1500 there were millions of books in Europe. People started new libraries. Many people learned new ideas by reading books. Many Christians who could read were now able to have their own Bibles at home.

William Shakespeare was an important writer during the English Renaissance. He wrote many wonderful plays. Some plays were very funny, and some were very sad. Shakespeare's plays are about 400 years old. They are part of the world's great literature.

The Renaissance brought lasting changes to Europe. Science and learning became more important. New ideas about art and literature were spread across Europe. Art, music, and plays were created that are still enjoyed today.

Changes in religion also took place during the Renaissance. Why was religion changing? Read the next chapter to find the answer.

Queen Elizabeth I (1533–1603)

Elizabeth I was the daughter of King Henry VIII of England and his second wife, Anne Boleyn. Elizabeth was born in England in 1533. As a child she learned to be a gifted speaker, artist, and musician. In 1558, a few years after King Henry VIII died, Elizabeth I became queen of England. She never married. She ruled as England's monarch until her death in 1603.

Elizabeth made many changes in England during her rule. She made the Church of England the main church of the nation. Queen Elizabeth also worked to end money problems in England. She did this by building up England's trade with other countries. She also ended an expensive war with France.

Queen Elizabeth encouraged people to explore other parts of the world for England. People from England went to North America to set up colonies. An English trade company set up trade between England and parts of Asia, including India. England grew rich through trade.

Queen Elizabeth I

Queen Elizabeth also helped England build a powerful navy. During Queen Elizabeth's rule, England's navy defeated the strong Spanish navy. The strong English navy helped the nation become a leading world power.

Elizabeth encouraged the growth of ideas during the Renaissance. During her rule, new music and works of art were created. Important literature was written. William Shakespeare wrote his poems and plays during this time.

Queen Elizabeth helped England gain wealth, power, and culture. Her rule has been called the Golden Age of England.

Using Vocabulary

Match Up Finish the sentences in Group A with words from Group B. Write on your paper the letter of each correct answer.

Group A

1. Religion was very important before the Renaissance, so most artists painted only _____ pictures.

2. *Renaissance* means "_____," or "to be born again."

3. Books, plays, and other written works are all types of _____.

4. The _____ was a time of many discoveries and inventions.

Group B

a. rebirth

b. Scientific Revolution

c. literature

d. religious

Read and Remember

Finish the Sentence Write on your paper the word or words that best complete each sentence.

1. The pictures painted by _____ told about stories from the Bible.

    Mona Lisa   Michelangelo   Tarquinia Molza

2. The Renaissance began in _____.

    England   France   Italy

3. _____ used movable type to print books during the Renaissance.

    Leonardo da Vinci   Johannes Gutenberg   Michelangelo

4. William Shakespeare wrote some of the world's best _____.

    literature   Bible stories   science experiments

5. Queen Elizabeth helped end England's money problems by encouraging _____.

    religion   trade   wars

Journal Writing

Write a paragraph that explains how Europe changed during the Renaissance. Tell at least three ways that Europe changed.

Skill Builder

Reading a Flow Chart   A **flow chart** shows you facts in the correct order they occur. This flow chart shows how a book is **bound**, or put together. Read the chart. Then write on your paper the words that complete the sentences.

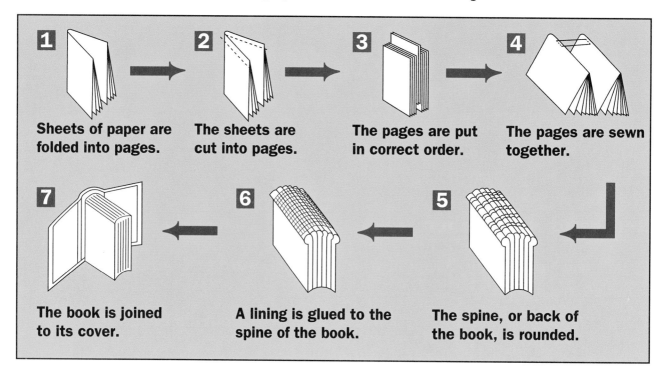

1. Sheets of paper are folded into pages.
2. The sheets are cut into pages.
3. The pages are put in correct order.
4. The pages are sewn together.
5. The spine, or back of the book, is rounded.
6. A lining is glued to the spine of the book.
7. The book is joined to its cover.

1. In the first step, the sheets of paper are _____ into pages.

    sewn   torn   folded

2. After the pages are put in the correct order, they are _____.

    glued to the cover   sewn together   cut in half

3. In step 5 the spine of the book is _____.

    rounded   flattened   glued

4. In the last step, the book is joined to its _____.

    lining   cover   needle

The Reformation

The Roman Catholic Church was rich and powerful during the Middle Ages. In western Europe all Christians belonged to the Roman Catholic Church. About the year 1500, some Catholics wanted to make changes in the Church. These people started the **Reformation**.

The Reformation was a movement to change the Roman Catholic Church. People tried to change some teachings and practices of the Church.

Why did some Catholics work to make changes in the Church? They thought that the pope and the Catholic Church had too much power, land, and wealth. They thought that the leaders of the Catholic Church were **abusing** their power. Peasants, nobles, and kings had to obey the pope and pay taxes to the Church. Much of the tax money was sent to the pope in Rome. Some Catholics were unhappy because

NEW WORDS

♦ Reformation
♦ abusing
♦ indulgences
♦ forgiven
♦ 95 Theses
♦ divorce
♦ Counter-Reformation

PEOPLE & PLACES

♦ Martin Luther
♦ Germany
♦ Pope Leo X
♦ Protestants
♦ Queen Catherine
♦ Jesuits

Martin Luther nailed to a church door a list called the 95 Theses. This list told about the bad practices of the Church.

they had to pay taxes to the Church in Rome. Others felt that the leaders of the Church no longer cared about religion.

Many Catholics were also unhappy because the Church was selling **indulgences**. An indulgence was a paper that said a person's sins were **forgiven**. People thought these indulgences would help them go to heaven when they died. At first, a person had to earn an indulgence by praying and by doing good work. Later, anyone could buy an indulgence. Some priests sold indulgences so that they could earn money for themselves. Many people thought that the Church should not sell indulgences.

Martin Luther

Martin Luther was a Catholic priest in Germany. In 1517 he wrote a list of statements about the bad practices of the Church. This list was called the **95 Theses**. Luther's list told people that it was wrong for the Church to sell indulgences. Luther nailed the 95 Theses to the doors of a church in Germany. Martin Luther became a leader of the Reformation. He did not want to leave the Catholic Church. Instead, he hoped to change the Church.

Martin Luther wanted everyone to read the Bible. He said that the Bible told people how to be good Christians. Luther said that people did not need a pope to tell them what the Bible said or how to be good Christians.

Pope Leo X

The pope and other Church leaders told Martin Luther to stop speaking out against the Catholic Church. But Luther would not stop spreading his ideas. So in 1520 Pope Leo X told Luther that he could no longer be a member of the Catholic Church.

Many people listened to Martin Luther's ideas. They started new churches. These Christians were no longer Catholics. They were called Protestants. Many Protestant churches were built in Europe. Today there are millions of Protestants around the world.

People in England also did not want to pay taxes to the Catholic Church. The Church held much land

Queen Catherine

King Henry VIII

Anne Boleyn

and power in England. England's king did not want to obey a pope in Rome.

King Henry VIII of England worked against the Catholic Church. Henry was a Catholic. He was married to Queen Catherine. Henry wanted to marry Anne Boleyn. Henry asked the pope to end his marriage to Catherine. But the pope said no. The pope was very powerful.

Henry was angry. Henry and Parliament made two new laws. In 1529 a law was passed that said that the pope had no power in England. In 1534 another law said that the king, not the pope, was the leader of the Church of England. King Henry VIII became the leader of the Church of England. He became a Protestant. The Church of England became a Protestant church. The Catholic Church and the pope had lost power in England. Henry got a **divorce** from Queen Catherine. He married Anne Boleyn. Their daughter, Elizabeth, would one day become one of England's greatest queens. You read about Queen Elizabeth in Chapter 16.

The pope and the other leaders of the Catholic Church did not want people to become Protestants. They wanted people to stay or to become Catholics. The pope and the other leaders of the Church started the **Counter-Reformation**. This was a time when the Catholic Church made changes. The Church

This Protestant minister was one of the important leaders of the Reformation. Here he is speaking to a group of nobles.

Jesuit priest

Page from the Gutenberg bible

stopped selling indulgences. More Catholic priests began to travel across Europe to teach people how to be Catholics. These priests were called Jesuits. They started many schools in Europe. The Jesuits taught many people about the Catholic religion.

After the Reformation, religious wars began in Europe. Catholics believed their religion was the only true religion. They wanted all people to be Catholics. Protestants believed their religion was the only true religion. They wanted all people to be Protestants. All over Europe, Protestants and Catholics fought about religion. They would continue to fight for hundreds of years.

The Reformation brought many changes to Europe. During the Middle Ages, few people knew how to read. Protestants believed that everyone should be able to read the Bible. Many new schools were started. Many people learned to read and write. The Roman Catholic Church was no longer the only church in western Europe. Europe now had many Protestant churches. The pope had less power. The monarchs of Europe had become more powerful. The Reformation caused many changes that can still be felt today.

Using Vocabulary

Find the Meaning   Write on your paper the word or words that best complete each sentence.

1. The **Reformation** was a movement to change the _____.

   Roman Catholic Church   Crusades   Renaissance

2. An **indulgence** said that a person's sins were _____.

   good   bad   forgiven

3. The **95 Theses** was a list that told people that it was wrong for the Roman Catholic Church to sell _____.

   indulgences   Bibles   goods

4. A **divorce** allowed Henry VIII to end his _____.

   marriage   taxes   Church of England

Read and Remember

Choose the Answer   Write the correct answers on your paper.

1. Who told Martin Luther he could no longer be a member of the Church?
   Pope Leo X   Henry VIII   God

2. What did Martin Luther want people to read?
   the Koran   the Bible   Greek plays

3. Who did Henry VIII's law of 1529 say had no power in England?
   the pope   the queen   the middle class

4. Who traveled across Europe to teach people about being Catholics?
   Protestants   Anne Boleyn   Jesuits

5. Which group became more powerful in Europe after the Reformation?
   monarchs   popes   Catholic priests

Finish the Paragraph   Number your paper from 1 to 5. Use the words in dark print to finish the paragraph below. Write on your paper the words you choose.

Protestants   taxes   abusing   indulgences   Martin Luther

___1___ wrote the 95 Theses about the bad practices of the Roman Catholic Church. He believed that the pope and other Church leaders were ___2___ their power. Many Catholics did not like paying ___3___ to the Church in Rome. They also believed that the Church should not sell ___4___ . For these reasons many Catholics chose to become ___5___ during the Reformation.

Journal Writing

Both Martin Luther and King Henry VIII were unhappy with the Catholic Church. Write a few sentences that tell why each was unhappy with the Church.

Think and Apply

Cause and Effect   Write sentences on your paper by matching each cause on the left with an effect on the right.

Cause

1. Catholics wanted to go to heaven when they died, so _____

2. The pope would not allow King Henry VIII to divorce Catherine, so _____

3. The Church did not want Catholics to become Protestants, so _____

4. Both Catholics and Protestants believed that their religion was the only true religion, so _____

Effect

a. Henry VIII made the Church of England a Protestant church.

b. it started the Counter-Reformation.

c. they fought religious wars.

d. they bought indulgences.

Explorers Find New Lands

Would you have wanted to sail across the ocean in the year 1500? You would have sailed slowly in a small ship. Your ship might have been destroyed by strong winds. You might have gotten lost and never returned home. Hundreds of years ago, many explorers bravely sailed across oceans to look for new lands.

Exploration was very important during the Renaissance. Inventions, such as better ships and an improved **compass**, made it easier to explore other lands. The explorations of the Renaissance were the beginning of a time period known as the Age of Exploration.

There were many reasons why people became explorers. Some people became explorers because of trade. They wanted to bring silks and spices from Asia back to Europe. But the land routes to Asia were difficult. Also, merchants who traded goods

On his voyage around Africa to India, Vasco da Gama visited this African king.

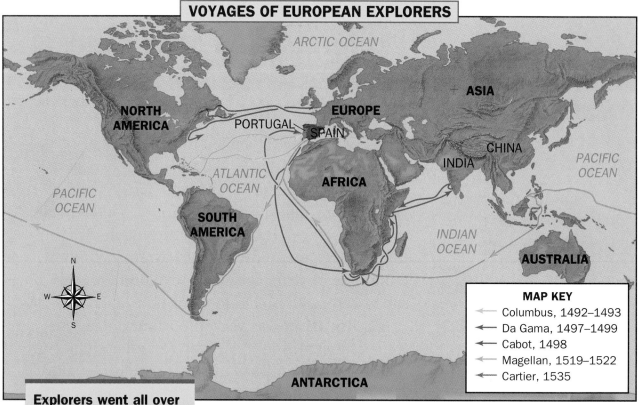

VOYAGES OF EUROPEAN EXPLORERS

MAP KEY
- Columbus, 1492–1493
- Da Gama, 1497–1499
- Cabot, 1498
- Magellan, 1519–1522
- Cartier, 1535

Explorers went all over the world. Which explorer on the map was the only one to sail on the Pacific Ocean?

Vasco da Gama

along the routes increased the prices. So explorers wanted to find new ways to go to Asia.

Some people became explorers because they wanted to find gold. Other people wanted to spread Christianity to people in far-off lands. Some people became explorers for their kings. Many kings in Europe wanted to rule more land. These kings paid explorers to find new lands for them to rule.

Vasco da Gama was an explorer from Portugal. He wanted to find a new way to go to India. In 1497 he left Portugal with four ships. Vasco da Gama and his crew were the first Europeans to go to Asia by sailing all the way around Africa to India. Find da Gama's route on the map above. Da Gama and his crew bought spices in India and sailed back to Portugal. The **voyage** took two years. Da Gama sold the spices for a lot of money. Soon many ships from Portugal sailed around Africa to trade in India.

Christopher Columbus also wanted to find a way to sail from Europe to Asia. At that time many people believed that the world was flat. But Columbus

Christopher Columbus met American Indians when his three ships landed off the coast of the Americas.

Christopher Columbus

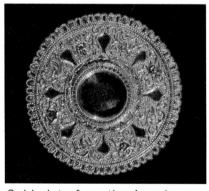
Gold plate from the Americas

believed that the world was round. He thought he could find a shorter way to reach Asia by sailing west across the Atlantic Ocean. King Ferdinand and Queen Isabella of Spain helped Columbus. They gave him three small ships.

In 1492 Columbus sailed across the Atlantic Ocean. The voyage was long and slow. After many weeks Columbus and his crew saw land. They did not know that there was land between Europe and Asia. Columbus thought they had reached India. But they were not in India. They had landed on islands off the coast of the Americas. Columbus and his crew were some of the first people from Europe to see the Americas. Europeans called this land the **New World**.

There were people already living in the New World. Columbus called them Indians because he thought he was in India. Today they are called American Indians, or Native Americans. The American Indians had many different civilizations at the time Columbus and other explorers reached the Americas.

Other explorers from Spain explored the lands in North America and South America. The Spanish explorers looked for gold in the New World. The king

Ferdinand Magellan

Jacques Cartier

John Cabot arriving in North America

of Spain said that most of South America belonged to Spain. He said that part of North America also belonged to Spain.

Ferdinand Magellan was another explorer who tried to go to Asia. He thought he could reach Asia by sailing around South America. In 1519 he sailed west from Spain with five ships. He and his crew sailed around South America to the Pacific Ocean. The voyage was hard, and most of the men died. Magellan died on an island in the Pacific. Only one ship was able to sail west to Africa and return to Spain. The 18 men on the ship had sailed all the way around the world in three years. The voyage proved that the world is round.

The French also wanted to find new ways to reach Asia. Jacques Cartier was a French explorer. He thought he could find a short cut to Asia through North America. He wanted to find a river in North America that would go all the way to Asia.

In 1534 Jacques Cartier sailed from France to North America. Cartier and his crew explored the St. Lawrence River in an area that Cartier called Canada. Cartier claimed land in Canada for France. Cartier explored part of the St. Lawrence River from 1535 to 1536. When the river became very narrow, Cartier knew that it was not a short cut to Asia.

The English also wanted to find a short cut to Asia. In 1497 John Cabot sailed west from England. He explored part of North America. Like Cartier, Cabot did not find a new way to Asia. But the king of England said that all of the land Cabot explored in North America belonged to England.

The world learned many things from the explorers of long ago. The explorers showed that ships could sail around Africa to reach Asia. Explorers proved that the world was round and not flat. The Europeans learned about other lands and civilizations. In the next chapter, you will learn about some of the different civilizations in Africa and the Americas.

Using Vocabulary

Analogies   Use the words in dark print to best complete the sentences. Write the correct answers on your paper.

compass   voyage   New World   exploration

1. Marco Polo is to China as Christopher Columbus is to the _____ .

2. Artist is to paintbrush as sailor is to _____ .

3. Invent is to invention as explore is to _____ .

4. Battle is to fight as journey is to _____ .

Read and Remember

Find the Answer   Find the sentences below that tell something true about why people in Europe became explorers. Write on your paper the sentences you find. You should find four sentences.

1. Europeans wanted to find a shorter route to Asia.

2. People in Europe wanted to see Martin Luther.

3. People wanted to find gold.

4. People wanted to spread Christianity to other lands.

5. People wanted to live in England.

6. People wanted to live on manors.

7. People wanted to help their kings rule more land.

Journal Writing

There were many explorers during the Age of Exploration. Pick one of the five explorers mentioned in this chapter. Write a few sentences that explain why this explorer was important.

Think and Apply

Sequencing Events   Number your paper from 1 to 5. Write the sentences to show the correct order.

Vasco da Gama left Portugal in 1497 and sailed around Africa to India.

Ferdinand Magellan set sail in 1519 on the voyage that proved the world is round.

Jacques Cartier claimed new land in Canada for France in 1534.

In 1492 Columbus sailed across the Atlantic Ocean to find a shorter way to Asia.

Magellan's crew returned to Spain after three years of sailing all around the world.

Skill Builder

Reading a Historical Map   A **historical map** shows information about events and places during a certain time period. The historical map on page 118 shows the routes of some explorers in the 1400s and 1500s. Study the map. Number your paper from 1 to 8. Then write on your paper the answer to each question below.

1. When was da Gama's voyage?

2. What color is used on the map to show Columbus' route?

3. Which three explorers sailed only in the Atlantic Ocean?

4. What land did da Gama sail around?

5. Which explorer sailed around South America?

6. Who sailed farthest south?

7. Which explorer sailed down the east coast of North America in 1498?

8. Which explorer sailed later than the other explorers did?

Skill Builder

Reading a Double Bar Graph
A **double bar graph** compares facts by using two different colored bars. This double bar graph shows how much gold and silver was shipped to Spain from the Americas from 1531 to 1560. The blue bar shows how much gold was shipped to Spain. The green bar shows how much silver was shipped to Spain. Study the bar graph. Number your paper from 1 to 5. Then write on your paper the numbers, dates, or words that best complete the sentences below.

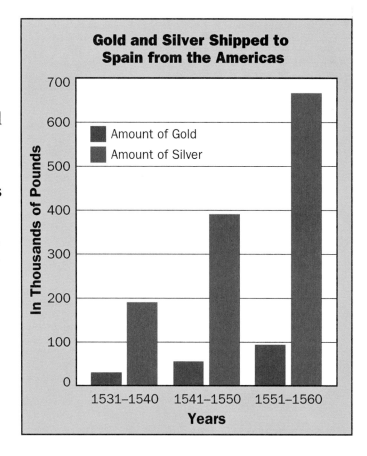

1. The bar graph shows that more _____ was shipped to Spain from the Americas from 1531 to 1560.

   gold   silver   copper

2. The largest amount of gold was shipped to Spain during the years _____ .

   1531–1540   1541–1550   1551–1560

3. During the years 1531–1540, Spain received about _____ pounds of silver.

   100 thousand   200 thousand   400 thousand

4. The amounts of both gold and silver being shipped to Spain _____ from 1531 to 1560.

   increased   decreased   stayed about the same

5. Spain received about _____ pounds more silver in 1541–1550 than in 1531–1540.

   100 thousand   200 thousand   400 thousand

Civilizations in Africa and the Americas

Archaeologists have found many Stone Age bones and tools in Africa and in the Americas. After the Stone Age, many civilizations developed on these continents. You have already read about the great civilization of ancient Egypt in Africa.

Africa is a land of gold and many other natural resources. Africa also has forests, meadows, and deserts. The Sahara is the world's largest desert. It is in northern Africa. To trade gold and salt in northern and western Africa, many people crossed the Sahara on camels in large **caravans**.

Between A.D. 300 and 1600, great trading empires began in Africa. Some of these empires developed in western Africa, just south of the Sahara. One trading empire in western Africa was Ghana. It developed in the 300s. The rulers of Ghana taxed the goods that passed through the empire. The Ghana Empire became wealthy from these taxes.

These buildings of the city of Zimbabwe were first built in Africa around A.D. 1000.

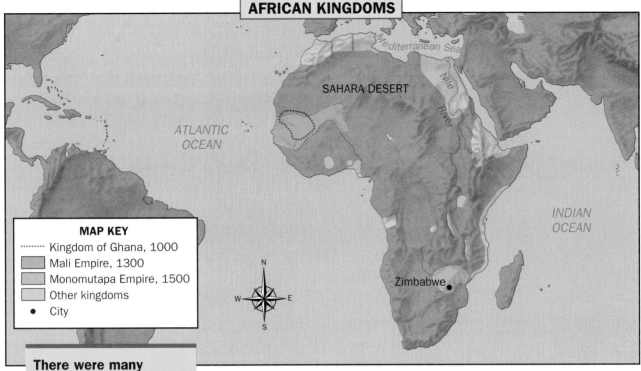

MAP KEY
········ Kingdom of Ghana, 1000
▢ Mali Empire, 1300
▢ Monomutapa Empire, 1500
▢ Other kingdoms
• City

There were many African civilizations all over the continent. What was one empire near the Indian Ocean?

African woman at a market

The people of Ghana were among the first in Africa to use iron to make tools and weapons. These strong weapons helped the people of Ghana conquer other groups of people. By the year 1000, Ghana was a very strong empire. But soon other people conquered Ghana. During the 1200s Ghana became part of the Mali Empire.

Other empires began in southeastern Africa. The city of Zimbabwe was built around A.D. 1000. The word *zimbabwe* means "house of stone." During the 1400s Zimbabwe became part of a rich and powerful empire. This empire was the Monomutapa Empire. The empire gained most of its wealth from the mining and trading of gold. Like Ghana, the Monomutapa Empire taxed all the goods that passed through its lands. Many stone buildings from the Monomutapa Empire have been found in the modern country of Zimbabwe.

Many of the customs from these and other African civilizations are still followed today. Many people in Africa make items that other Africans made hundreds of years ago. One such item is jewelry. Some people also wear clothing that is like the clothing worn in Africa long ago. Customs are very important all over Africa.

While civilizations were developing in Africa, other civilizations were beginning in the Americas. Two of the most advanced American Indian civilizations were in Mexico and in South America. One was the Aztec. The Aztec civilization began in Mexico around the year A.D. 1200. By the 1400s the Aztec had a wealthy empire with a strong government. Religion was very important to the Aztec. They believed in many gods. They went to war to capture people that they could **sacrifice** to the gods.

The Aztec had many skills. They created land for farms by digging up mud from the bottom of a nearby lake. They used the mud to form islands. They grew crops such as corn on the islands. The Aztec also developed a written language in which pictures stood for ideas. They invented a calendar. They made works of art out of gold and stones. Many Aztec foods such as chocolate and tacos are still enjoyed today.

Aztec calendar stone

CIVILIZATIONS IN AFRICA AND THE AMERICAS

Civilization	Location	Dates	Interesting Facts
Ghana	West Africa	about A.D. 300–1076	Made iron weapons. Controlled caravan routes through the Sahara.
Monomutapa	Southeast Africa	about 1450– early 1500s	Made buildings using stones without clay.
Aztec	Mexico in North America	about 1200–1521	Developed written language and calendar. Sacrificed people to the gods.
Inca	Andes Mountains in South America	about 1200–1532	Built roads and bridges. Built large temples.
Algonquin	Eastern Woodlands region of North America	?–present	Used wood and animal skins to build homes. Used canoes, snowshoes, and sleds for travel.
Hopi	Southwest region of North America	?–present	Grew cotton and wove it into cloth. Built homes with adobe.

The Inca built their cities in the tall mountains of the Andes.

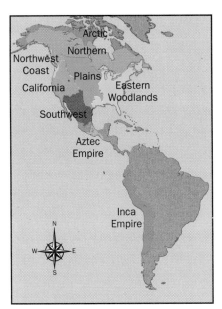
American Indians, 1500

American Indians adapted to their regions.

The Inca in South America were developing their own empire at about the same time as were the Aztec. Their civilization began around 1200 in the Andes Mountains of South America. They made their civilization larger by conquering nearby groups of people. By the 1400s the Inca had formed an empire.

Religion was an important part of the Inca way of life. The Inca believed in many gods. The Inca also made beautiful cloth and works of art. They irrigated their farms. They did not have a system of writing.

The Inca were known for their building skills. They built many temples and government buildings. They built thousands of miles of roads. They also built bridges that went across rivers and between mountains to connect roads.

Many American Indian groups lived in different **regions** of North America. Each group **adapted** to the different resources and climates of the regions where they lived. Different groups within the same region often developed similar cultures. The map on this page shows some of the different regions in North America.

One group of American Indians who lived in the Eastern Woodlands region was the Algonquin. Many Algonquin also lived in the southeast part of

Many American Indians living in the Southwest region of North America used adobe to build their homes.

Algonquin village

Hopi today

Canada. There are many forests, lakes, and rivers in the areas where they lived. The Algonquin fished and hunted to get food. They also gathered berries and wild plants for food. They used animal skins for their clothes and homes. The Algonquin also used wood from trees to make their homes. They had their own religion. There are still Algonquin living in North America today.

The Hopi were a peaceful group of American Indians who lived in the Southwest. Religion was very important to the Hopi. The climate where the Hopi lived is hot and dry. Few plants and animals live there. However, there are some large rivers in the Southwest. The Hopi hunted animals and gathered nuts and seeds. They also used river water to grow crops. They grew cotton to make their clothing. There is little wood in the Southwest. So the Hopi used **adobe** to make their houses. Adobe is a mixture of desert clay and straw. Today many Hopi still live in the Southwest.

What happened to the civilizations in Africa and the Americas after Europeans arrived? The next chapter provides the answer to this question.

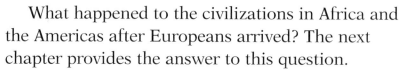

Mansa Musa (1297?–1332)

The Mali Empire began in western Africa during the early 1200s. Ghana became part of the Mali Empire. Mali was a strong, large empire. It gained much wealth by controlling the gold and salt trade. Mali became a center of trade.

In 1307 Mansa Musa became king of Mali. He was a great ruler. Mansa Musa made the Mali Empire a center of culture in western Africa. He also made the Mali Empire much larger. He did this by conquering people in nearby lands. Mansa Musa also used peaceful ways to gain more land.

Mansa Musa was a Muslim. He spread Islam throughout the empire. He had mosques built in many cities in the empire. Like all Muslims he was required to visit Mecca. So in 1324 Mansa Musa began a pilgrimage to Mecca. It took him more than a year to travel the 3,500 miles. Thousands of his people went with him. Hundreds of camels carried gold. Mansa Musa gave away gold to poor people he met on his pilgrimage.

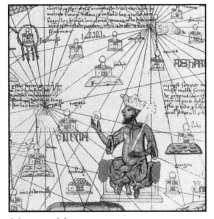

Mansa Musa

Mansa Musa brought back to Mali teachers and builders he met on his pilgrimage. He had the builders construct a school in the Mali city of Timbuktu. Timbuktu became a great center of learning. People in Timbuktu could study Islam and law. Timbuktu also became a center of trade.

Mansa Musa ruled Mali until 1332. During his rule, Mali was a large and powerful empire. The rulers who came after Mansa Musa were weak. They could not control the large empire. About one hundred years after Mansa Musa's death, Mali was conquered by people in another empire. The great Mali empire came to an end.

Using Vocabulary

Finish Up   Choose the words in dark print to best complete the sentences. Write on your paper the words you choose.

sacrifice   caravans   adobe   regions   adapted

1. Many _____ of people and animals crossed the Sahara to trade in northern Africa.

2. The Hopi _____ to the resources in their area by using river water to grow crops in the hot, dry climate.

3. Different _____ of a continent often also have different natural resources and climates.

4. The Aztec sometimes killed people because the Aztec believed they should _____ people to the gods.

5. The Hopi used _____, a mixture of desert clay and straw, to build their houses.

Read and Remember

Finish the Sentence   Write on your paper the word or words that best complete each sentence.

1. The _____ Empire became wealthy from the taxes on goods that passed through the empire.

   Aztec   Ghana   Inca

2. The rich and powerful Monomutapa Empire included the great city of _____ .

   Zimbabwe   Sahara   Timbuktu

3. The _____ are known for building bridges that reached across rivers and between mountains.

   Monomutapa   Aztec   Inca

4. The Algonquin Indians lived in the _____ region.

Southwest   Plains   Eastern Woodlands

5. Mansa Musa made a pilgrimage to Mecca from the _____ Empire.

Ghana   Inca   Mali

Think and Apply

Distinguishing Relevant Information   Imagine that you want to explain to a friend about life in early civilizations in Africa and the Americas. Read each sentence below. Decide which sentences are relevant to what you will say. Write the relevant sentences on your paper. There are four relevant sentences.

1. Religion was an important part of many civilizations in Africa and the Americas.

2. The Sahara is the world's largest desert.

3. The people of Ghana used iron to make their tools and weapons.

4. People could go to school in Timbuktu.

5. The Aztec made works of art out of gold and stones.

6. Many Hopi and Algonquin live in North America today.

7. The Andes are very tall mountains.

Skill Builder

Reading a Chart   Read the chart on page 126 about civilizations in Africa and the Americas. Then write on your paper the answer to each question.

1. What is one interesting fact about the Ghana Empire?

2. Where was the Monomutapa Empire located?

3. When did the Aztec civilization exist?

4. Which civilization lived in the Southwest region?

5. Which civilization sometimes had snow?

CHAPTER 20

Colonies for Europe

As you read in Chapter 18, European explorers traveled to many far-off lands. European countries began to start colonies  in Africa and the Americas. They also built up trade with India and China. The map on page 134 shows the American lands ruled by European countries.

Why did European countries want to rule colonies in the Americas? One reason was that the **ruling countries** wanted to find gold and silver in their colonies. Another reason was that colonies helped trade. They were good places for merchants to sell their goods. A third reason was that colonies gave the ruling countries **raw materials** that they did not have at home. Metals, cotton, and wood were important raw materials from the colonies. Colonies sent goods like coffee, sugar, and chocolate to their ruling countries. A fourth reason was that ruling countries also wanted to spread Christianity to the American Indians.

THINK ABOUT AS YOU READ

1. **Why did countries in Europe want to rule colonies?**
2. **How did ruling countries hurt their colonies?**
3. **What was the French and Indian War?**

NEW WORDS

♦ **ruling countries**
♦ **raw materials**
♦ **plantations**
♦ **trading posts**
♦ **freedom of religion**

PEOPLE & PLACES

♦ **Brazil**
♦ **Quebec**
♦ **Mississippi River**
♦ **Pilgrims**
♦ **Great Britain**
♦ **British**

European countries started colonies in the Americas.

Spain, Portugal, and England brought people from Africa to work as slaves in the colonies.

An American Indian dying from a European disease

In many ways the ruling countries hurt their colonies. Colonies were only allowed to trade with their ruling country. Colonies were not allowed to make many things they needed. The colonies needed cloth, guns, and tools. They had to buy these things from the ruling countries. The ruling countries became richer from this trade.

There were other ways that ruling countries hurt their colonies. The ruling countries wanted the people in the colonies to work for them. But the countries did not want to pay workers much money. Ruling countries wanted slaves to work in their colonies in mines and on large farms called **plantations**. Spain and Portugal forced American Indians to work as slaves. Spain, Portugal, and England also brought people from Africa to work as slaves in the colonies.

As more Europeans came to America, thousands of American Indians died. Many died from the hard, dangerous work they were forced to do as slaves. But even more died as a result of disease. Many Europeans brought diseases that had never before been in the Americas. Sometimes diseases killed entire groups of American Indians. Then the cultures of these American Indians were also destroyed.

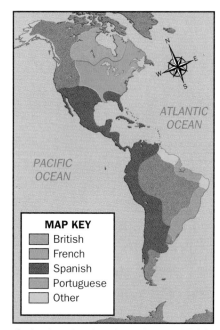

Colonies in the Americas, 1700

MAP KEY
British
French
Spanish
Portuguese
Other

Spanish soldiers conquered the Aztec in 1521.

Which European countries had colonies? Portugal had **trading posts** in India and China. It ruled colonies in Africa. In South America, Portugal also ruled a large colony called Brazil.

Spain also built a large empire. Spanish soldiers conquered the Aztec and Inca empires. Spain also conquered other lands in North America and in South America. Many Spanish colonies began. People in the Spanish colonies sent gold and silver to Spain.

France ruled colonies in North America. The French ruled Quebec and most of eastern Canada. They ruled land around the Mississippi River in North America.

The French came to North America to trade. The American Indians hunted many animals for their furs. The French traded with the American Indians for furs. In France the French sold these furs for a lot of money.

English people came to live in North America beginning in 1607. Some English people came to North America to find gold. Other English people came to North America because they wanted **freedom of religion**. Freedom of religion means that people can belong to any religious group they choose. Everyone in England had to belong to the Church of England. Many English people did not

The French traded with the American Indians for fur.

Many American Indians helped the French fight the British during the French and Indian War.

Pilgrims landing in North America

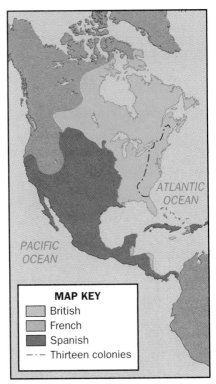
North America in 1763

MAP KEY
British
French
Spanish
— · — Thirteen colonies

PACIFIC OCEAN

ATLANTIC OCEAN

like the Church of England. Some of these people were called the Pilgrims. In 1620 the Pilgrims moved to North America. There they had religious freedom.

In 1707 England joined with two smaller nations to become part of a larger nation called Great Britain. The people of Great Britain became known as the British. The colonies of England were now called British colonies.

Great Britain did not want France to rule any colonies in North America. France did not want Great Britain to have colonies in North America. In 1754 the French and the British fought over who would rule North America. Their fight was called the French and Indian War. Many American Indians helped the French fight the British. The British army was stronger. In 1763 Great Britain won the war. France lost its colonies in North America. Now Great Britain and Spain ruled most of North America.

Great Britain ruled 13 colonies in America. But soon the people in these colonies decided they did not want to be ruled by Great Britain. You will learn about the American fight for freedom in Chapter 21.

Using Vocabulary

Finish the Paragraph   Number your paper from 1 to 4. Use the words in dark print to finish the paragraph below. Write on your paper the words you choose.

ruling countries   diseases   plantations   freedom of religion

Some Europeans came to the Americas because they were sent by their ___1___ to start colonies. Some English people who did not want to belong to the Church of England came to the Americas because they wanted ___2___. But the colonies hurt many American Indians and Africans. Many were forced to work as slaves on large farms called ___3___. Many American Indians became sick and died from European ___4___.

Read and Remember

Write the Answer   Write one or more sentences on your paper to answer each question.

1. Which ruling countries had both American Indians and African slaves in the colonies?

2. Which empires did the Spanish soldiers conquer in the Americas?

3. When did England become a part of Great Britain?

4. How did France lose its colonies in North America?

Journal Writing

Imagine that you were a colonist living in the Americas. Write a short letter to your king or queen. In your letter explain some of the ways the ruling country was hurting your colony.

Think and Apply

Exclusions   One word or phrase in each group does not belong. Find that word or phrase and write it on your paper. Then write on your paper a sentence that tells how the other words are alike.

1. Portugal
Spain
Brazil
France

2. find gold
increase trade
spread Christianity
get sick from diseases

3. coffee
sugar
land
chocolate

4. destroyed the Aztec Empire
settled in Quebec
traded for furs
went to war against Great Britain

Skill Builder

Reading a Circle Graph   A **circle graph** shows how all of something is divided into parts. Most often a circle graph shows **percent**, or parts per one hundred. This circle graph shows how the population of the world in 1650 was divided among the continents. Study the circle graph. Then write the correct answers on your paper.

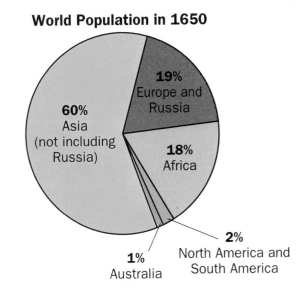

World Population in 1650

60% Asia (not including Russia)

19% Europe and Russia

18% Africa

2% North America and South America

1% Australia

1. Which continent had the largest population in 1650?

Europe   Asia   Africa

2. Which continent had about 1% of the world population in 1650?

Antarctica   Australia   Africa

3. Which continent had about the same percent of the world population as Europe and Russia?

North America   Asia   Africa

Unit 4   Revolutions

People were angry and unhappy. They did not like their rulers or the laws of their government. They decided to fight for their freedom. Their wars were called revolutions.

Many nations had revolutions between 1775 and 1850. Freedom became an important idea. The fight for freedom began with the 13 British colonies in America. Other nations joined the fight for freedom. Their revolutions changed the world.

What caused these revolutions? For hundreds of years, most monarchs had full power to make all laws. Things began to change. Many people did not want powerful monarchs to be their rulers. People in colonies did not want to be ruled by other countries. People wanted laws that would be fair to the rich and to the poor. They wanted the freedom to make laws for their nations. They wanted to vote for their leaders. People in many lands fought for these ideas.

You will be reading about important revolutions that happened between 1775 and 1850. How did the fight for freedom begin in the 13 American colonies? Why did the people of France fight against their king? How did countries in Latin America win their freedom? As you read Unit 4, think about how different

the world would be if people had not fought in revolutions. Think about why people feel that freedom is worth fighting for.

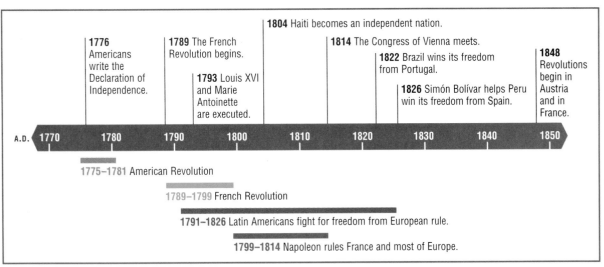

1804 Haiti becomes an independent nation.

1776 Americans write the Declaration of Independence.

1789 The French Revolution begins.

1793 Louis XVI and Marie Antoinette are executed.

1814 The Congress of Vienna meets.

1822 Brazil wins its freedom from Portugal.

1826 Simón Bolívar helps Peru win its freedom from Spain.

1848 Revolutions begin in Austria and in France.

A.D. 1770   1780   1790   1800   1810   1820   1830   1840   1850

1775–1781 American Revolution

1789–1799 French Revolution

1791–1826 Latin Americans fight for freedom from European rule.

1799–1814 Napoleon rules France and most of Europe.

The American Revolution

Many people from countries in Europe came to live in America. They came from such countries as Great Britain, France, Germany, Sweden, and Holland. People came to America for many reasons. Some people came because they wanted freedom of religion. Some people came to own land and become rich. Some British people came to America because they did not like the king or the laws of Great Britain.

Great Britain started 13 American colonies along the Atlantic Ocean. The colonies belonged to Great Britain. Americans had to obey the laws and the king of Great Britain.

You read in Chapter 20 that Great Britain and France fought a war about which nation would rule in America. Great Britain spent a lot of money fighting for America in the French and Indian War. Great Britain wanted the American **colonists** to help

There were many battles between the British and the Americans during the American Revolution.

Americans became angry when King George III passed new tax laws.

King George III

British tax stamp

pay for the war. So in 1764 Parliament and the king of Great Britain, George III, passed a tax law called the **Sugar Act**. The Sugar Act said that Americans had to pay taxes for certain goods that were brought to the American colonies. Some of the taxed goods were sugar and coffee.

In 1765 Parliament and King George III passed another tax law for the American colonies. This new law, the **Stamp Act**, said that Americans had to pay taxes on newspapers and other printed items.

The Sugar Act and the Stamp Act made the colonists angry. In Great Britain, voters helped make their tax laws in Parliament. But Americans were not allowed to help Parliament write tax laws for the colonies. King George said that Americans must obey laws that were made for them in Great Britain.

Americans said that it was unfair for the British to write tax laws for the colonies. The colonists wanted to send American **representatives** to Parliament. They wanted the right to help write their own tax laws. People in Great Britain had this right.

King George removed the Stamp Act in 1766. But in 1767 King George and Parliament wrote more tax laws for America. The new laws taxed such things

This battle near Boston in 1775 was one of the major battles of the American Revolution.

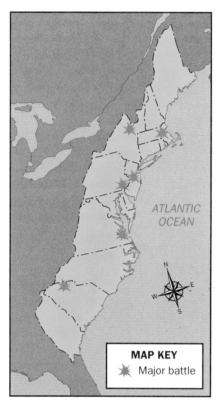
Battles of the American Revolution

MAP KEY
✹ Major battle

ATLANTIC
OCEAN

Thomas Jefferson

as tea and paper. Americans did not want to obey laws that were made in Great Britain. Some angry Americans decided to fight. They would fight for the right to make their own laws.

In 1775 a war began between Great Britain and America. The war was called the **American Revolution**. British soldiers and American soldiers fought each other in America. At first, Americans fought because they wanted King George to let them write their own laws. But then their goals changed. In 1776 Americans decided that they did not want to be ruled by Great Britain. They wanted America to become an **independent** nation. Americans were fighting for their freedom.

In 1776 Americans decided to tell the world that America was a free country. American leaders asked Thomas Jefferson to write a paper called the **Declaration of Independence**. Jefferson used some of John Locke's ideas about democracy in the Declaration of Independence. This paper told the world that the 13 American colonies had the right to make laws for themselves. It said that the colonies no longer belonged to Great Britain and would no longer obey King George. The Declaration

An American woman named Deborah Sampson dressed as a male soldier so that she could fight for her country.

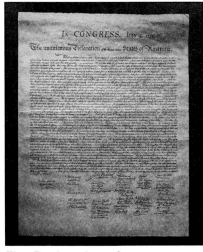

The Declaration of Independence

of Independence told the world that America was an independent country.

The American soldiers fought many battles against the British. General George Washington was the leader of the American army. He had fought in the French and Indian War. Washington was a strong leader. He lost many battles, but he kept on fighting for American freedom.

Many different Americans fought together to win the American Revolution. African Americans and women fought against the British. Protestants, Catholics, and Jews fought together in the war. People from other nations also helped the Americans fight in the war.

In 1781 Americans won the American Revolution. In 1783 Great Britain signed a **peace treaty** that said that Great Britain no longer ruled the American colonies. But Great Britain did not lose all of its land in North America. It still ruled parts of Canada. Americans were free from British rule. However, independence from Great Britain did not mean freedom for African American slaves.

American leaders wrote the United States Constitution in 1787.

The Constitution

President George Washington

The American Revolution brought about many changes in America. The 13 colonies were now 13 states. Americans called their nation the United States of America. The nation needed its own laws and plan of government. In 1787 American leaders wrote laws for their new nation. The leaders also used ideas about law and democracy from people such as John Locke. They also used ideas from the Magna Carta and from Great Britain's Parliament. All these ideas helped the leaders write the **Constitution**.

The Constitution gave the United States a strong government. This government ruled all the states. The laws helped the nation become a democracy. It was also a republic. The new nation would not have a monarch. Americans would choose a President to be their leader. George Washington became the first President of the United States in 1789.

The American Revolution also brought changes to Europe. The people in Europe learned how Americans fought to become an independent nation and a democracy. Soon people in some parts of Europe would also fight for their rights and freedom.

Using Vocabulary

Match Up   Finish the sentences in Group A with words from Group B. Write on your paper the letter of each correct answer.

Group A

1. American colonists had to pay taxes on printed materials after Parliament passed a tax law called the _____ .

2. Americans wanted to be free, or _____ , of British rule.

3. The American colonists fought the _____ so that they could form a new nation.

4. At the end of the war, Great Britain signed a _____ saying that it no longer ruled the 13 colonies.

5. The _____ was a set of laws that was written for the new United States government.

Group B

a. American Revolution

b. peace treaty

c. independent

d. Constitution

e. Stamp Act

Read and Remember

Write the Answer   Write one or more sentences on your paper to answer each question.

1. Why did the Sugar Act and the Stamp Act make Americans angry?

2. What were two things the Declaration of Independence said?

3. What was the American government like after the Constitution was written?

4. Who was the first President of the United States?

5. How did the American Revolution affect Europe?

Think and Apply

Cause and Effect   Write sentences on your paper by matching each cause on the left with an effect on the right.

Cause

1. Some British people did not like the laws of Great Britain, so _____

2. Great Britain had spent a lot of money to fight for America in the French and Indian War, so _____

3. Americans were not represented in Parliament, so _____

Effect

a. they thought tax laws written for the colonies were unfair.

b. they came to live in America.

c. Great Britain wanted America to help pay for the war.

Skill Builder

Understanding a Political Cartoon   A **political cartoon** is a drawing that shows what an artist thinks about a certain person, event, or **issue**. An issue is something that people have different opinions about. Sometimes political cartoons seem funny, but they are usually about serious ideas. Benjamin Franklin drew this political cartoon to help unite the American colonies against Great Britain. Study the cartoon. Then write on your paper the answer to each question.

1. What is the title of the political cartoon?

2. What animal is used to stand for the American colonies?

3. What did Franklin believe would happen to the colonies if they did not unite against Great Britain?

4. Imagine you were an American colonist. Would Franklin's political cartoon have made you want to help fight the British? Explain.

Journal Writing

Do you think the colonists had a right to be angry about the tax laws? How would you have felt if you had been an American colonist? Write a paragraph that tells how you would have felt about the tax laws.

Riddle Puzzle

Number your paper from 1 to 7. Choose the words in dark print to best complete the sentences. Write the correct answers on your paper.

represented   **fight**   **Magna Carta**   **earn**

Europe   **obey**   **Declaration**

1. Angry colonists decided to _____ for the right to make their own laws.

2. The Americans wanted to be _____ in Parliament.

3. The American Revolution brought many changes to _____.

4. To pay for its wars, Great Britain tried to _____ money by getting tax money from the colonists.

5. The _____ of Independence said that the American colonies no longer belonged to Great Britain.

6. King George said that Americans must _____ laws made for them in Great Britain.

7. The Constitution included ideas from the _____.

Now look at your answers. Circle the first letter of each answer you wrote on your paper. The letters you circle should spell a word. The word answers the riddle below.

RIDDLE: What is the goal for many people who start revolutions?

Write on your paper the answer to the riddle.

The French Revolution

THINK ABOUT AS YOU READ

1. **Why did the French Revolution begin?**
2. **How did the National Assembly change France's government?**
3. **How did the French Revolution change France?**

NEW WORDS

- French Revolution
- absolute rule
- estate
- National Assembly
- Bastille
- "Liberty, Equality, Fraternity"
- royal

PEOPLE & PLACES

- King Louis XVI
- Paris
- Jacobins
- Marie Antoinette
- Napoleon Bonaparte
- Austria

Imagine a time when the people in France were so angry that they killed their king and queen and thousands of other people. This was the time of the **French Revolution**. It began in 1789. The revolution was a ten-year fight to change old laws and to gain more rights.

Before 1789 the French monarchs had been very powerful. They had **absolute rule**. They made all the laws. People had few rights. The French people learned how Americans had won freedom in the American Revolution. Many French people wanted more freedom, too. They also wanted more rights.

There were three groups of people in France before the French Revolution. Each group was called an **estate**. People who worked for the Roman Catholic Church were in the First Estate. Rich nobles were in the Second Estate. People such as peasants,

In 1789 the French people gained power by capturing a prison called the Bastille.

city workers, lawyers, doctors, and merchants were in the Third Estate. Only a very small part of the French population was in the First and Second Estates. Most French people were in the Third Estate.

The people of the First and Second Estates owned much of the land in France. Most were very wealthy. The people in the First and Second Estates did not pay taxes. The Third Estate was forced to pay very high taxes. The people in the Third Estate wanted the other estates to pay taxes. They wanted to change the laws of France.

King Louis XVI was the king of France in 1789. He wanted both the Second and Third Estates to pay taxes because France needed money. The French had spent too much money fighting long wars against other nations. They had fought in the French and Indian War. The French had also spent a lot of money helping Americans fight in their war for freedom.

People in the Third Estate

King Louis XVI

The people of the Second Estate said they would not pay taxes. Most people in the Third Estate did not have enough money to pay more taxes. The Third Estate felt that the king had too much power and wealth. The Third Estate started the **National Assembly**. They said they spoke for all the people of France. People from the First and Second Estates also met with the National Assembly. The people of the National Assembly told King Louis that they would make new laws for France. They said that absolute rule in France was over. The French Revolution had begun!

King Louis did not want the National Assembly to make new laws. The king called soldiers to Paris, the capital of France. Many French people became very angry. They started many riots in Paris. There was fighting and killing in the city's streets. Fighting also began in other parts of France.

The **Bastille** was an old prison in Paris. For many years French kings had sent many people to the Bastille. On July 14, 1789, angry French people attacked the Bastille. They were looking for guns and other weapons inside. The French people freed the prisoners. The fall of the Bastille meant that King Louis had less power. It also made the National Assembly stronger. July 14 is now a French holiday called Bastille Day. Each year France celebrates its independence on this day.

"Liberty, Equality, Fraternity" became very important words during the revolution. People shouted these words. They carried signs and flags with these words on them. The words meant that all people should have freedom and equal rights.

On August 27, 1789, the National Assembly signed a paper called the Declaration of the Rights of Man and of the Citizen. This important paper said that everyone had freedom and equal rights. It also said that people had freedom of speech and freedom of religion. By 1791 the National Assembly had also written a new constitution. The National Assembly said all laws must be fair to the rich and to the poor. Everyone had to pay taxes and obey the new constitution.

French soldiers

The National Assembly

The National Assembly said Louis would still be the king of France. But King Louis lost most of his power. The National Assembly, not the king, would make laws for France.

King Louis did not want to fight the angry people in France. So he agreed to both the Declaration of the Rights of Man and the new constitution. But then in 1791, King Louis and his family tried to escape from France. Louis wanted rulers from other countries to help him have absolute rule in France again. The **royal** family was captured by French soldiers and put in prison.

In 1792 some French people decided they did not want another king. Like the Americans in the United States, the French started a republic. People called Jacobins became the rulers of the French Republic. The Jacobins then tried to kill everyone who was

The angry people of France rioted outside the palace of King Louis XVI and his family.

Napoleon Bonaparte

against the French Revolution and the new republic. Thousands of French people, including both nobles and peasants, were executed. In 1793 King Louis and his wife, Marie Antoinette, were also executed.

The French hated the Jacobins because they killed so many people. So in 1794 people began to fight the Jacobins. The Jacobins lost power. In 1795 a new group of people became the rulers of the French Republic. They wrote a new constitution. But they could not bring peace to France. Riots continued in the nation's streets.

The French Revolution ended in 1799. It ended when Napoleon Bonaparte became the ruler of France. He started a strong government. He brought peace to France and war to the rest of Europe. You will read about Napoleon in Chapter 23.

Thousands of people died during the long years of the French Revolution. But the revolution also brought some good changes to France. The people of France had more freedom. They all had to pay taxes. They all had equal rights. The old laws of France were gone.

Marie Antoinette (1755–1793)

Marie Antoinette was born to a royal family in the country of Austria in 1755. She married the prince of France when she was just 14 years old. In 1774 her husband became King Louis XVI of France. Marie Antoinette became the queen of France at age 19.

Marie Antoinette was not well liked in France. She was from Austria, an enemy of France. She also did not seem to care that France was having money problems. She did not seem to worry that many people in France were starving. She spent large amounts of France's money on clothes and other items for herself. She also spent money on her friends. This made the French people angry.

As you have read, the French Revolution began in 1789. In October 1789 Marie Antoinette, King Louis XVI, and their children were forced to move to Paris. They were treated like prisoners. Marie asked for help from her brother, the ruler of Austria. She and Louis wanted her brother and other rulers to help them fight for more power. Finally, Marie Antoinette and her family tried to escape from France. The royal family was caught and returned to Paris. The people of France were angry that Marie Antoinette and the king had tried to leave France.

Marie Antoinette continued to try to get help from other European countries. In 1792 she was caught trying to give Austria secret information about the French armies. Marie and her husband were sent to prison. In 1793 the French people used a special machine to chop off the heads of Marie and Louis. Neither Marie nor Louis showed any fear as they were executed.

Marie Antoinette

The palace of Louis XVI and Marie Antoinette

Using Vocabulary

Analogies   Use the words in dark print to best complete the sentences. Write the correct answers on your paper.

Rights of Man   National Assembly   estate   French Revolution

1. The American Revolution was to America as the _____ was to France.

2. A caste was to ancient India as an _____ was to France.

3. The House of Commons was to Great Britain as the _____ was to France.

4. The Declaration of Independence is to the United States as the Declaration of the _____ is to France.

Read and Remember

Finish the Sentence   Write on your paper the word or words that best complete each sentence.

1. People who worked for the Roman Catholic Church were in the _____ Estate.

   First   Second   Third

2. Rich nobles were in the _____ Estate.

   First   Second   Third

3. The National Assembly made new _____ for France.

   buildings   prisons   laws

4. Marie Antoinette asked for help from her brother, the ruler of _____.

   Spain   Austria   France

5. The Jacobins _____ King Louis and Marie Antoinette.

   saved   liked   executed

6. The French Revolution ended when _____ became the ruler of France.

   Charlemagne   Napoleon   King Louis XVI

Journal Writing

The French Revolution was started by people in the Third Estate of France. Pretend you are a French peasant in the Third Estate. Write a paragraph that tells why you want a revolution. Give at least two reasons.

Think and Apply

Drawing Conclusions   Read each pair of sentences. Then look in the box for the conclusion you might make. Write on your paper the letter of the conclusion you choose.

1. The French people wanted new laws.
   The French people decided they did not want another king.

2. France spent a lot of money on wars with other nations.
   France spent a lot of money helping Americans in the American Revolution.

3. In 1791 the National Assembly wrote new laws that gave people in France equal rights.
   In 1792 the National Assembly said that France would not be ruled by a king.

 4. Marie Antoinette spent large amounts of France's money on items for herself and for her friends.
   Marie Antoinette did not seem to care that many people in France were poor and hungry.

5. The Jacobins killed thousands of French people.
   The French people hated the Jacobins.

   a. France needed money.
   b. The National Assembly helped end absolute rule in France.
   c. The French people did not like Marie Antoinette.
   d. The French people started to fight against the Jacobins.
   e. The French people started a republic.

CHAPTER 23

Napoleon Bonaparte

Napoleon Bonaparte was a famous leader of the army of France. He became the emperor of France. He won many lands for France. Yet Napoleon died as a prisoner far from home.

Napoleon was born in 1769. His parents came from noble Italian families. Napoleon joined the French army at the age of 16. Later, he became an important leader of the French army.

In 1796 Napoleon led the French army against its enemy, the Austrians. The Austrian army was in northern Italy. The French conquered the Austrians in Italy. Napoleon went on to win other battles. He soon became a famous French hero.

Napoleon wanted to rule France. The government of France was in Paris. In 1799 Napoleon went to the city of Paris with a group of French soldiers. Napoleon and his soldiers forced the leaders of the French

THINK ABOUT AS YOU READ

1. **How did Napoleon become the ruler of France?**
2. **What changes did Napoleon bring to France?**
3. **How did the Russians defend themselves against Napoleon?**

NEW WORDS

- order
- Code Napoléon
- dictator
- censored
- defended
- allies
- allied nations

PEOPLE & PLACES

- Russia
- Russians
- Moscow
- Elba
- Waterloo
- Belgium
- St. Helena

Napoleon Bonaparte carefully planned his attacks on the countries of Europe.

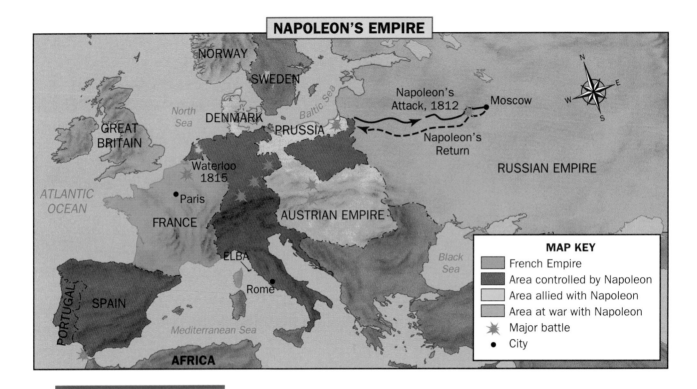

NORWAY

SWEDEN

North Sea

DENMARK

Baltic Sea

GREAT BRITAIN

PRUSSIA

ATLANTIC OCEAN

Waterloo 1815

•Paris

FRANCE

Napoleon's Attack, 1812   •Moscow

Napoleon's Return

RUSSIAN EMPIRE

AUSTRIAN EMPIRE

ELBA

Black Sea

Rome

PORTUGAL

SPAIN

Mediterranean Sea

AFRICA

MAP KEY
French Empire
Area controlled by Napoleon
Area allied with Napoleon
Area at war with Napoleon
✳ Major battle
• City

The map shows major battles fought by Napoleon. Which battle took place in the French Empire?

Republic to leave the government. Napoleon became the ruler of France.

The people of France wanted peace. They wanted the French Revolution to end. Napoleon was able to bring **order** to France. He helped solve France's money problems. Under Napoleon's rule, France built many new roads, buildings, and schools.

Napoleon made many fair laws. His system of laws was called the **Code Napoléon**. Some of his laws were based on the goals of the French Revolution. The laws gave religious freedom to all. The laws also said that all French people were equal. All people had to pay taxes.

Napoleon set up a strong French government. He became a **dictator**. A dictator is a ruler who has full power. All the laws of France were made by Napoleon. Napoleon also **censored** newspapers. The newspapers were not allowed to say things against Napoleon. People did not have freedom of speech.

Much of the power of the Roman Catholic Church had been taken from the Church during the French Revolution. In order for the Church to help

Napoleon made himself emperor of France. Here he is crowning his wife empress.

Soldiers of Napoleon

him control France, Napoleon made changes that gave the Church more power. But Napoleon did not return land that was taken from the Church during the French Revolution.

Napoleon wanted more power. So in 1804 Napoleon made himself the emperor of France. As the emperor he ruled all the nations France had conquered. But Napoleon wanted still more power. He wanted to rule all of Europe. He led the French army to war against many countries. By 1810 Napoleon controlled most of Europe. Look at the map of Napoleon's empire on page 156.

Napoleon wanted to conquer Russia. In 1812 he led a large army into Russia. This army had over 400,000 soldiers. Most of the soldiers were from the lands France had already conquered.

The Russians knew that Napoleon was coming. They did not have enough soldiers to win a war against France. They knew they could not defeat Napoleon by fighting. So the Russians **defended** themselves in a different way. They did not want French soldiers to use their homes or to eat their food. The Russians burned their homes and farms. They also burned Moscow, their capital city. They moved into eastern Russia.

Cold winter and snow led to the defeat of Napoleon in Russia.

Napoleon and his soldiers in the burning city of Moscow

Napoleon and his soldiers came to Russia. They found burned cities and burned houses. There were few Russians for the French soldiers to fight. Soon winter came to Russia. There was a lot of snow. The weather was very, very cold. The French soldiers did not have enough food or warm clothing. Napoleon knew he could not conquer Russia. So he decided to return to France with his army. Most of the cold, hungry soldiers died on the way back to France. The Russians and their cold winter had defeated Napoleon.

The conquered people of Europe hated Napoleon. He had forced the conquered people to pay a lot of taxes to France. He had forced conquered men to become soldiers in the French army. The conquered nations learned that Napoleon was defeated in Russia. His army was now very weak. The conquered nations decided to fight to be free again. These and other nations joined together as **allies** in a war against Napoleon. Some of the **allied nations** were Great Britain, Russia, and Austria.

The allied nations invaded France. They captured Paris. In 1814 the allies defeated Napoleon. Napoleon no longer ruled Europe. The allied nations forced Napoleon to leave France. They sent him to a small island called Elba. Elba is near Italy. The allied nations told Napoleon that he could never return to France.

Napoleon was captured by the allies after he lost the battle at Waterloo.

Napoleon on the island of St. Helena

Napoleon escaped from Elba and went back to Paris. He became emperor of France again. He was emperor for only 100 days. In 1815 Napoleon and his soldiers fought the allied nations again at Waterloo. Today Waterloo is a town in the country of Belgium. Find Waterloo on the map on page 156. Napoleon and his soldiers were defeated at Waterloo. Waterloo was Napoleon's last battle. Napoleon became a prisoner of the allies. The allies took Napoleon to St. Helena, a small island near southern Africa. Napoleon died there in 1821.

Napoleon was a strong ruler. He made laws to carry out some of the French Revolution's ideas about democracy. French soldiers spread the idea of "Liberty, Equality, Fraternity" to many parts of Europe. But Napoleon also took away the right to freedom of speech that people had won in the French Revolution. As a dictator and an emperor, Napoleon ruled with full power.

Napoleon had brought years of war to Europe. After Napoleon was defeated, the nations of Europe wanted peace. They wanted Europe to be the way it was before the French Revolution. You will read about Europe after Napoleon in the next chapter.

Using Vocabulary

Finish Up   Choose the words in dark print to best complete the sentences. Write on your paper the words you choose.

order   **defended**   **allied nations**

dictator   **censored**

1. As _____ of France, Napoleon ruled with complete power.

2. Napoleon _____ newspapers so that they could not say things against him.

3. Instead of fighting Napoleon's soldiers to save Russia, the Russians _____ their country by burning their homes and farms.

4. The nations that fought Napoleon were called _____.

5. A nation that has _____ is a nation in which people obey laws and rules.

Read and Remember

Finish the Paragraph   Number your paper from 1 to 7. Use the words in dark print to finish the paragraph below. Write on your paper the words you choose.

equal   **schools**   **food**   **Code Napoléon**

fight   **allies**   **Europe**

Napoleon became the ruler of France in 1799. He was a strong ruler. Under Napoleon's rule, new __1__ were built in France. The laws made by Napoleon were called the __2__. These laws said that all French people were __3__. Napoleon wanted to rule all of __4__. He tried to conquer Russia, but the French army did not have enough warm clothing or __5__. After that, the other conquered nations of Europe decided to __6__ against Napoleon. At Waterloo, Napoleon and his soldiers were defeated by the __7__.

Find the Answer Find the sentences below that tell something true about Napoleon. Write on your paper the sentences you find. You should find four sentences.

1. Napoleon was the leader of the French army.

2. Napoleon was caught trying to give secrets about France to Austria.

3. Napoleon became emperor in 1804.

4. Napoleon was a good emperor to all the people he ruled.

5. After he became emperor, Napoleon took away all of the Roman Catholic Church's power in France.

6. In 1812 Napoleon led over 400,000 soldiers into Russia.

7. Napoleon died on the island of St. Helena in 1821.

Think and Apply

Categories Read the words in each group. Decide how they are alike. Choose the best title for each group from the words in dark print. Write the title on your paper.

Russians   Waterloo   Dictator   Allied Nations

1. Great Britain, Russia, and
   Austria
   defeated Napoleon
   took Napoleon to St. Helena

2. censored newspapers
   made all laws
   had full power

3. burned Moscow
   burned houses and farms
   defended themselves against
   Napoleon

4. Napoleon's last battle
   1815
   allies won

Journal Writing

Do you think Napoleon was a good ruler? Write a paragraph to explain your answer.

Riddle Puzzle

Number your paper from 1 to 8. Choose words in dark print to best complete the sentences. Write the correct answers on your paper.

empire	religious	island	Russia
Paris	newspapers	southern	order

1. In 1799 Napoleon and his soldiers went to _____ to force the leaders of the French Republic to leave the government.

2. The winter attack on _____ in 1812 made Napoleon's army very weak.

3. In 1814 the allies defeated Napoleon and sent him to the _____ of Elba.

4. After Waterloo, the allies took Napoleon to St. Helena, an island near _____ Africa.

5. Napoleon helped bring _____ to France and helped solve many of France's money problems.

6. During Napoleon's rule, _____ were not allowed to say anything against the emperor.

7. By 1810 Napoleon's _____ included most of Europe.

8. The Code Napoléon gave the people of France _____ freedom.

Now look at your answers. Circle the first letter of each answer you wrote on your paper. The letters you circle should spell a word. The word answers the riddle below.

RIDDLE: What was Napoleon to the allies after the battle at Waterloo?

Write on your paper the answer to the riddle.

CHAPTER 24

Europe After Napoleon

THINK ABOUT AS YOU READ

1. Who were the members of the Quadruple Alliance?
2. How did the Congress of Vienna change Europe?
3. Why did some countries in Europe have revolutions?

NEW WORDS

♦ borders
♦ Congress of Vienna
♦ Quadruple Alliance
♦ balance of power
♦ secret police

PEOPLE & PLACES

♦ Vienna
♦ Prussia
♦ Klemens von Metternich
♦ Netherlands
♦ Dutch
♦ Louis Napoleon

As Napoleon conquered more land in Europe, he changed the rulers and the **borders** of the different countries that he had conquered. After Napoleon was defeated, leaders from many European nations met to change again the rulers and the borders in Europe. The leaders met in Vienna, Austria. These meetings were called the **Congress of Vienna**.

The Congress of Vienna began in 1814. It ended in 1815. The leaders of the Congress of Vienna wanted Europe to be the way it was before the French Revolution. They wanted peace. The Congress of Vienna wanted to stop all revolutions. Four important nations led the Congress of Vienna. The four powers were called the **Quadruple Alliance**. Great Britain, Russia, Austria, and Prussia were in the Quadruple Alliance. Later, France joined the Quadruple Alliance.

Leaders met at the Congress of Vienna to make changes in the rulers and the borders of the nations of Europe.

Klemens von Metternich was a leader of the Congress of Vienna. He represented Austria. He was against the ideas of the French Revolution. He thought the ideas of liberty, equality, and fraternity would bring more wars to Europe. He thought that democracy led to wars.

Metternich said that only strong kings could keep peace. He wanted all laws to be made by kings. He said people should have less freedom and should not be equal. The other leaders at the Congress of Vienna agreed with Metternich. They began to take away the freedom and the equality that people had won after the French Revolution. The Congress of Vienna helped the old kings become the rulers of their nations again. The old kings again had full power to make all laws in their countries.

The leaders of the Congress of Vienna changed the sizes of some nations in Europe. They did this because they wanted a **balance of power**. A balance of power means that one nation should not be strong enough to conquer other nations. The leaders thought a balance of power would keep peace in Europe. Some nations, such as Russia, became larger. Others became smaller. France lost all land that Napoleon had conquered. The nations around France also became stronger to prevent France from trying to take again the land of other countries.

Many **secret police** worked for the Quadruple Alliance. They looked for people who might start revolutions. The secret police looked for people who talked against the kings. The people they found were sent to prison. Thousands of people went to prison.

The Congress of Vienna helped Europe in one important way. No big wars were fought for almost forty years. But the Congress of Vienna could not make people forget the ideas of the French Revolution. Europe had many rich merchants in the middle class. These people no longer wanted powerful kings. These

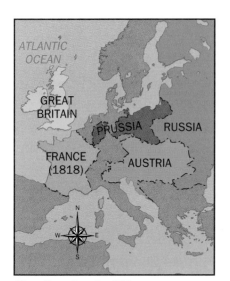

The Quadruple Alliance

Klemens von Metternich

people wanted freedom. They wanted to help make their laws. Revolutions began to occur in many European nations.

The first revolutions were in Spain and in northern Italy in 1820. Soldiers from the Quadruple Alliance nations went to Spain and Italy and stopped the revolutions.

There was also a revolution in Belgium. This revolution was a success. Belgium had been ruled by the Netherlands. The people of the Netherlands are the Dutch. The people of Belgium wanted to rule themselves. In 1830 the people of Belgium fought for their freedom. They fought their Dutch rulers and won. The Quadruple Alliance could not stop this revolution.

Revolution in Austria in 1848

In 1830 and in 1848, revolution came again to France. Both times the French forced their king to leave France. In 1848 the French started another republic. The people of France voted for Louis Napoleon to become the president of the Second French Republic. Napoleon Bonaparte had been Louis's uncle. Like his uncle, Louis became a dictator. Later, Louis made himself emperor. By 1870 this new French empire fell apart.

In 1848 revolution came to Austria, where Metternich lived. Angry people began to fight for freedom. Metternich left Austria and went to Great Britain. After that Metternich had no power. The Quadruple Alliance fell apart.

Louis Napoleon

The Congress of Vienna could not stop new revolutions in Europe. The French Revolution had brought new ideas about freedom and equal rights to many parts of Europe. Europe also changed because Europeans learned about the growth of democracy in Great Britain and in America. In the years ahead, people in other parts of the world would also fight for freedom.

Using Vocabulary

Find the Meaning   Write on your paper the word or words that best complete each sentence.

1. **Borders** are the lines that separate _____ .

   people   time periods   nations

2. The **Congress of Vienna** was a set of meetings between _____ .

   European leaders   Napoleon and his army   French merchants

3. The **Quadruple Alliance** was a group of nations that included Great Britain, Austria, Prussia, and _____ .

   Russia   Spain   Belgium

4. A **balance of power** means that nations have _____ amounts of power.

   equal   different   large

5. The **secret police** were people who looked for other people who might start _____ .

   businesses   colonies   revolutions

Read and Remember

Choose the Answer   Write the correct answers on your paper.

1. Which was Klemens von Metternich against?

   the Congress of Vienna   the ideas of the French Revolution   old kings

2. Which group worked to stop revolutions in Europe?

   merchants   middle class   Quadruple Alliance

3. Which nation did Belgium revolt against in 1830?

   Netherlands   Austria   Russia

4. What did Louis Napoleon rule in 1848?

   Congress of Vienna   Second French Republic   most of Europe

Skill Builder

Reading a Political Map
A **political map** shows how areas of land are divided. Some political maps show how a continent is divided by nations. Thin lines are used to show the borders between nations. Different colors are used to show different nations. Sometimes colors are used more than once. Look at this map of Europe. It shows how Europe was divided after the Congress of Vienna. Study the map. Number your paper from 1 to 7. Then write on your paper the answer to each question.

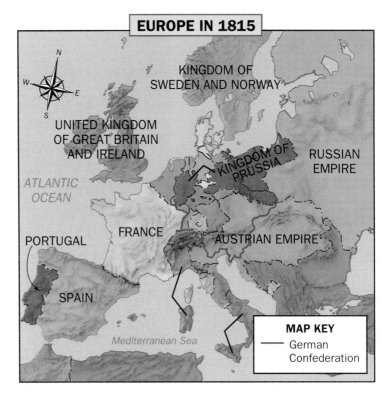

EUROPE IN 1815

KINGDOM OF SWEDEN AND NORWAY

UNITED KINGDOM OF GREAT BRITAIN AND IRELAND

ATLANTIC OCEAN

KINGDOM OF PRUSSIA

RUSSIAN EMPIRE

PORTUGAL

FRANCE

AUSTRIAN EMPIRE

SPAIN

Mediterranean Sea

MAP KEY
— German Confederation

1. What country shares Spain's northeast border?

2. Which had more land: the Austrian Empire or the Russian Empire?

3. Which were two nations that shared a border with the Austrian Empire?

4. What island nation was located northwest of France?

5. What is one nation that has the same color as Portugal?

6. Which nation was east of the Kingdom of Sweden and Norway?

7. Which country shares a border with Portugal?

Journal Writing

The Congress of Vienna hoped to bring peace to Europe. Do you think the Congress of Vienna reached this goal? Write a few sentences to explain your answer.

CHAPTER 25

Latin Americans Win Freedom

THINK ABOUT AS YOU READ

1. Why did the people of Latin America decide to fight for freedom?
2. Which people led some of the revolutions in Latin America?
3. How did Brazil become a free country?

PEOPLE & PLACES

♦ Latin America
♦ Haiti
♦ Hispaniola
♦ Caribbean Sea
♦ Saint Domingue
♦ Toussaint L'Ouverture
♦ Father Miguel Hidalgo
♦ Mexicans
♦ José de San Martín
♦ Simón Bolívar
♦ Argentina
♦ Chile
♦ Peru
♦ Dom Pedro
♦ Venezuela
♦ Bolivia

The countries to the south of the United States are called Latin America. For more than 300 years, Spain ruled most of Latin America. France, Portugal, and some other European nations also held colonies in Latin America. The Latin American colonies were only allowed to trade with their ruling countries. In the 1800s many Latin American colonies wanted to be free of European rule. Latin Americans wanted to rule themselves. They wanted to be able to trade with all nations. They wanted to write their own laws.

Latin Americans knew that American colonists had won their independence from Great Britain during the American Revolution. Latin Americans knew that the French people had fought for their rights during the French Revolution. These two

Father Miguel Hidalgo led Mexico's fight for independence from Spain in 1810.

Slaves in Haiti fought against their French owners and won independence.

Toussaint L'Ouverture

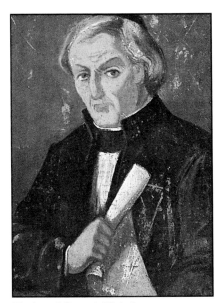
Father Miguel Hidalgo

revolutions helped the people of Latin America decide to fight for their independence.

Haiti is a country on the island of Hispaniola. Hispaniola is in the Caribbean Sea to the north of South America. Haiti is a small Latin American country. It was once a French colony. The French called this colony Saint Domingue. Most of the people in Saint Domingue were slaves on plantations owned by French people. In 1791 a leader of the slaves, Toussaint L'Ouverture, led a revolution against French rule. He was captured by the French in 1799. But the slaves continued to fight. They won the revolution in 1804. They named their new independent country Haiti.

In 1808 Napoleon Bonaparte of France conquered Spain. Napoleon let his brother become the ruler of Spain and of Spain's colonies in Latin America. The people of Latin America did not want to obey a French king. Many Latin Americans decided to fight for their freedom.

Mexico was the first Spanish colony in Latin America to fight to be free. Father Miguel Hidalgo was a Catholic priest in Mexico. He became the leader of Mexico's war against Spain. Father Hidalgo started an army. Most of the soldiers were poor

José de San Martín led an army across the Andes Mountains to help Chile win freedom.

José de San Martín

A Spanish general meets with Simón Bolívar.

American Indians. In 1810 they began to fight. Father Hidalgo and his soldiers won some battles. But in 1811 Father Hidalgo was captured. He was killed by Spanish soldiers. Father Hidalgo became a Mexican hero. But the revolution failed. The Mexicans were not free.

In 1814 the French were driven from Spain. Napoleon's brother no longer ruled Spain. Spain was again ruled by a Spanish king. The Spanish army was weak after fighting against the French. The new Spanish government was weak, too. Because Spain was weak, many Latin American colonies thought they could defeat Spain.

The Mexicans began to fight again for their freedom. In 1821 the Mexicans won their war with Spain. Mexico became an independent nation.

The colonies in South America also wanted to be free. José de San Martín and Simón Bolívar were two great leaders in the fight for freedom in South America. They helped many colonies become independent nations. José de San Martín began the fight for freedom in Argentina. He helped Argentina win its independence from Spain in 1816.

Dom Pedro

Independence in Latin America

San Martín decided to also help Chile become free. He formed an army to fight for Chile. The Andes Mountains separated Chile and Argentina. These mountains are some of the tallest mountains in the world. San Martín led his army across the Andes. The trip across the Andes was slow and hard.

At last San Martín and his army came to Chile. The Spanish never thought San Martín would cross the Andes Mountains to fight for Chile. The Spanish soldiers were not ready to fight. San Martín and his army defeated the Spanish. In 1818 Chile became an independent nation. The nations in the southern part of South America were free.

By 1822 Peru was Spain's only colony in South America. It took four more years for this colony to become free. San Martín and Simón Bolívar both fought for freedom in Peru. In 1820 San Martín invaded Peru with his army. He fought there for two years. Then in 1823 Bolívar led the fight for freedom in Peru. Many battles were fought. At last in 1826, Peru became an independent nation. Spain had lost all of its colonies in South America.

Brazil is the largest country in South America. Brazil had been a colony of Portugal. In 1807 Napoleon conquered Portugal. The king of Portugal went to live in Brazil. After Napoleon was defeated, the king went back to Portugal to rule. Dom Pedro, the king's son, became the new ruler of Brazil in 1821.

The people of Brazil wanted to be free. In 1822 Dom Pedro told Portugal that Brazil wanted to rule itself. Portugal did not want to fight against Brazil. Portugal allowed Brazil to be free. Brazil became independent without fighting.

Thousands of people had fought to win freedom for Latin America. By 1826 most of the Latin American colonies had won their freedom. The new nations would work hard to protect their independence. Such freedom is an important part of many nations all over the world.

Simón Bolívar (1783–1830)

Simón Bolívar was born in Venezuela. His parents died when he was young. They left a large amount of money to him. As a young man, Bolívar visited Europe. While in Europe, Bolívar saw the changes brought about by the French Revolution. He read books on freedom by people such as John Locke. In 1805 he made a promise to help Venezuela become a free country.

Bolívar became a leader of the revolutions against the Spanish in Latin America. Bolívar led the fight for freedom in the northern part of South America. He is sometimes called the "George Washington of South America." This is because he helped so many colonies become free. He led the fight for freedom for more than ten years.

Simón Bolívar's army won many battles against the Spanish. He helped free five Latin American nations. One of these nations was Venezuela. In 1823 Bolívar fought to help Peru become independent of Spanish rule. In 1824 one of Bolívar's generals won a major battle that freed most of Peru. Finally in 1826 the defeat of the remaining Spanish army in Peru ended Spanish rule in South America. The northern part of Peru formed a new country called Bolivia. This new country was named after Simón Bolívar.

Simón Bolívar

Simón Bolívar hoped that the new countries in Latin America would become republics. He wanted the people to make their own laws. He hoped that all the countries in Latin America could work together to make Latin America strong. But Bolívar did not ever get to see a united Latin America. Over the years the independent nations would struggle with many problems.

Read and Remember

Write the Answer   Write one or more sentences on your paper to answer each question.

1. Why did Latin Americans decide to fight for their independence?

2. Who was the ruler of Spain and of Spain's colonies in Latin America in 1808?

3. What happened in 1814 that led to new revolutions in Latin America?

4. How did San Martín and his army defeat the Spanish in Chile?

5. Which colony became independent without fighting?

 6. Which colony's independence marked the end of Spanish rule in South America?

 7. Which Latin American country was named after Simón Bolívar?

Who Am I?   Read each sentence. Then look at the words in dark print for the name of the person who might have said it. Write on your paper after each sentence the name of the person you choose.

Father Miguel Hidalgo	**Dom Pedro**	**Toussaint L'Ouverture**
Simón Bolívar	**Napoleon**	**José de San Martín**

1. "In 1791 I led the slaves in the fight for freedom from French rule in Saint Domingue."

2. "I was the French emperor who conquered Spain."

3. "My army of poor American Indians fought for Mexico's freedom from Spain in 1810."

4. "I led an army to fight for Chile's freedom."

5. "I told Portugal that Brazil wanted to rule itself."

 6. "Some people have called me the 'George Washington of South America,' because I helped so many nations become free."

Think and Apply

Understanding Different Points of View   The Spanish and the Latin Americans had different points of view about the fight for independence in Latin America. Read each sentence below. Write **S** on your paper for each sentence that might show the Spanish point of view. Write **LA** on your paper for each sentence that might show the Latin American point of view.

1. Spanish kings should rule Latin America.

2. Latin Americans should rule themselves.

3. Latin American colonies should be able to trade with all countries.

4. Spanish colonies in Latin America should trade only with Spain.

5. Father Miguel Hidalgo was a hero.

6. Our army is safe from an attack from people crossing the Andes Mountains.

7. We can defeat their soldiers by planning a surprise attack from the Andes Mountains.

Skill Builder

Reading a Historical Map   The historical map on page 171 shows the dates that different countries in Latin America won their independence. It also shows from which European country each Latin American country won its independence. Study the map and the key. Then write on your paper the answer to each question.

1. Which country became independent from Portugal?

2. Which nation ruled Chile before 1818?

3. Which five countries fought for freedom against Spain?

4. Which two nations became independent in 1821?

5. Which country was the last to become independent?

6. Which country once ruled the country that is now called Haiti?

Journal Writing

You have read about many interesting people in Latin American history. Of all the people in this chapter, whom would you most like to meet? Write a few sentences that explain why you would like to meet this person.

Riddle Puzzle

Number your paper from 1 to 7. Choose a word in dark print to complete each sentence. Write the correct answers on your paper.

Latin   **Domingue**   **European**   **Spain**
Argentina   **revolution**   **end**

1. _____ Americans knew that people had fought for freedom during the American and French revolutions.

2. Many _____ nations had colonies in Latin America.

3. José de San Martín began the fight for freedom in _____.

4. Most of the people in Saint _____ were slaves.

5. Simón Bolívar and José de San Martín helped to _____ Spanish rule in Latin America.

6. Mexico's _____ ended in 1821.

7. Latin American nations began their fight for independence during the time that _____ was weak.

Now look at your answers. Circle the first letter of each answer you wrote on your paper. The letters you circle should spell a word. The word answers the riddle below.

RIDDLE: What were L'Ouverture, Hidalgo, San Martín, and Bolívar to the people of Latin America?

Write on your paper the answer to the riddle.

Unit 5   A Changing World

The years between 1700 and 1900 were years of great change in the world. During this time there were many revolutions. Some revolutions were wars for independence. But other revolutions were not wars. The agricultural revolution of the 1700s was a change in the way farmers grew food. New machines were invented that helped farmers grow much more food. Fewer people were hungry.

During this time there was another kind of revolution. This revolution was a change in the way goods were made. The Industrial Revolution caused great changes in the ways people lived and worked. Many kinds of new machines were made. The new machines made work faster and easier. Many people were needed to run these new machines. People began to work in factories in cities. More and more people moved to cities. Cities grew larger.

The factories had many new problems. They were not always safe places to work. People had to work long, hard hours. As time passed, workers found ways to solve their problems. They worked together to get better pay, better hours, and safer factories.

What new machines were made in the years between 1700 and 1900? What changes did they bring? How did workers solve their problems? As you read Unit 5, think about some of the ways that the world changed between 1700 and 1900. Think about how the inventions and the changes of the Industrial Revolution affect our lives today.

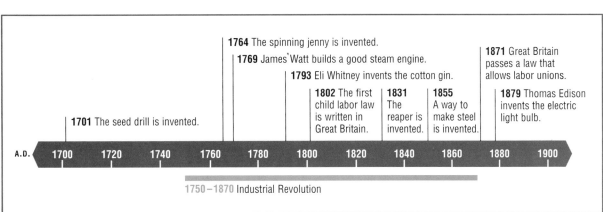

1764 The spinning jenny is invented.

1769 James Watt builds a good steam engine.

1793 Eli Whitney invents the cotton gin.

1802 The first child labor law is written in Great Britain.

1831 The reaper is invented.

1855 A way to make steel is invented.

1871 Great Britain passes a law that allows labor unions.

1879 Thomas Edison invents the electric light bulb.

1701 The seed drill is invented.

A.D. 1700 1720 1740 1760 1780 1800 1820 1840 1860 1880 1900

1750–1870 Industrial Revolution

CHAPTER 26

The Industrial Revolution

THINK ABOUT AS YOU READ

1. **How did the Industrial Revolution change the way things were made?**
2. **Why did the Industrial Revolution begin in Great Britain?**
3. **What were some of the inventions made during the Industrial Revolution?**

NEW WORDS

- Industrial Revolution
- seed drill
- factories
- industry
- spinning wheels
- spinning jenny
- spinning mule
- power loom
- cotton gin
- steam engine
- reaper

PEOPLE & PLACES

- Eli Whitney
- James Watt

Have you ever thought about how your clothes are made? Who sewed the clothes? Who made the cloth? Most people today buy clothes that were made by machines. However, just 250 years ago, most people had to make their clothes by hand. Then about the year 1750, people began to invent new machines to help them make clothes. These new machines could do work that people had always done by hand. This change is known as the **Industrial Revolution**. The Industrial Revolution was not a war. It was a change in the way goods were made.

The Industrial Revolution began with another revolution. This revolution was an agricultural revolution. The agricultural revolution was a change in the way farmers grew food. You have learned about the agricultural revolution that happened thousands of years ago during the Stone Age. Stone

During the Industrial Revolution, people began to use machines in factories. Here workers are using power looms to weave cloth.

Age people learned to plant seeds to grow food. They no longer had to move from place to place to hunt animals. The first agricultural revolution changed the way of life for Stone Age people.

For thousands of years, farmers had done most work by hand. They had planted seeds by throwing them on top of the ground. The wind blew away most of the seeds. So most of the seeds never grew. It was hard for farmers to grow enough food.

Then in 1701 the **seed drill** was invented in Great Britain. The seed drill was a machine that pushed the seeds into the soil. More seeds grew into plants. The seed drill helped farmers grow much more food. The invention of the seed drill led to the invention of many other farm machines. The seed drill was the beginning of the agricultural revolution of the 1700s and 1800s. Before long, there were also other changes. People started to have larger farms. They learned better ways to grow crops. They also raised better farm animals.

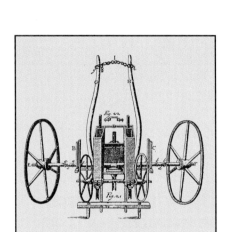
Seed drill

The agricultural revolution helped the Industrial Revolution begin in Great Britain. The revolution began in Great Britain for five main reasons. One reason was that Great Britain had a large population. There were many British people who were interested in science and inventions. There were also many people who could work in new **factories**. Because one farmer could grow more food, fewer farmers were needed. People moved to cities to work.

A second reason was that Great Britain had many natural resources. Many resources were needed to start the Industrial Revolution. Great Britain had a lot of iron, coal, rivers, and streams. Iron was needed to make machines. Coal was needed to provide power to run machines. Rivers and streams were needed to provide water power to run machines. Great Britain also had a lot of sheep for wool cloth.

People used sheep's wool to make cloth.

A third reason the Industrial Revolution began in Great Britain was that there were no wars on British

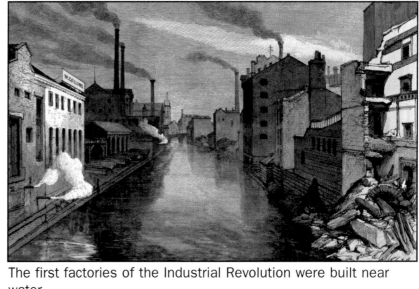

The first factories of the Industrial Revolution were built near water.

Woman using a spinning wheel

Spinning jenny

land. Years of peace in Great Britain gave people more time and money to invent new machines.

A fourth reason the Industrial Revolution began in Great Britain was that Great Britain had a good banking system. The banking system helped people have more money. Many people had money to buy goods. Rich merchants used their money to buy machines and build factories. They also bought ships. They used their ships to take goods to far-off places.

A fifth reason was Great Britain's good location. The British could move goods to and from many other lands easily by sea. Great Britain also has many harbors. British ships left the harbors to carry goods to other countries for trade.

The cloth **industry** was the first business to change because of the Industrial Revolution. People all over the world wanted to buy more wool and cotton cloth. Most cloth was made at home. Workers who made cloth at home could not make enough cloth. For a long time, the British had used **spinning wheels** at home to make thread. A spinning wheel could only spin one thread at a time. It took a long time to make thread on a spinning wheel at home.

About 1764 a machine called the **spinning jenny** was invented in Great Britain. This machine could

Many machines today are similar to those invented during the Industrial Revolution. These machines are weaving cloth.

Cotton

Cotton gin

spin up to eight threads at one time. A worker turned a wheel to make the jenny spin. The spinning jenny was much faster than the spinning wheel. Then in 1779 the **spinning mule** was invented. This new machine used water power to spin thread. The spinning mule was better than the jenny because it could spin much more thread more quickly.

People made cloth by weaving many threads together on a loom. For thousands of years, weaving had been done by hand. The British wanted a loom that could weave thread into cloth quickly. In 1785 a machine called the **power loom** was invented in Great Britain. The power loom used water power to weave cloth. People could now make a lot of cloth quickly. They began to need more natural resources, such as cotton. Many people used cotton to make cloth. Farmers could not grow enough cotton.

Large cotton crops were grown in the United States. Seeds had to be pulled out of the cotton plant. Then the cotton could be used to make cloth. Workers used to pick the cotton seeds out of the plant by hand. This was slow work. Then in 1793 an American named Eli Whitney invented a machine called the **cotton gin**. The cotton gin quickly pulled the seeds from the cotton. One cotton gin could do the work of fifty people. Farmers began to grow

James Watt

Watt's steam engine

A reaper

larger cotton crops. Soon the United States had more cotton to sell to Great Britain.

The Industrial Revolution changed the ways that people lived and worked. For hundreds of years, most families had worked together at home. The new spinning and weaving machines were too big to be used at home. Merchants built factories for the new machines. The factory owners hired many people to work in the factories.

At first, water power was used to run the new spinning and weaving machines. Water power made the machines work. Factories that needed water power had to be built close to rivers and streams. It was not always easy to build factories near water.

People tried to find better ways to run machines so that factories could be built away from rivers and streams. People learned that they could burn coal to make hot water for steam power. In 1769 James Watt built a good **steam engine** in Great Britain. By 1800 this steam engine was being used to run machines in factories. Factories could be run by steam power instead of by water power. A steam engine could be used anywhere. Factories did not have to be built near streams or rivers.

People continued to invent other machines. For thousands of years, wheat has been used to make bread. Before the Industrial Revolution, farmers had cut wheat by hand. In 1831 an American invented the **reaper**. This new machine cut wheat quickly. Farmers began to grow a lot more wheat. People soon had more bread to eat.

As time passed, more and more people left farms to work in factories. Many factories were in cities. More people moved to the cities to find jobs in factories. Cities grew larger. As you read the next chapter, you will learn more about the Industrial Revolution. You will learn more about how it changed the ways people lived and worked.

Using Vocabulary

Finish the Paragraph   Number your paper from 1 to 6. Use the words in dark print to finish the paragraph below. Write on your paper the words you choose.

spinning mule   **power loom**   **Industrial**
cotton gin   **factories**   **spinning jenny**

The __1__ Revolution was a change from making goods by hand to making goods by machine. Some of the first new machines were made for the cloth industry. The __2__ was the first machine that could spin several threads at the same time. The __3__ was a machine that used water power to spin thread. The __4__ used water power to weave threads into cloth. These machines were very big. People began to use the machines in places called __5__. Soon people needed more cotton for cloth. The __6__ helped farmers grow more crops.

Read and Remember

Find the Answer   Find the sentences that tell why the Industrial Revolution began in Great Britain. Write on your paper the sentences you find. You should find four sentences.

1. Great Britain had a large population.

2. Great Britain had a lot of natural resources, such as iron and coal.

3. Great Britain had a very rainy climate.

4. Great Britain had a good banking system.

5. Great Britain was the largest island in Europe.

6. There were no wars on British land.

7. The British used spinning wheels to make thread by hand.

Journal Writing

Write a few sentences about an invention from this chapter that you feel was the most important invention during the Industrial Revolution.

Riddle Puzzle

Number your paper from 1 to 8. Choose a word in dark print to complete each sentence. Write the correct answers on your paper.

agricultural   **natural**   **steam**   **Eli**
inventions   **money**   **harbors**   **cloth**

1. Great Britain's banking system helped merchants have more _____ to buy machines and build factories during the Industrial Revolution.

2. The Industrial Revolution actually began with an _____ revolution.

3. The _____ industry was the first business to change because of the Industrial Revolution.

4. Great Britain shipped goods from its many _____ to other countries.

5. The seed drill and the reaper were two _____ that helped farmers grow more food.

6. One of Great Britain's most important _____ resources was coal.

7. The cotton gin was invented by a American named _____ Whitney.

8. In 1769 James Watt invented a good _____ engine that provided power for machines in factories.

Now look at your answers. Circle the first letter of each answer you wrote on your paper. The letters you circle should spell a word. The word answers the riddle below.

RIDDLE: What changed people's lives during the Industrial Revolution?

Write on your paper the answer to the riddle.

The Industrial Revolution Brings Change

The Industrial Revolution began in Great Britain. The new inventions helped many British people earn more money. At first, the British tried to keep their inventions a secret. But they could not stop the Industrial Revolution from spreading to other parts of the world. Soon it spread to the rest of Europe and to the United States. Later, it spread to other parts of the world. The Industrial Revolution changed the ways people all over the world lived and worked. Some changes made life better. Other changes caused problems.

The Industrial Revolution gave people better ways to travel. Before the revolution, people had traveled on horses or by ships. Then in 1804 the first **steam locomotive** was built in Great Britain. The steam locomotive was a train car with a steam engine. The

THINK ABOUT AS YOU READ

1. **How did the Industrial Revolution change the way people traveled?**
2. **What other changes did the Industrial Revolution bring?**
3. **What were some of the problems caused by the Industrial Revolution?**

NEW WORDS

♦ **steam locomotive**
♦ **steamboat**
♦ **canals**
♦ **vaccine**
♦ **smallpox**
♦ **bacteria**
♦ **working class**
♦ **standard of living**
♦ **elements**
♦ **radiation**

PEOPLE & PLACES

♦ **Suez Canal**
♦ **Red Sea**
♦ **Elijah McCoy**
♦ **Thomas Edison**
♦ **Louis Pasteur**
♦ **Marie Curie**
♦ **Pierre Curie**

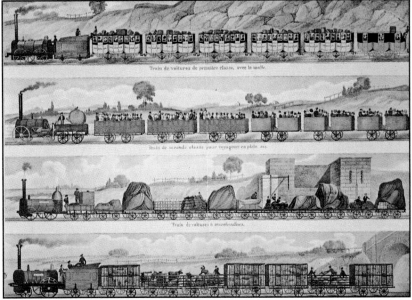

The steam locomotive changed the ways that people traveled and sent goods on land.

The first train in Japan

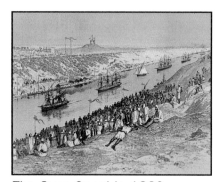
The Suez Canal in 1869

A steel factory

The steamboat was a fast way to travel because it did not need wind to move.

locomotive was strong enough to pull other train cars. The trains traveled on rails. Steam locomotives moved faster than horses. Soon many people traveled in trains pulled by locomotives. It cost less money to send goods on trains than on carts pulled by horses. The railroads also helped other industries grow.

People also wanted to travel in faster ships. For hundreds of years, people had traveled in ships with sails. The wind blew these ships across the sea. Then in 1807 a good **steamboat** was built. The steamboat had a steam engine that moved the ship. People no longer had to wait for wind to move their ships.

As people invented better ways to travel, they began to find other ways to help them travel more quickly. They began to build better roads. They also built **canals**. Canals are water routes that connect rivers, lakes, and oceans. The canals cross land to connect these bodies of water. By using the canals, merchants no longer had to move their goods from a ship, then across land, and then to another ship. One important canal is the Suez Canal, which was built in 1869. This canal connects the Mediterranean Sea with the Red Sea near Egypt. Better roads and new canals helped people save time and money.

Strong metal was needed to build machines, factories, and railroads. Great Britain had a lot of iron. For a while, iron was used to build machines, factories, and railroads. But iron is not as strong as

Elijah McCoy

Thomas Edison

Louis Pasteur

the metals we use today. In 1855 a way to change iron into a stronger metal was invented in Great Britain. First, the iron was made very clean and very hot. Then some materials were added to the hot, clean iron to change it into steel. Steel is a very strong metal. Steel railroads last longer than iron railroads. People began to use steel to build new machines and steam locomotives.

People found other ways to improve their machines and factories. In the 1870s an African American named Elijah McCoy invented a way to help trains and other machines run better. In the past, people had to stop their machines to oil them. Businesses lost a lot of time and money while the machines were turned off. McCoy invented a better way for people to oil machines without having to turn them off.

Other inventions of the Industrial Revolution made life easier. One of these was the electric light bulb. For hundreds of years, people had used candles to light their homes. In 1879 an American named Thomas Edison invented the electric light bulb. Soon electric light bulbs were being used in homes and in factories. Electricity would become a very important part of other inventions.

There were many other advances in science during the revolution. New discoveries in medicine helped people stay healthy. In 1796 a **vaccine** was developed to prevent **smallpox**. Smallpox was a disease that had killed millions of people.

In the 1860s the French scientist Louis Pasteur studied tiny living things called **bacteria**. He found that bacteria caused many diseases. Pasteur also discovered that bacteria could be killed through heat. Pasteur's ideas were used to make milk safer to drink. Many of Pasteur's ideas were used to solve other problems in medicine.

During the Industrial Revolution, two groups of people became very important. These groups were

A crowded city during the Industrial Revolution

Pollution from factories

the **working class** and the middle class. The people of the working class worked in mines and factories. The working class grew larger as more factories were built. The middle class included factory owners and merchants. The Industrial Revolution helped the middle class become a very large and powerful group. People in the middle class had more money than people in the working class had.

The Industrial Revolution helped improve the **standard of living**. Many people earned more money. They were able to buy the things they needed or wanted. People could travel more easily. More people had jobs. People had better food and better medicine. But the Industrial Revolution also caused new problems.

As people created more machines, factories were built very quickly. Many factories were not safe places to work. The new factories and the need for many workers made cities grow too quickly. The cities were not planned very well. Many factories and other buildings were built too close together. Cities were very crowded. Diseases and fires spread very quickly through the crowded cities.

The factories also caused pollution. The factories put a lot of smoke into the air. They also put dirty liquids into rivers and streams. There was a lot of garbage created by factories and by the large populations in the cities.

The Industrial Revolution changed the way of life for millions of people. As time passed, more and more inventions would be made. Inventions such as the telegraph, the telephone, and the automobile would soon be made. But with the changes came problems, too. Cities were crowded, and pollution increased. As you read the next chapter, you will learn that life for working-class people was hard. You will also read how working-class people worked to solve their problems.

Marie Curie (1867–1934)

The Industrial Revolution led to many changes in farming, industry, and science. People continued to make many new discoveries in the late 1800s and the early 1900s. The discoveries changed the way that scientists thought about nature. An important scientist during this time was Marie Curie.

Marie was born in Warsaw, Poland, during the Industrial Revolution. Her name was Marie Sklodowska. From a young age, Marie enjoyed math and science. After high school, Marie went to the University of Paris in France. She became a Doctor of Science in 1903.

Marie married Pierre Curie while she was at the university. Pierre Curie was a teacher and a scientist. The Curies worked together on science experiments. Together they found two new **elements**. Everything in nature is made up of different elements. The Curies discovered that one of these two elements releases a powerful energy called **radiation**. In 1903 Marie and Pierre Curie and another scientist received the Nobel Prize for their work.

In 1906 Pierre Curie died. The University of Paris asked Marie Curie to take the place of her husband as a teacher at the school. Marie Curie became the first woman teacher at the University of Paris.

Marie Curie continued to study radiation. In 1911 Curie received another Nobel Prize for her work with radiation and the two elements. The study of radiation has led to great changes in medicine. Today radiation is used to treat cancer and to make x-rays. Marie Curie's work with radiation helped make people's lives better.

Marie Curie

Pierre and Marie Curie at work

Using Vocabulary

Match Up   Finish the sentences in Group A with words from Group B. Write on your paper the letter of each correct answer.

Group A

1. A _____ was a train that used a steam engine for its power.

2. The _____ was a large group of people who worked in mines and in factories.

3. A _____ is a water route that crosses land to connect bodies of water.

4. A _____ is medicine that prevents people from getting a disease.

5. A _____ shows how well a person is able to buy the things that he or she wants or needs.

 6. Nature is made up of many _____ .

Group B

a. canal

b. standard of living

c. vaccine

d. working class

e. elements

f. steam locomotive

Read and Remember

Who Am I?   Read each sentence. Then look at the words in dark print for the name of the person who might have said it. Write on your paper the name of the person you choose.

Marie Curie   **Thomas Edison**   **Elijah McCoy**   **Louis Pasteur**

1. "I invented a better way for people to oil machines."

2. "I won two Nobel Prizes for my work in science."

3. "I found a way to use electricity to light homes and factories."

4. "I discovered that bacteria cause many diseases."

Write the Answer Write one or more sentences on your paper to answer each question.

1. What are three things from the Industrial Revolution that helped people travel more quickly?

2. How is steel made?

3. Which people were part of the working class?

4. In what ways did the Industrial Revolution help improve the standard of living?

5. What were some of the problems that were caused by the Industrial Revolution?

 6. How did Marie Curie's work help modern medicine?

Think and Apply

Categories Read the words in each group. Decide how they are alike. Find the best title for each group from the words in dark print. Write the title on your paper.

Inventors   Middle Class   Working Class   Ways to Travel

1. owned factories
   often had a lot of money
   became powerful

2. carts
   steamboats
   steam locomotives

3. worked in mines
   worked in factories
   had a hard life

4. Elijah McCoy
   Thomas Edison
   Eli Whitney

Journal Writing

Elijah McCoy, Thomas Edison, and Louis Pasteur were three important people of the Industrial Revolution. Choose one of these three people. Write a paragraph that tells how the work of this person affects our lives today.

Skill Builder

Reading a Chart   The chart below shows facts about some of the inventions made during the Industrial Revolution. Study the chart. Then write on your paper the answer to each question.

SOME INVENTIONS MADE DURING THE INDUSTRIAL REVOLUTION

Invention	Inventor	Year Invented	Purpose of Invention
Spinning jenny	James Hargreaves	1764	To spin many threads at one time.
Steam engine	James Watt	1769	To be a source of power to run machines.
Cotton gin	Eli Whitney	1793	To pull the seeds from cotton.
Smallpox vaccine	Edward Jenner	1796	To prevent people from dying from the smallpox disease.
Steam locomotive	Richard Trevithick	1804	To move people and goods across land.
Steamboat	Robert Fulton	1807	To move people and goods across water.
Electric light bulb	Thomas Edison	1879	To provide light for homes and factories.

1. Who invented the spinning jenny?

2. What was invented in 1769?

3. What invention could pull the seeds from cotton?

4. What invention did Thomas Edison make?

5. What two inventions were made to move people and goods?

6. When was the smallpox vaccine invented?

7. What was the purpose of the steam engine?

8. Who invented the steam locomotive?

9. Who invented a way to light homes and factories without candles?

Workers Solve Some Problems

**THINK ABOUT
AS YOU READ**

1. **Why was life hard for the working class?**
2. **What kinds of changes did the working class want?**
3. **How do labor unions work to make changes?**

NEW WORDS

♦ **immigrants**
♦ **wages**
♦ **working conditions**
♦ **cotton mills**
♦ **labor unions**
♦ **strike**

What was it like to be a factory worker in Great Britain about the year 1800? Many factories were dirty and dangerous. Many workers had to work 14 hours every day. People had to work hard, but they were paid very little money.

Life was hard for the working class during the Industrial Revolution. Parents often could not earn enough money for their families by working in factories. Children often had to work, too. Some children who were as young as six years old went to work in factories. Factory owners paid women and children less money than they paid men.

Thousands of children worked in factories. Other poor children were sent to dig for coal in coal mines. Children worked at least six days a week in factories

Many children were forced to work long hours in factories. Often the factories were dangerous places to work.

One of the first labor laws said that children were no longer allowed to be coal workers.

and coal mines. They often worked more than ten hours a day. They could not go to school. They had no time for play. The factories and the coal mines were dirty and dangerous. Factory owners often beat children if they did not like the work the children did. Children became sick from working in factories and coal mines. Many children died.

Factory workers had other problems. Sometimes there was not enough work in a factory for all the workers. Then some workers would lose their jobs. Many factory workers were hurt while doing dangerous work. If they were hurt and could not work, they lost their jobs. People without jobs did not earn money. They did not have money to buy food for their families.

Many working-class people in Europe thought that they could solve their problems by moving to the United States. They thought they would have a better life in the United States. The invention of the steamboat made it possible for millions of people to move to the United States. These **immigrants** came from Great Britain and other countries in Europe.

Immigrants from Europe

People in the working class began to demand changes.

An immigrant family arriving in the United States

Women working in a glove factory

But the Industrial Revolution also changed life in the United States. Immigrants found life in the United States hard, too.

Other working-class people tried to make changes in their own countries. The working class wanted many changes. They wanted better pay, or **wages**. They wanted to work fewer hours each day. They wanted new laws to say that women and children could not work in the mines. They also wanted better **working conditions**. This means that they wanted factories and mines to be cleaner and safer. It also means they wanted to be paid if they were hurt on the job and could not work.

Many countries wrote labor laws to help their workers. Great Britain was the first country to write such laws. This was because the first factories of the Industrial Revolution began there. Then laws to help workers were written in other countries.

How did the new laws help the workers? In 1802 the first child labor law was written in Great Britain. This law said that certain children who were less than nine years old could not work in **cotton mills**. The law also said that children could not work more than 12 hours a day. Then more labor laws were written. Women and children were not allowed to work in coal mines. Children who were less than 18 years old could not work in factories. A law in 1847 said that women and children should not work more than ten hours a day in factories. Laws were also written to make factories safer.

There were still many problems for workers in factories and in mines. Workers started **labor unions**. A labor union is a group of workers that join together to solve problems. Workers in a union are called union members. Every union has leaders.

The first unions began in Great Britain in the early 1800s. But Great Britain used laws to prevent workers from starting labor unions. In 1871 the laws were changed, and labor unions were able to help the workers. Soon unions became important in the United States and in Europe. Unions began in India and Japan in the 1890s. Labor unions soon started in countries in many parts of the world.

How do labor unions help workers solve their problems? Union members might want better wages. They might want better working conditions. The union leaders talk with the factory owners. The leaders ask the factory owners to give workers better wages or better working conditions.

Sometimes factory owners agree to make changes. But sometimes they say no. If union leaders and factory owners do not agree, then union members sometimes **strike**. A strike means that union members stop working until owners and union members agree on a way to solve a problem.

Factories cannot make goods when workers are on strike. Factory owners do not want their workers to strike. So many times factory owners will give their workers better wages and working conditions. In this way unions help their members. Labor unions have been helping their members for many years.

There are still some countries in the world today that allow children to work in factories. But most countries have laws that protect their workers. Factories are safer. Working conditions are better. Today most people have a better life because of the Industrial Revolution and the work of labor unions.

Many people were injured during this strike in 1892.

Modern labor union strike in Germany

Using Vocabulary

Finish Up   Choose the word or words in dark print to best complete each sentence. Write on your paper the word or words you choose.

> **immigrants**   **working conditions**   **strike**
> **labor unions**   **wages**

1. Workers formed _____ because they wanted to work together for better labor laws.

2. People who move to one country from another are _____ .

3. Many factory workers wanted better pay, or _____ .

4. A _____ is when union members stop working until owners agree to make changes.

5. Safe factories and high wages are examples of good _____ .

Read and Remember

Choose the Answer   Write the correct answers on your paper.

1. Factory owners paid women and children _____ they paid men.

   more money than   less money than   the same amount as

2. Workers wanted _____ .

   longer hours   lower wages   safer factories

3. The invention of the _____ made it possible for millions of people to move from Europe to the United States.

   railroad   seed drill   steamboat

4. In 1802 the first child labor law was written for children in _____ .

   schools   cotton mills   coal mines

5. In 1871 British laws were changed to allow workers to start _____ .

   labor unions   their own factories   working with machines

Think and Apply

Drawing Conclusions   Read each pair of sentences. Then look in the box for the conclusion you might make. Write on your paper the letter of the conclusion you choose.

1. Parents often could not earn enough money to feed their families.
   Many factory owners beat children who worked for them.

2. Factories in Europe had poor working conditions.
   Workers thought life in the United States would be better.

3. Factory workers wanted better pay and a shorter workday.
   Factory workers needed to work together to get changes made.

4. Union members might strike if factory owners will not make changes.
   Factories cannot make goods when workers are on strike.

5. Children in Great Britain often had to work long hours in dangerous factories and mines.
   Today British children are not allowed to work in factories and in mines.

6. Labor unions in Great Britain helped improve working conditions.
   People in other nations liked the effects that British labor unions caused.

   a. Factory workers started labor unions to help solve their problems.
   b. Life was hard for the working class.
   c. Many European workers moved to the United States.
   d. Great Britain passed child labor laws.
   e. Labor unions started in countries in many parts of the world.
   f. Factory owners will sometimes agree to make changes to keep workers from striking.

Journal Writing

Life was hard for the working class before labor laws were passed. Write a paragraph that tells at least four problems that factory workers had during the Industrial Revolution.

Skill Builder

Reading a Line Graph   The line graph below shows how many people worked in British coal mines from 1831 to 1871. Study the graph. Then write on your paper the words or dates that best complete the sentences below.

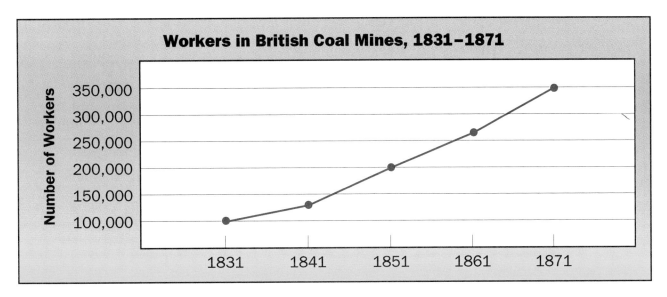

Workers in British Coal Mines, 1831–1871

1. The graph shows the number of coal miners in _____.

   the United States   Great Britain   France

2. The graph shows the number of coal miners from 1831 to _____.

   1821   1871   1881

3. The year with the fewest coal miners was _____.

   1831   1841   1861

4. There were about 200,000 coal miners in _____.

   1841   1851   1861

5. There were about 350,000 coal miners in _____.

   1851   1861   1871

6. From 1831 to 1871, the number of coal miners _____.

   grew smaller   grew larger   stayed the same

Unit 6   Nationalism, Imperialism, and War

Are you very proud of your nation? When people feel great pride for their nation, that pride is called nationalism. Nationalism can unite the people of a nation. It can help people work together to make changes for their nation. They might fight to protect their nation from invading armies. They might want their nation to grow in size and to gain power. Nationalism has led to many changes in the world.

During the 1800s and the early 1900s, nationalism became very strong in many countries. People in different Italian states fought to unite their states into one nation. This also happened in Germany. Many people helped their nations to conquer and control other lands in places like Asia and Africa. Nations built strong armies because of nationalism. Nationalism has led to terrible wars.

Other changes also occurred during this time period. The sizes of many nations changed at the end of wars. A major revolution occurred in Russia. Some nations started new kinds of governments. New dictators came to power. The Great Depression hurt nations all over the world.

How did Italy and Germany become new nations? Why did nations want to conquer other lands? How did the ideas of a few people affect millions of people in the world? As you read Unit 6, think about the good and bad effects of nationalism. Think about the conditions in the world that led to a world war and to new dictators.

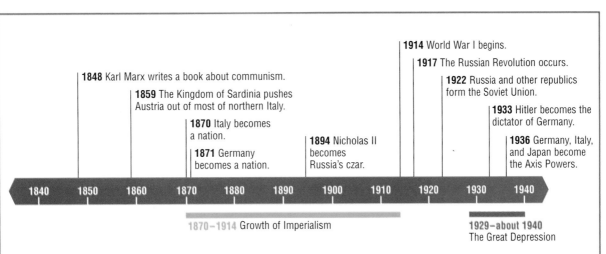

1848 Karl Marx writes a book about communism.

1859 The Kingdom of Sardinia pushes Austria out of most of northern Italy.

1870 Italy becomes a nation.

1871 Germany becomes a nation.

1894 Nicholas II becomes Russia's czar.

1914 World War I begins.

1917 The Russian Revolution occurs.

1922 Russia and other republics form the Soviet Union.

1933 Hitler becomes the dictator of Germany.

1936 Germany, Italy, and Japan become the Axis Powers.

| 1840 | 1850 | 1860 | 1870 | 1880 | 1890 | 1900 | 1910 | 1920 | 1930 | 1940 |

1870–1914 Growth of Imperialism

1929–about 1940 The Great Depression

CHAPTER 29

The Unification of Germany and Italy

Italy and Germany became nations in the 1870s. Before that, Italy and Germany were divided into many independent states. Each state had its own ruler and laws. But people wanted the states to unite. They had strong feelings of **nationalism**. Nationalism means love and pride for one's nation. Nationalism helps unite people. Feelings of nationalism helped the Italian and German states to become new nations.

It was not easy for the Italian states to become one nation. After the Congress of Vienna, there were nine Italian states. Austria controlled many of the northern states of Italy. Southern Italy was ruled by a king. Between northern Italy and southern Italy were the Papal States. The Papal States belonged to the Roman Catholic Church.

A man named Count Camillo di Cavour helped unite Italy. He was the **prime minister** of the

The people of Italy celebrated the nation's unification in 1870.

ITALY BEFORE UNIFICATION

FRANCE
SAVOY
SWITZERLAND
AUSTRIA
LOMBARDY
VENETIA
Venice
KINGDOM
OF SARDINIA
TUSCANY
CORSICA
(French)
PAPAL
STATES
Rome
Adriatic Sea
Mediterranean
Sea
KINGDOM
OF THE
TWO SICILIES
AFRICA

ITALY AFTER UNIFICATION

FRANCE
SWITZERLAND
AUSTRIA
Venice
CORSICA
(French)
ITALY
1870
SARDINIA
Rome
Adriatic Sea
Mediterranean
Sea
AFRICA
SICILY

Many Italian states united to become the nation of Italy. Which two states included large islands?

Count Camillo di Cavour

Kingdom of Sardinia, one of the nine Italian states. Cavour hoped that all the states of Italy would unite. But he knew that first the northern states of Italy had to be freed from Austria.

Cavour asked other European nations to help the Italians fight the Austrians. France agreed to help the Kingdom of Sardinia. When Austria **declared war** on Sardinia in 1859, French and Italian soldiers went to fight. They pushed the Austrians out of most of northern Italy. By 1860 most of the northern states had joined with the Kingdom of Sardinia. Austria still ruled the northern state of Venetia.

Once the northern states had united, an Italian named Giuseppe Garibaldi sailed to southern Italy. In 1860 Garibaldi and his army captured southern Italy. Then Garibaldi and Cavour's soldiers conquered the Papal States. They did not conquer Rome because France was protecting the city. Except for Venetia and Rome, most of the Italian states were united. In 1861 these united states became known as the Kingdom of Italy.

Giuseppe Garibaldi

Pope Pius IX, the pope during Italy's unification

In 1866 Italy joined Prussia in a war against Austria. Austria lost the war. As part of the peace treaty, Austria had to give the state of Venetia to Italy. Then in 1870 France and Prussia went to war against each other. So France removed its soldiers from Rome. The Italian army then conquered Rome. The pope was allowed to rule a small part of Rome. The **unification** of Italy was complete. Italy had become one nation.

The new Italian government had problems. It needed money. Also, the pope was angry that he had lost control of Rome and of the Papal States. He told Roman Catholics not to support the new government. But Italy remained **unified**. It slowly grew stronger.

Like Italy, the 39 German states did not easily become a nation. The Congress of Vienna had joined the 39 states together to form a group called the **German Confederation**. But the 39 states had independent governments. The strongest German states were Austria and Prussia. Each of the 39 states was ruled by a prince or a king.

Otto von Bismarck led the unification of Germany. He was the prime minister of the state of Prussia. Bismarck said that wars with other countries would unite the German people. He believed that winning wars would help the growth of German nationalism.

Bismarck led the Germans in three wars. The first war was in 1864. Prussia and Austria fought together against Denmark. They won the war. They then controlled two states of Denmark.

Bismarck wanted to force Austria to leave the German Confederation. In 1866 Prussia went to war against Austria. After seven weeks, Prussia won the war. The two states from Denmark and small areas of Austria then belonged to Prussia. It was during this war that Austria lost Venetia to Italy. After the war, northern Germany was united as a new North German Confederation. Austria was no longer a German power. It became Austria-Hungary.

GERMANY BEFORE UNIFICATION

DENMARK
HANOVER
NETHERLANDS
PRUSSIA
PRUSSIA
Berlin
SAXONY
BAV.
BAVARIA
LORRAINE
ALSACE
AUSTRIA
SWITZ.
FRANCE

MAP KEY
— German Confederation

GERMANY AFTER UNIFICATION

DENMARK
NETHERLANDS
Berlin
GERMANY
BELGIUM
AUSTRIA-HUNGARY
LORRAINE
ALSACE
SWITZ.
FRANCE
ITALY

Germany became united by 1871. Did the new nation include all of the areas that were part of the German Confederation?

Otto von Bismarck

Bismarck decided that a war against France would unite all Germans. In 1870 southern Germans helped the North German Confederation defeat the French. In 1871 the southern Germans joined the confederation and formed one nation. This new nation was called the German Empire. A new **kaiser,** or emperor, ruled the empire. The kaiser said that Bismarck would run the German government.

As a result of the war in 1870, Bismarck forced France to give most of two small French states to Germany. The two French states were Alsace and Lorraine. Alsace and Lorraine had coal and iron. Bismarck wanted this coal and iron for German factories. France was also forced to pay a lot of money to Germany. France hated Germany for many years after the war.

Bismarck worked to make the German Empire strong. He also tried to find European nations that would help protect the new nation.

Nationalism was very strong in Europe for many years. Feelings of nationalism would make nations want to rule colonies in many parts of the world. How did nations conquer and rule colonies? You will learn the answer in Chapter 30.

Using Vocabulary

Find the Meaning   Write on your paper the word or words that best complete each sentence.

1. If one nation **declares war** on another nation, then the two nations are _____ in battle.

   allies   enemies   equal

2. The **prime minister** is the _____ of a nation.

   government leader   monarch   Church leader

3. The **unification** of Italy meant that Italy was _____.

   one nation   several states   smaller in size

4. The **German Confederation** was a group of German states that were joined together by _____.

   imperialism   Cavour   the Congress of Vienna

5. The **kaiser** was the German _____.

   army   government   emperor

Read and Remember

Finish the Paragraph   Number your paper from 1 to 5. Use the words in dark print to finish the paragraph. Write on your paper the words you choose.

Lorraine   nationalism   states   wars   Austria

It was difficult for Germany and Italy to become nations. They each had to unite their many __1__. For Italy to become unified, the Italians first had to free the northern states from __2__. In Germany, Otto von Bismarck said that __3__ with other countries would increase German __4__. This would help unite the German people. After a war with France, the German Empire gained most of the land of the two states of Alsace and __5__.

Think and Apply

Compare and Contrast   Read each sentence below. Decide whether it tells about Germany, Italy, or both nations. Write **G** on your paper for each sentence that tells about Germany. Write **I** on your paper for each sentence that tells about Italy. Write **GI** on your paper for each sentence that tells about both Germany and Italy.

1. There were 39 states that united to form this nation.

2. Cavour and Garibaldi led the unification of this nation.

3. The Kingdom of Sardinia pushed Austria out of the northern states to help the unification of this nation.

4. Feelings of nationalism helped the unification of the states.

5. This nation gained Venetia after helping Prussia defeat Austria in 1866.

6. Wars against Denmark, Austria, and France helped unite this nation.

7. Much of the fight for unification took place during the 1860s.

Skill Builder

Using Map Directions   Study the map on page 203 that shows Italy before its unification. Then write on your paper the word **north, south, east,** or **west** to finish each sentence below.

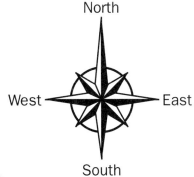

1. Austria is _____ of Switzerland.

2. Lombardy and Venetia are _____ of the Papal States.

3. The island that is part of the Kingdom of Sardinia is _____ of France.

4. Tuscany is _____ of Lombardy.

5. Savoy is _____ of Corsica.

6. To get to Rome from Venice, you could go south on the Adriatic Sea and then _____ across land.

Imperialism

THINK ABOUT AS YOU READ

1. **What were some of the reasons for the growth of imperialism?**
2. **Where were most of the colonies located?**
3. **How did imperialist nations gain trade rights in Japan and in China?**

NEW WORDS

♦ **imperialism**
♦ **imperialist**
♦ **expand**
♦ **sepoys**
♦ **discrimination**
♦ **Spanish-American War**
♦ **opium**
♦ **Opium War**

PEOPLE & PLACES

♦ **South Africa**
♦ **Queen Victoria**
♦ **Hawaii**
♦ **Puerto Rico**
♦ **Guam**
♦ **Japanese**

Imperialism means one nation wins control of colonies or other nations. A nation that controls colonies is called an **imperialist** nation. Imperialism occurred in ancient times. The ancient Persians and ancient Greeks were imperialists. The Roman Empire was imperialist. Between 1870 and 1914, many European and Asian nations became imperialist nations.

There were four main reasons for the growth of imperialism. One reason was that the Industrial Revolution created a need for raw materials. Many European nations needed cotton, iron, and other raw materials for their factories. They got many raw materials from countries in Africa, Asia, the Middle East, and Latin America.

Another reason for the growth of imperialism was that many merchants wanted new markets in which to sell their goods. There were millions of people in

For many years, the British controlled the land and the people of India. The British used many Indians as servants.

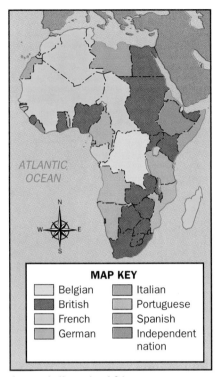
Imperialism in Africa

British soldiers in Africa

Africa and in Asia. Imperialist nations hoped to sell many goods to these large populations.

A third reason was that many European nations felt that they had a right to conquer lands in Asia and in Africa. The Industrial Revolution had not reached many of these areas. Europeans felt that they were bringing new machines and ideas to their colonies. Colonies in Africa and Asia became good places to build factories. Many people in these colonies worked for low wages.

A fourth reason for the growth of imperialism was nationalism. Great Britain was the first nation to rule many colonies in Africa and Asia. As Great Britain's empire grew, other nations began to want new lands, too. Countries such as France, Germany, the United States, and Japan were eager to **expand** their empires. People felt proud when their nation ruled a large empire. They thought that the colonies would make their nations greater and stronger.

By 1914 most of Asia and Africa was ruled by a few nations in Europe. Look at the maps on this page and on page 211. The maps show the areas in Africa and Asia that imperialist nations ruled in 1914.

The imperialist nations often sent soldiers to capture land and to make people work for them. In Africa, Europeans used weapons to make millions of Africans work in mines and on plantations. They also forced people in the colonies to pay high taxes. Africans had to work for Europeans in order to pay these high taxes.

Great Britain ruled more land and more people than any other nation ruled. Its empire included India, Egypt, South Africa, and many other colonies. By controlling South Africa, Great Britain controlled ninety percent of the world's diamond trade. Queen Victoria was the ruler of Great Britain during much of its imperialism. She ruled from 1837 to 1901.

The British controlled a lot of land and people in Africa. They also controlled India. India provided

The sepoys began to fight against the British in India in 1857.

Queen Victoria

Hawaii was an island colony of the United States.

raw materials to Great Britain. It was also a good place for British merchants to sell their goods. Great Britain made a lot of money by controlling India.

At first, India was controlled by a British trade company. The British used many Indians as servants. They made the Indians pay high taxes. They also had an army of Indian soldiers called **sepoys**. Then in 1857 the sepoys began to fight against the British trade company. The British won the war against the sepoys. At this time the British government took control of India. The British ruled India until 1947.

In some ways the British helped India. They built canals, railroads, bridges, and new buildings. But the Indians did not like being ruled by the British. They were forced to work hard at low-paying jobs. They were treated as a lower class of people in their own country. In many parts of India, there were signs that read "For Europeans only." The Indians were angry about this **discrimination**. Many Indians felt that they did not have any rights. Discrimination also happened in other European colonies.

The United States was also an imperialist nation. The United States ruled island colonies in the Pacific Ocean and in the Caribbean Sea. One island colony was Hawaii. The United States gained more colonies

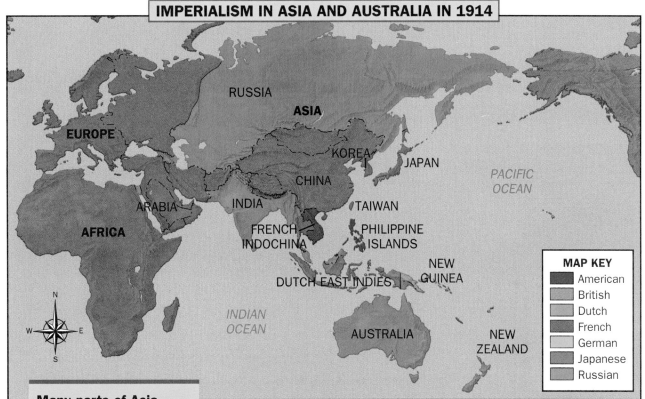

MAP KEY

- American
- British
- Dutch
- French
- German
- Japanese
- Russian

Many parts of Asia were controlled by imperialist nations. How many imperialist nations had colonies in Asia?

The Opium War of 1839 was fought mostly at sea.

after winning the **Spanish-American War** in 1898. Puerto Rico and Guam were two of these colonies.

Many countries wanted to control the businesses and trade in Latin America. But the United States said that it would fight to prevent other nations from starting colonies in Latin America. In this way the United States protected its own interests in Latin American businesses.

Many nations wanted to control China, a large nation in Asia. China was able to make most of the goods it needed. So China did not want to trade with other countries. Europeans wanted to find something that the millions of Chinese people would want to buy. Finally, the British began to sell a drug called **opium** to the Chinese. Many Chinese wanted this dangerous drug. The Chinese government tried to stop the opium trade. This led to the **Opium War** between China and Great Britain in 1839. This war was fought mostly at sea. China lost the war because it could not defeat the powerful British navy.

When four large United States ships came to Japan, the Japanese felt they had to agree to trade with the Americans.

Imperialist nations wanted to control China's trade.

Great Britain gained many trade rights in China. Soon other nations, including France, Germany, Japan, and Russia, controlled cities along China's coast. The United States wanted to trade in China. It encouraged open trade in China for all nations.

The Industrial Revolution did not reach Japan until the late 1800s. Japan did not want to trade with other countries. But in 1853, four large United States ships entered a Japanese harbor. Americans asked that Japan start to trade with the United States. The Japanese felt that they had to agree to trade with the Americans. But the Japanese did not want to be ruled by other nations. They decided to make Japan a modern industrial nation. Soon the Japanese built railroads, machines, and many factories. Japan also became an imperialist nation. The Japanese conquered parts of Asia in order to get raw materials for their factories.

Imperialism helped the imperialist nations gain raw materials and wealth. The people in the colonies were hurt by high taxes, low-paying jobs, and discrimination. Imperialism also caused wars. Nations fought one another to rule colonies. In 1914 a terrible war began in Europe. Why did this war begin? You will learn the answer in Chapter 31.

Using Vocabulary

Match Up   Finish the sentences in Group A with words from Group B. Write on your paper the letter of each correct answer.

Group A

1. A nation that controls colonies or other nations is an _____ nation.

2. Indian soldiers that worked for a British trade company were called _____.

3. When a nation gains control over more land, it _____ its empire.

4. Laws that treat a group of people unfairly are examples of _____.

Group B

a. sepoys

b. expands

c. discrimination

d. imperialist

Read and Remember

Finish the Sentence   Write on your paper the word or words that best complete each sentence.

1. Europeans used weapons and _____ to force Africans to work for them in mines and on plantations.

   canals   taxes   raw materials

2. The nation with the largest empire was _____.

   Great Britain   Japan   Portugal

3. By controlling _____, Great Britain controlled ninety percent of the world's diamond trade.

   India   Latin America   South Africa

4. The United States won the colonies of _____ during a war with Spain.

   Japan and China   Puerto Rico and Guam   India and South Africa

Write the Answer   Write one or more sentences on your paper to answer each question.

1. What were four reasons that imperialism grew in the 1800s?

2. Why did Great Britain want to control India?

3. What was life like for Indians during British rule in India?

4. How did the United States protect its interests in Latin America?

5. How did Japan change after 1853?

Think and Apply

Fact or Opinion   Write **F** on your paper for each fact below. Write **O** for each opinion. You should find three sentences that are opinions.

1. Nations such as France and Germany wanted to expand their empires during the late 1800s.

2. Africa, Asia, Latin America, and the Middle East are rich in raw materials.

3. It was not fair that the Indians were treated as a lower class of people in their own country.

4. Queen Victoria was the greatest ruler in the world.

5. The trade of a drug led to the Opium War of 1839 between Great Britain and China.

6. The British built railroads and bridges in India.

7. It is important for a nation to expand its empire.

8. The United States wanted open trade in China.

Journal Writing

China had not wanted to trade with other nations in the early 1800s. How do you think the Chinese felt about the British and the results of the Opium War? Write a paragraph to explain your answer.

Skill Builder

Using Map Keys   Look at the map about imperialism in Asia and Australia on page 211. Study the map and the map key. Then write on your paper the answer to each question below.

1. What color shows the land controlled by Germans?

2. What are two nations on the map that were controlled by the British in 1914?

3. Which nation controlled Korea?

4. Did France or Great Britain control more land in Asia?

5. Which land did the Dutch control?

6. Which nation controlled Australia?

Understanding a Political Cartoon   The political cartoon on page 212 is about imperialism. Study the political cartoon. Then write on your paper the answer to each question below.

1. What nation does the pie represent?

Russia   China   India

2. The people in the drawing are from different nations. What are they doing to the pie?

dividing it   eating it   cooking it

3. The woman on the left is a woman you read about in this chapter. What is her name?

Marie Curie   Empress Theodora   Queen Victoria

4. A Chinese man is standing behind the other people in the cartoon. How do you think he feels?

glad   angry   sleepy

5. Do you think the artist was pleased about what the other nations were doing to China? Explain your answer on a separate piece of paper.

World War I

THINK ABOUT AS YOU READ

1. **What were the causes of World War I?**
2. **Why did the United States enter the war?**
3. **What were some of the results of the war?**

NEW WORDS

- World War I
- military
- technology
- alliances
- tension
- neutral
- Central Powers
- submarines
- poison gas
- trenches
- surrendered
- Fourteen Points
- Treaty of Versailles
- League of Nations

PEOPLE & PLACES

- Archduke Francis Ferdinand
- Serbia
- Woodrow Wilson
- Edith Cavell
- Brussels

The late 1800s to the early 1900s was a time of great hope in Europe. Democracy was growing in some nations. The Industrial Revolution increased the food supply and helped people get jobs. Then in 1914 Austria-Hungary's Archduke Francis Ferdinand and his wife were shot by a person from Serbia. Suddenly many nations in Europe and other parts of the world were at war. This was the beginning of **World War I**. This war was also called the Great War.

The war was fought all over Europe. It was fought in Africa and in the Middle East. People from more than thirty nations fought in World War I. Millions of people were killed or wounded.

The deaths of the archduke and his wife were not the real causes of World War I. The four main causes began in the 1800s. Nationalism was one cause. People were united by pride for their nation. They wanted their nation to gain land, money, and power.

Airplanes were used for the first time in war during World War I.

The deaths of Austria-Hungary's archduke and his wife sparked World War I in 1914.

Kaiser Wilhelm II, the ruler of Germany during World War I

A second cause of World War I was an increase in **military** strength. Each nation wanted to be the strongest. The nations of Europe had built large armies. Germany had built the strongest army. Great Britain had built the strongest navy. But by 1898 Germany also had a strong navy. This made Germany a danger to Great Britain. By 1914 nations all over Europe had new military **technology**. New ships and weapons made the nations ready for war.

Imperialism was a third cause of World War I. The nations of Europe wanted more colonies. France was still angry that Germany had taken Alsace and Lorraine. France wanted these lands again. Serbia wanted land that was ruled by Austria-Hungary.

A fourth cause of World War I was that many nations had made **alliances**. This means that the nations had promised to fight for one another in a war. Austria-Hungary and Germany promised to fight for each other. Great Britain, France, and Russia also promised to help one another during a war.

These four causes created anger and **tension** between nations in Europe. So when Archduke Ferdinand was killed, Austria-Hungary went to war against Serbia. Then Germany promised to help

French soldiers during a battle in World War I

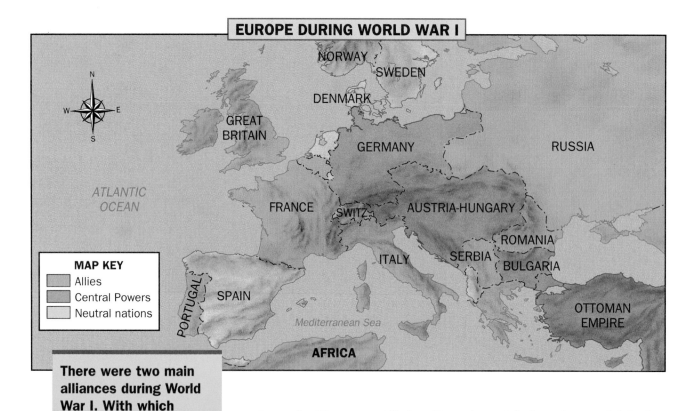

EUROPE DURING WORLD WAR I

MAP KEY
- Allies
- Central Powers
- Neutral nations

NORWAY
SWEDEN
DENMARK
GREAT BRITAIN
GERMANY
RUSSIA
ATLANTIC OCEAN
FRANCE
SWITZ
AUSTRIA-HUNGARY
ROMANIA
ITALY
SERBIA
BULGARIA
PORTUGAL
SPAIN
Mediterranean Sea
OTTOMAN EMPIRE
AFRICA

There were two main alliances during World War I. With which alliance was Bulgaria?

Women built weapons and machines during World War I.

Austria-Hungary fight. Russia said that it would help Serbia fight. So Germany declared war on Russia. Germany also declared war on its old enemy, France.

Then Germany invaded Belgium. Belgium was a **neutral** country. It did not want to fight in a war. Germany's attack on Belgium made Great Britain angry. Great Britain declared war on Germany. Soon there was fighting all over Europe. The fighting spread to Africa and the Middle East.

Germany and Austria-Hungary were the two main nations of an alliance called the **Central Powers**. Great Britain, Russia, France, Serbia, and many other nations were known as the Allies. There were also several neutral nations in Europe.

The Central Powers and the Allies both thought that they would win the war quickly. But the war did not end quickly. It lasted four years.

The German army fought in Russia and in France. In 1917 the Germans were winning in Russia. The Russians did not have enough guns. They did not have enough food. People in Russia had also begun a revolution. The Russians decided to stop fighting.

Soldiers from many nations fought in World War I. These Canadian soldiers are leaving a trench.

German submarine

Soldiers wore masks to avoid poison gas.

In 1917 the Russians signed a peace treaty with the Germans. Russia promised to stop helping the Allies.

New military technology was used during World War I. The Germans built new powerful ships called **submarines**. The German submarines could travel underwater to sneak up on and sink an enemy ship. The Germans also used **poison gas** to kill enemy soldiers. Airplanes, tanks, and new types of guns were also used for the first time in a war.

German soldiers fought the Allies in France for a long time. Soldiers fought one another from **trenches,** or long, deep ditches. Although millions of German soldiers and Allied soldiers were killed, neither side could defeat the other. The war also continued in other areas of Europe and Africa.

At first, Americans did not want to fight in World War I. Woodrow Wilson was the President of the United States during the war. He wanted the United States to be a neutral nation. But in 1915 Germany began to use its submarines to sink many ships that carried food and other goods to Great Britain. A submarine sank the *Lusitania*, a large British ship. More than a thousand people died, including 128 Americans. By 1917 the German navy had also sunk several American ships that were carrying goods to the Allies. Americans also found out that Germany

Many cities were completely destroyed during World War I.

Woodrow Wilson

A German submarine sank the *Lusitania* in 1915.

had tried to get Mexico to declare war on the United States. Wilson called for war against Germany. The United States entered World War I in April 1917.

American soldiers helped the Allies win World War I. The Allies and the Americans fought against the Germans in France. They also fought Austria-Hungary. At last in 1918, the Central Powers **surrendered** to the Allies. The war was over. The Allies had won.

Before the war was over, Wilson had begun to work for world peace. He had written a peace plan called the **Fourteen Points**. He wanted this plan to be used for the peace treaty after the war. These Fourteen Points told how German soldiers should leave Allied lands. The plan also included ways to prevent future wars. The Allies used some of the Fourteen Points when they wrote the **Treaty of Versailles** at the end of World War I.

The Treaty of Versailles punished Germany for its role in World War I. Germany had to pay billions of dollars to the Allies. Germany also lost some of its land and colonies. Another treaty punished Austria-Hungary. Austria-Hungary lost most of its land and became Austria. Austria and Germany were not allowed to have large armies and navies. The map on page 221 shows how Europe looked after the war.

The Treaty of Versailles also started the **League of Nations**. President Wilson planned the League of

EUROPE AFTER WORLD WAR I

NORWAY

FINLAND

SWEDEN

DENMARK

GREAT BRITAIN

ATLANTIC OCEAN

GERMANY

POLAND

SOVIET UNION (U.S.S.R.)

LORRAINE

ALSACE

CZECHOSLOVAKIA

SWITZ.

AUSTRIA

HUNGARY

FRANCE

ROMANIA

YUGOSLAVIA

PORTUGAL

SPAIN

ITALY

BULGARIA

Mediterranean Sea

TURKEY

AFRICA

N W E S

The size and names of many nations changed at the end of the war. Compare this map to the map on page 218. What happened to the nation of Austria-Hungary?

Leaders at the signing of the Treaty of Versailles

Nations when he wrote the Fourteen Points. The League was a group of nations that worked for world peace. It began in 1920 with 42 nations. The United States did not join the League. Many Americans believed that by joining the League they might have to fight in another war.

After World War I, the countries of the world faced new problems. Millions of people had been killed or wounded during the war. Some cities and towns had been completely destroyed. Many people in Europe were left without jobs, homes, or money. European countries needed money for new buildings and roads. But many nations had spent most of their money on the war. Many countries had borrowed money to pay for their weapons and armies. After the war, these nations could not pay back the money they had borrowed.

The Treaty of Versailles made many people angry. The treaty made the Germans hate the Allies. The Germans wanted their nation to be strong again. Would the Germans live in peace with the Allies? You will find the answer in Chapters 33 and 34.

Edith Cavell (1865–1915)

Women were not soldiers in World War I, but they played a very important part in the war. Many worked in factories to build weapons. Others became nurses to help care for wounded soldiers. One of the greatest World War I nurses was Edith Cavell.

Edith Cavell was born in England in 1865. For her first job, she moved to Belgium where she cared for a family's children. While she was in Belgium, her father became ill. Cavell returned to England to help nurse her father back to health. Cavell realized that she enjoyed nursing.

In 1895 Cavell was accepted by the London Hospital in England to be trained as a nurse. After that she worked as a nurse in England for several years. In 1907 Cavell became the head nurse in a teaching hospital in Brussels, Belgium. She started the nursing system in Belgium.

Edith Cavell

Soon after World War I began, German soldiers took control of the city of Brussels. Edith Cavell began working to help Allied soldiers escape from Belgium to Holland, a neutral nation. Cavell nursed injured soldiers and let them hide in the hospital until they were well enough to leave. Then the soldiers were given money and a guide to show them their escape route.

Within a few months, Cavell had helped several hundred soldiers escape. However, Cavell was caught by the Germans. On October 12, 1915, the Germans executed her for helping the Allied soldiers.

Cavell with nurses during World War I

After the war, Cavell's body was brought back to England and buried there. A statue was built in London to honor Cavell. Many books have been written about Edith Cavell. People still admire this fine nurse for her courage during World War I.

Using Vocabulary

Find the Meaning   Write on your paper the word or words that best complete each sentence.

1. The **Central Powers** was an alliance that included Austria-Hungary and _____ .

   Great Britain   Serbia   Germany

2. A **neutral** nation is a nation that does not want to _____ .

   fight in a war   lose   win

3. Soldiers in World War I fought in **trenches,** or long _____ .

   submarines   tanks   ditches

4. To **surrender** means to _____ .

   fight   give up   win

5. The **League of Nations** was a group that worked for _____ .

   world peace   military technology   wars

Read and Remember

Find the Answer   Find the sentences that tell the causes of World War I. Write on your paper the sentences you find. You should find four sentences.

1. Nationalism was strong in many nations.

2. Many nations in Europe wanted to expand their empires.

3. The League of Nations was part of Woodrow Wilson's Fourteen Points.

4. Many nations had made alliances with one another.

5. The Industrial Revolution increased the supply of food and jobs.

6. German submarines sank the *Lusitania*.

7. Many nations were increasing their military strength with new technology and large armies.

Finish the Paragraphs   Number your paper from 1 to 8. Use the words in dark print to finish the paragraphs below. Write on your paper the words you choose.

Versailles	neutral	Ferdinand	technology
tension	Allies	Serbia	Germany

There was much ___1__ between nations in 1914. That is why the deaths of Archduke ___2__ and his wife sparked World War I. When Austria-Hungary declared war on ___3__, the allies of the two nations also began to fight. The two alliances in World War I were the Central Powers and the ___4__. New war ___5__ included submarines, tanks, airplanes, and poison gas.

At first, Americans wanted the United States to be ___6__. Then in 1917 the United States declared war on ___7__. The Americans helped the Allies win the war in 1918. At the end of the war, the leaders of the Allies wrote the Treaty of ___8__, which punished Germany.

Skill Builder

Reading a Historical Map   The historical map on page 218 shows the Central Powers, the Allies, and the neutral countries in Europe during World War I. Study the map and the map key. Then write on your paper the answer to each question.

1. What color is used to show the Allies?

2. What were two nations that were part of the Central Powers?

3. What were two nations that were part of the Allies?

4. Was Romania a neutral country?

5. Was Switzerland allied with France?

6. Which Allied nation was east of Germany?

Journal Writing

 Write a paragraph that explains why people honor Edith Cavell for her courage.

Think and Apply

Cause and Effect Write sentences on your paper by matching each cause on the left with an effect on the right.

Cause

1. Each nation in Europe wanted to be the strongest, so _____

2. Russia did not have enough food and weapons, so _____

3. German submarines kept sinking American ships, so _____

4. Germany knew it could not win World War I, so _____

5. Many cities were completely destroyed during World War I, so _____

6. Nations had spent most of their money during the war, so _____

Effect

a. many people in Europe did not have homes after the war.

b. the nations built strong armies and navies.

c. in 1918 it surrendered to the Allies.

d. the United States went to war against Germany.

e. after the war they could not pay back the money they had borrowed.

f. it signed a peace treaty with Germany in 1917.

Sequencing Events Number your paper from 1 to 4. Write the sentences to show the correct order.

In 1917 Russia signed a peace treaty with Germany.

The League of Nations was formed after World War I ended.

The deaths of Austria-Hungary's archduke and his wife sparked World War I.

The Central Powers surrendered in 1918.

Revolutions in Russia

Russia is the world's largest country in size. It covers parts of Europe and Asia. The Industrial Revolution that changed Western Europe did not come to Russia until the 1860s. Most Russians remained poor farmers. They had to obey absolute rulers. These rulers were called **czars**. In 1917 Russia had two major revolutions. After the revolutions, Russia was no longer ruled by a czar. Why did these revolutions happen?

In the years before 1917, many Russians were unhappy. They had little freedom. Most people were peasants called **serfs**. The serfs worked on land that belonged to nobles. The serfs were not free. They were often treated very cruelly. They did not have enough food. They could not go to school to learn to read and write. Some peasants became factory

Vladimir Lenin and the Bolsheviks led the Russian Revolution of 1917.

Russian peasants were forced to work as slaves. These serfs are using hammers to crush rocks between their feet.

workers. They were paid very low wages. Most of the peasants were very hungry.

The czars made all the laws. Many czars were very cruel. They were often hated by their people. There was no freedom of speech. Some czars made a few changes to improve life for the peasants. One czar freed the serfs. But the serfs were not given any land. The czars also involved Russia in several wars. Many Russians were killed during the wars.

Some people tried to start revolutions in order to change Russia. The revolutions that took place before 1917 failed to bring changes to Russia.

A group of Russians called the Bolsheviks wanted Russia to become a **Communist** nation. They used many ideas from a German named Karl Marx. In 1848 Karl Marx wrote a book about **communism**. He said that workers should start a revolution against business owners. Marx said that workers would be the rulers in a Communist government. Marx's ideas brought new hope to Russia's poor, hungry peasants. The peasants believed that a Communist government would improve life for them.

In 1894 Nicholas II became Russia's czar. During his rule, people continued to be poor and unhappy. Many peasants starved because of bad crops. Factory workers wanted better wages and better working conditions. In 1905 thousands of workers went to

Czar Nicholas II with his son Alexis

the czar's palace to ask for changes. Government soldiers shot hundreds of these workers. People were very angry. Soon revolutions began all over Russia. But Nicholas II continued to rule Russia. He refused to make changes to help the poor.

Then World War I began. The Russians fought against the Central Powers. Almost two million Russian soldiers died during the war. Railroads carried military supplies and food to the Russian soldiers. But at home the Russian people were starving. The Russian people wanted peace. But the czar would not let Russia leave the war. Russian soldiers continued to fight and die.

In March 1917 an important revolution began in Russia. Angry Russians began to march and riot in the streets of Petrograd, Russia's capital city. Other Russians began to strike. People demanded bread. They wanted coal to heat their homes. They wanted Russia to stop fighting in World War I. Nicholas II lost his control of Russia. He was forced to leave his position as czar. He and his family were then put in prison. Later, they were executed by the Bolsheviks. Nicholas II was the last czar of Russia.

A new government controlled Russia after the March revolution. A parliament was started. The new government was weak. People were still poor and hungry. Russian soldiers continued to die in World War I. People became unhappy with the new government. Another revolution began in November. This was the **Russian Revolution** of 1917. It was started by the Bolsheviks.

A man named Vladimir Lenin led the Bolsheviks during the Russian Revolution. Lenin promised to give the Russians peace, land, and bread. These were the three things the Russians wanted. The Bolsheviks captured the capital city of Petrograd. They soon controlled the Russian government. Lenin was the leader of the government. In 1918 the city of Moscow became the capital of Russia.

Vladimir Lenin

The Soviet Union was formed in 1922. What were two cities in the Soviet Union?

SOVIET UNION (U.S.S.R.)

Leningrad

Moscow

URAL MOUNTAINS

Ob River

Volga River

EUROPE

ASIA

AFRICA

INDIAN OCEAN

PACIFIC OCEAN

N W E S

A poster asking people to join the Bolsheviks

As soon as Lenin became ruler, he took Russia out of World War I. Lenin ruled as a dictator. He had full power to make laws. Lenin's government took control of most farms and factories. The government also took away the power of Russia's church.

Many Russians did not want the new government. Some of them wanted Russia to be ruled by a czar again. These people were called White Russians. The White Russians began to fight against the Bolsheviks. A **civil war** began. During a civil war, people of the same nation fight against one another. The civil war lasted three years. In 1920 the Bolsheviks won.

In 1922 the Bolsheviks created a new Communist nation. They called the new nation the Union of Soviet Socialist Republics, or U.S.S.R. It was also called the Soviet Union. The Soviet Union was the union of Russia and many small republics. The Bolsheviks called themselves the Communist party.

Lenin ruled the Soviet Union until he died in 1924. By that time the government owned most farms and industries. Lenin had promised to give land to the peasants. But the peasants never got their land. The government owned the land. Lenin had promised more food. But for many years there was not enough food in the Soviet Union.

Joseph Stalin was the dictator of the Soviet Union for 25 years.

People on a collective farm in the Soviet Union

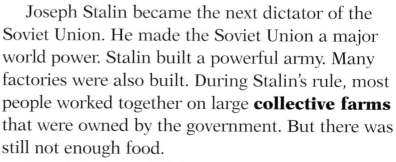
Flag of the Soviet Union

Joseph Stalin became the next dictator of the Soviet Union. He made the Soviet Union a major world power. Stalin built a powerful army. Many factories were also built. During Stalin's rule, most people worked together on large **collective farms** that were owned by the government. But there was still not enough food.

Joseph Stalin ruled for 25 years. His government had total control of life in the Soviet Union. People were told not to believe in any religion. Many people were afraid of Stalin. His secret police **arrested** many people who spoke out against his government. Millions of people in the Soviet Union were killed or sent to prison by Stalin.

Many people fight revolutions to get freedom. The American and French revolutions in the 1700s were fought for freedom. But the Russian Revolution of 1917 did not bring freedom to the people of Russia. The revolution only changed the absolute rulers of Russia from czars to dictators. Communists ruled the Soviet Union for almost seventy years. But many people in the Soviet Union did not like communism. In Chapter 44 you will learn how communism ended in the Soviet Union.

Karl Marx (1818–1883)

Karl Marx was a German who had many ideas about government and workers. His ideas were used to bring Communist governments to many nations.

Marx was born in 1818 in what was then Prussia. At college he studied history, government, and law. He also studied different ways of thinking. He shared many ideas with teachers and students who did not like the government of Prussia.

Karl Marx became a writer. He wrote about governments and businesses. He also wrote about bad working conditions in factories. Marx believed that business owners unfairly used working-class people to gain wealth. He said that in this way rich people became richer and poor people became poorer. Marx believed that the differences between the rich and the poor led to problems. He thought that problems would end if people were no longer divided into classes.

Marx and a close friend wrote about these ideas in a short book called *The Communist Manifesto*. In this book the two men told the working class to start a revolution against the ruling class. They wrote that businesses should be owned by all workers. All people should share wealth. Then there would be very few rich people or poor people. Many people, including the Bolsheviks in Russia, used Marx's ideas to start revolutions in their nations.

Karl Marx

Marx's ideas were used to develop communism. Communism is a system that allows the government to own all farms and industries. Many nations used Marx's ideas to form Communist governments. In this way Karl Marx affected governments, businesses, and people in countries all over the world.

Using Vocabulary

Finish Up   Choose the word or words in dark print to best complete each sentence. Write on your paper the word or words you choose.

civil war	**communism**	**serfs**
Russian Revolution	**collective**	**czars**

1. After the year 1500, the rulers of Russia were called _____ .

2. Peasants called _____ were not allowed to leave the land on which they worked.

3. The _____ was fought in 1917 because people in Russia were unhappy with the new government.

4. Under the system of _____ , the government owns all farms and industries.

5. During a _____ , people of the same nation fight against one another.

6. During Stalin's rule, most people worked together on large _____ farms.

Read and Remember

Choose the Answer   Write the correct answers on your paper.

1. On which two continents is Russia?

   Europe and Australia   Asia and Africa   Europe and Asia

2. Who was Russia's last czar?

   Nicholas II   Vladimir Lenin   Joseph Stalin

3. Which people were shot at the czar's palace in 1905?

   government soldiers   serfs   factory workers

4. Who did Karl Marx say would be the rulers in a Communist government?

   czars   presidents   workers

5. Which group wanted Russia to become a Communist nation?

   Bolsheviks   White Russians   Germans

6. Which leader took Russia out of World War I?

Nicholas II   Vladimir Lenin   Joseph Stalin

7. When did the Bolsheviks create the Soviet Union?

1894   1917   1922

8. Who believed that all people should share wealth?

White Russians   czars   Karl Marx

Think and Apply

Drawing Conclusions   Read each pair of sentences. Then look in the box for the conclusion you might make. Write on your paper the letter of the conclusion you choose.

1. Russian peasants often did not have enough food.
Russian factory workers were paid very low wages.

2. The Russian people hated the czar.
The Russian people wanted changes.

3. Almost two million Russian soldiers were killed in World War I.
People in Russia were starving during the war because the food supplies were being sent to soldiers.

4. After the Russian Revolution, the Bolsheviks ruled Russia.
The White Russians wanted a czar to rule Russia.

5. Millions of people in the Soviet Union were killed or were sent to prison by Stalin.
People were arrested if they spoke out against Stalin.

---

a. People in the Soviet Union were afraid of Stalin.
b. Life was hard for peasants and factory workers in Russia.
c. They began to fight in a civil war.
d. People wanted Russia to stop fighting in the war.
e. The Russian people began a revolution.

Journal Writing

 Pretend you are Karl Marx. Write a short letter to a friend. Tell your friend how you feel about businesses and workers.

Riddle Puzzle

Number your paper from 1 to 9. Choose a word in dark print to complete each sentence. Write the correct answers on your paper.

nobles	**religion**	**demanded**	**Nicholas II**	**arrested**
land	**ended**	**Industrial**	**government**	

1. The Russian people wanted peace, _____, and bread.

2. Communism _____ in the Soviet Union after almost seventy years.

3. _____ would not let Russia leave World War I.

4. The _____ Revolution did not come to Russia until the 1860s.

5. Serfs worked on land that belonged to _____ .

6. The Bolsheviks began a Communist _____ .

7. During Stalin's rule, people were told not to believe in any _____ .

8. Stalin's secret police _____ and killed many people.

9. During the revolution in March 1917, people _____ bread.

Now look at your answers. Circle the first letter of each answer you wrote on your paper. The letters you circle should spell a word. The word answers the riddle below.

RIDDLE: When Lenin died in 1924, Soviet leaders changed the name of the city of Petrograd. What was Petrograd's new name?

Write on your paper the answer to the riddle.

CHAPTER 33

The Rise of Dictators

Europe had many problems after World War I. The war had cost nations millions of dollars. Millions of people did not have jobs, homes, or enough food. Italy, Germany, and other nations were angry about the Treaty of Versailles. People began to want strong leaders. In some nations, people believed that dictators could solve their problems.

You have read about Lenin and Stalin in the Soviet Union. Lenin gained strong control of the nation during his rule. Stalin was also a strong dictator. He increased the industries and the military strength of the Soviet Union. By the 1930s the Soviet Union was a major world power.

THINK ABOUT AS YOU READ

1. **How did dictators gain power after World War I?**
2. **How did the Great Depression affect nations in Europe and Asia?**
3. **Why did Italy, Germany, and Japan build large armies?**

NEW WORDS

♦ Great Depression
♦ concentration camps
♦ Axis Powers

PEOPLE & PLACES

♦ Benito Mussolini
♦ Ethiopia
♦ Adolf Hitler
♦ Nazis
♦ General Hideki Tojo
♦ Czechoslovakia

The 1930s brought new dictators to power. Mussolini and Hitler wanted their nations to be great empires.

Benito Mussolini

Germans selling tin cans during the 1929 depression

Adolf Hitler

During World War I, Italy had fought with the Allies against Germany. Like many European countries, Italy had money problems after the war. The people of Italy were also angry that their country did not gain much land from the Treaty of Versailles. They turned to a man named Benito Mussolini to solve their problems. Mussolini helped the growth of nationalism in Italy. He promised to help Italy become a great empire. People in Italy believed that Mussolini would help them.

In 1922 Benito Mussolini became Italy's dictator. Mussolini made all the laws. Soon the people of Italy had no freedom. Workers were not allowed to strike. Newspapers were censored. Mussolini's secret police arrested people who spoke out against the dictator. Some people were killed.

Mussolini wanted to conquer new land for Italy. He built a large army and prepared his nation for war. In 1935 Mussolini conquered Ethiopia, a country in Africa. The Allies and the League of Nations were angry with Mussolini for attacking Ethiopia. But they did nothing to stop Mussolini. They did not want another world war to begin.

In 1929 the **Great Depression** began in the United States. A depression is a time when business becomes very slow. A depression can last many years. During the Great Depression, many banks, factories, and other businesses closed. Millions of people lost their jobs and all of their money. This terrible depression soon spread to many parts of the world.

The Great Depression brought very hard times to Germany. The nation already had many money problems because of the Treaty of Versailles. The treaty said that Germany had to pay a very large amount of money to the Allies. But Germany did not have enough money to do this. People in Germany were poor. Many people were starving. By 1933 the depression was very bad in Germany. Factories and banks closed. Almost half of the working people did

Hitler often spoke to thousands of his soldiers to encourage them to fight for Germany.

Nazi soldiers

Secret police arrested many Jews in Germany.

not have jobs. People did not have money to buy food. The Germans blamed the Allies and the Treaty of Versailles for their many problems. They wanted Germany to be strong again.

Adolf Hitler knew that the German people were very unhappy. Hitler was the leader of a group of Germans called the Nazis. The Nazis had their own army. Hitler told the German people that he would make new jobs. He said that he would help Germany conquer and rule the world. Many Germans liked Hitler's ideas. He made people feel very proud to be Germans. Nationalism grew stronger in Germany. Many German people wanted Hitler and the Nazis to rule Germany.

In 1933 Adolf Hitler became Germany's dictator. He had complete power. The Nazis worked to keep Hitler as their nation's dictator. Soon there was no freedom at all in Hitler's Germany. The Nazis controlled all activities in Germany. They controlled newspapers, radios, literature, music, and art. There was no freedom of speech. Secret police arrested people who spoke out or wrote against the ideas of Hitler. Many people were sent to prisons called **concentration camps**.

Hitler believed that Germans were better than all other people in the world. He also strongly hated

Jews. In 1935 he said that Jews were no longer German citizens. Jews were no longer allowed to work in hospitals, banks, and many other places. Nazis beat many Jews and burned Jewish homes and temples. Many Jews were arrested and sent to concentration camps.

Hitler knew that most Germans were angry about the Treaty of Versailles. The Germans wanted to have a large, powerful army again. They wanted to rule all the land that had been part of the German Empire. The treaty would not let Germany do these things. Hitler said that he would not obey the treaty. He planned ways to make Germany strong again.

Hitler secretly built a strong German army. He had German factories make many weapons. The factories made guns, tanks, and airplanes. Soon Germany was ready for war.

Japanese soldiers

While Italy and Germany prepared for war, Japan also prepared for war. Japan was a strong nation after World War I. There had not been any fighting on Japanese land during the war. Japan's trade and industries had grown. Japan was the most powerful country in Asia. Nationalism in Japan grew. Military leaders took control of Japan's government.

The depression that had begun in 1929 hurt the Japanese. People in other countries did not have money to buy Japan's goods. Many factories and other businesses in Japan closed. Many people lost their jobs. Farmers could not sell their crops.

Japanese military leaders decided that Japan should conquer other nations in Asia. These nations would give Japan many raw materials and new places to sell goods. Japan's General Hideki Tojo strongly encouraged war. He and the other military leaders told the Japanese people that war would be good for Japan. Many Japanese trained to become soldiers. In 1931 the Japanese army attacked and conquered part of China. The League of Nations did little to stop Japan.

Hideki Tojo

The Japanese invaded China in 1937.

The Axis Powers in Europe in 1938

Nazi soldiers entering Prague, Czechoslovakia

Italy, Germany, and Japan built strong armies. They all hoped to expand their empires. In 1936 they formed an alliance. Germany, Italy, and Japan were called the **Axis Powers**. They agreed to help one another conquer other lands.

The Axis Powers tested their strength by fighting in a civil war in Spain in 1937. The same year Japan began a major attack on China. In 1938 Hitler was ready for Germany to conquer Europe. That year German soldiers went to Austria. The Austrians did not fight. They allowed Austria to be ruled by Hitler.

Then Hitler's soldiers took control of part of Czechoslovakia. Great Britain and France were angry. Hitler promised these two nations that he would not try to take over the rest of Czechoslovakia. Then later Hitler went against this agreement. He took control of all of Czechoslovakia. This might have started a major war. But Great Britain and France did not want another world war. To keep peace, they decided to allow Hitler to conquer Czechoslovakia. They hoped that this would keep Hitler from wanting to conquer other nations.

The Axis Powers continued to gain strength. They began to look at other lands to conquer. Soon Great Britain and France realized that Hitler and his allies would not keep peace. They began to prepare for war.

Using Vocabulary

Match Up Finish the sentences in Group A with words from Group B. Write on your paper the letter of each correct answer.

Group A

1. The _____ was the period after 1929 when many businesses and people lost all of their money.

2. In 1936 Germany, Italy, and Japan formed an alliance called the _____.

3. The Nazis forced many people to go to prisons called _____.

Group B

a. Axis Powers

b. concentration camps

c. Great Depression

Read and Remember

Finish Up Choose the word in dark print that best completes each sentence. Write on your paper the word you choose.

Jews	Ethiopia	citizens	money
Asia	Spain	Versailles	nationalism

1. After World War I, many nations needed _____.

2. Mussolini's soldiers conquered _____ for Italy in 1935.

3. Mussolini and Hitler helped _____ grow in their countries.

4. Hitler knew that the people of Germany were angry about the Treaty of _____.

5. Hitler said that Jews were no longer German _____.

6. Many _____ were sent to concentration camps.

7. Japan decided that it could solve its problems by conquering land in _____.

8. The Axis Powers tested their strength by fighting in a civil war in _____ in 1937.

Who Am I?   Read each sentence. Then look at the words in dark print for the name of the person who might have said it. Write on your paper the name of the person you choose.

Joseph Stalin   **Adolf Hitler**   **Benito Mussolini**
Vladimir Lenin   **Hideki Tojo**

1. "I was the first dictator in Russia after the revolution of 1917."

2. "As dictator of Italy, I prepared the nation for war."

3. "I was one of the Japanese military leaders who led Japan to attack China in the 1930s."

4. "After Lenin died, I helped the Soviet Union increase its industries and become a world power."

5. "I was the German dictator who led the Nazis to conquer Austria and Czechoslovakia."

Think and Apply

Categories   Read the words in each group. Decide how they are alike. Find the best title for each group from the words in dark print. Write the title on your paper.

Japan   **Great Depression**   **Dictators**   **Nazis**

1. Hitler
   Mussolini
   Stalin

2. hurt nations all over the world
   millions of people lost money
   factories and banks closed

3. kept Hitler in power
   arrested Jews
   controlled newspapers

4. Asian nation
   military leaders
   attacked China

Journal Writing

Hitler and Mussolini were very powerful dictators in Europe. Write a paragraph that tells at least three ways these dictators were alike.

Unit 7 World War II and Its Effects

People in many parts of the world wanted peace after World War I. The League of Nations was started to keep peace between nations. But the League of Nations could not stop nations from building strong armies. The League could not stop Italy, Germany, and Japan from starting the next world war.

World War II was the most terrible war the world had ever seen. More nations fought in this war than in any other war. More people died in this war than in any other war. The most powerful weapon ever invented was used during World War II. Nations learned that they would have to find new ways to keep peace.

The years after 1945 brought important changes to the world. A new, stronger peace-keeping organization was started after World War II. The United States and the Soviet Union became very powerful nations. Soon after the war, Communist leaders took control of many governments. The United States and other democracies tried to stop countries from becoming Communist nations. Sometimes wars were fought. But the nations were careful not to have another world war.

PACIFIC OCEAN

ATLANTIC OCEAN

PACIFIC OCEAN

INDIAN OCEAN

How did the Allies win World War II? What was the Cold War? How are nations working for peace? As you read Unit 7, think about how differences in governments can lead to wars. Think about how World War II, the Cold War, and the Vietnam War affected the world.

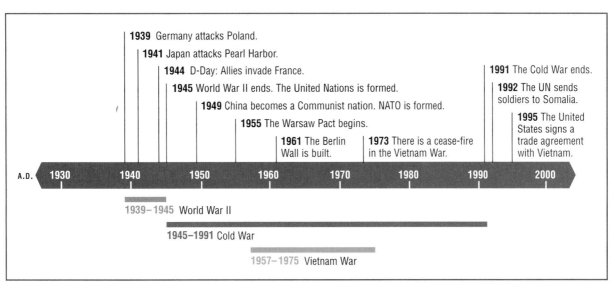

1939 Germany attacks Poland.

1941 Japan attacks Pearl Harbor.

1944 D-Day: Allies invade France.

1945 World War II ends. The United Nations is formed.

1949 China becomes a Communist nation. NATO is formed.

1955 The Warsaw Pact begins.

1961 The Berlin Wall is built.

1973 There is a cease-fire in the Vietnam War.

1991 The Cold War ends.

1992 The UN sends soldiers to Somalia.

1995 The United States signs a trade agreement with Vietnam.

A.D. | 1930 | 1940 | 1950 | 1960 | 1970 | 1980 | 1990 | 2000

1939–1945 World War II

1945–1991 Cold War

1957–1975 Vietnam War

CHAPTER 34

The Beginning of World War II

THINK ABOUT AS YOU READ

1. **Why did Germany, Italy, and Japan want another war?**
2. **Why did Germany lose the Battle of Britain?**
3. **What caused the United States to fight in World War II?**

NEW WORDS

- ♦ World War II
- ♦ Battle of Britain
- ♦ bombs
- ♦ bombed
- ♦ Battle of Stalingrad
- ♦ naval base

PEOPLE & PLACES

- ♦ Poland
- ♦ Dunkirk
- ♦ Winston Churchill
- ♦ Soviets
- ♦ Franklin D. Roosevelt
- ♦ Pearl Harbor

Great Britain and France wanted peace after World War I. But Adolf Hitler wanted war. He wanted Germany to rule the world. The other Axis Powers wanted to rule the world with Germany. Italy wanted to rule land in Europe and Africa. Japan wanted to rule Asia. Later, other countries would join the Axis Powers.

Great Britain and France were called the Allies. The Allies did not want to fight in another war. This is why the two nations allowed Hitler to conquer Austria and Czechoslovakia. Hitler promised that he would not conquer any more nations. He broke that promise. In 1939 Germany invaded Poland. This time the Allies said that they would fight for Poland. Great Britain and France declared war against Germany. **World War II** had begun.

Hitler salutes his soldiers as they march into Poland in 1939.

Allied soldiers wading out to boats at Dunkirk, France

Winston Churchill

The city of London during the Battle of Britain

The German army was strong. They conquered Poland in a few weeks. Then the German soldiers conquered northern Europe. In 1940 they attacked France. British soldiers and French soldiers fought the Germans in France.

Soon the Allies realized that France would be conquered. The British soldiers and French soldiers who were fighting there did not want to be captured. Great Britain sent hundreds of ships and small boats to Dunkirk, France, to help the soldiers escape. Thousands of soldiers went to Great Britain in the boats. These Allied soldiers would continue to fight against Hitler.

Germany conquered France. By 1940 the Axis Powers had conquered most of Europe. Then Adolf Hitler decided to conquer Great Britain. The prime minister of Great Britain was Winston Churchill. Winston Churchill said that Great Britain would never surrender to Hitler. Churchill was a strong leader. He gave the people of Great Britain hope that they could defeat the Germans.

The German fight against Great Britain was called the **Battle of Britain**. German airplanes dropped **bombs** on British cities. Germany **bombed** Great Britain for many months. Many people were killed. Many buildings were destroyed. But the British were brave. They did not surrender to the Germans. Great Britain's Royal Air Force shot down more than 2,000 German planes. Finally in 1941, the Germans stopped attacking Great Britain from the air. The battle was over. But World War II continued.

Other nations became involved in World War II. Six of these nations joined the Axis Powers. By the end of the war, almost 50 nations had joined the Allies. But the Axis Powers were very strong. They conquered most of Europe and parts of Asia and Africa. The Axis nations were winning World War II.

Then Hitler decided that the Soviet Union was an enemy. Hitler also wanted oil and wheat from the

The Axis Powers conquered most of Europe during World War II. Was Yugoslavia an area under Axis control?

Italian airplanes and British airplanes in battle above Egypt

Soviet Union. In 1941 Germany attacked the Soviet Union. This attack forced the Soviets to fight against the Germans. So the Soviet Union joined the Allies.

At first, the Germans won many battles in the Soviet Union. But the Soviets fought back. They remembered how they had fought Napoleon in 1812. They had burned their own farms and houses to defeat Napoleon. The Soviets did almost the same thing during World War II. They decided to burn everything the Germans might use. The Soviets burned houses, factories, and food. Then winter came. The weather was very cold. Snow covered the land. The Germans did not have enough food or warm clothing. Many Germans died. Then at the **Battle of Stalingrad** in 1943, the last Germans in the Soviet Union surrendered.

There was also fighting in the Atlantic Ocean. German submarines sank many ships that carried food, weapons, and other supplies to the British. But World War II brought new technology. Some of this new technology helped the Allies locate many of the German submarines that were underwater. When

On December 7, 1941, the Japanese dropped bombs on Pearl Harbor. The event brought the United States into World War II.

Franklin D. Roosevelt

Pearl Harbor, Hawaii

the submarines came up to the top of the water, the Allies dropped bombs on them from airplanes.

Across the Atlantic Ocean, the United States was a neutral nation. It did not want to fight in World War II. But Americans helped the Allies in other ways. Franklin D. Roosevelt was the President of the United States. He had American factories make weapons, tanks, and planes. American farmers grew extra food. The United States sent the food and weapons to Great Britain, the Soviet Union, and other Allies.

Americans hoped that they would not have to fight in World War II. But in 1941 General Hideki Tojo became the main military leader of Japan. On December 7, 1941, Tojo ordered Japanese soldiers to attack Pearl Harbor in the Pacific Ocean. Pearl Harbor was a large American **naval base** in Hawaii. The Japanese destroyed American ships and planes. They killed more than 2,000 Americans.

The people in the United States were very angry. They knew it was time for war. The next day, the United States declared war against Japan. Three days later, Germany and Italy declared war against the United States. Americans would help the Allies fight against the Axis Powers in Asia and in Europe.

Nations all over the world were now fighting in World War II. The war would continue for four more years. Who would win World War II? How would the war end? Read the next chapter to find out.

Using Vocabulary

Analogies   Use the words in dark print to best complete the sentences. Write the correct answers on your paper.

bomb   naval base   Battle of Britain   World War II

1. Central Powers is to World War I as Axis Powers is to _____ .

2. Airport is to airplane as _____ is to navy ships.

3. Japan is to the attack on Pearl Harbor as Germany is to the _____ .

4. Submarine is to ship underwater as _____ is to exploding weapon.

Read and Remember

Finish the Sentence   Write on your paper the word or words that best complete each sentence.

1. World War II started after Hitler invaded _____ .

China   France   Poland

2. Great Britain and France were part of the alliance called the _____ .

Axis Powers   Allies   Central Powers

3. _____ was the British prime minister during the Battle of Britain.

Franklin Roosevelt   Adolf Hitler   Winston Churchill

4. General _____ ordered the attack on Pearl Harbor in 1941.

Hideki Tojo   Benito Mussolini   Franklin Roosevelt

Write the Answer   Write one or more sentences on your paper to answer each question.

1. What happened at Dunkirk, France?

2. How did the Soviets stop the Germans from conquering the Soviet Union?

3. How did the United States help the Allies while it was a neutral nation?

Journal Writing

Imagine that you were living in Great Britain during the Battle of Britain. Write a paragraph about what it was like to live in Great Britain during the battle.

Skill Builder

Reading a Bar Graph   The bar graph below shows how many soldiers different countries sent to fight in World War II. The bar graph also uses colors to show whether the nations were part of the Allies or part of the Axis Powers. Study the bar graph. Then write on your paper the answer to each question.

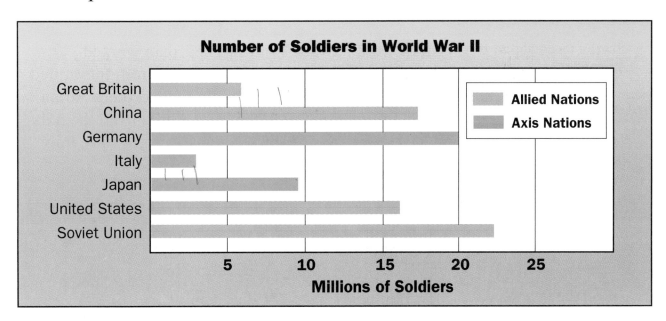

Number of Soldiers in World War II

Allied Nations
Axis Nations

Great Britain
China
Germany
Italy
Japan
United States
Soviet Union

5   10   15   20   25
Millions of Soldiers

1. What color are the bars that show Allied nations?

2. Which country sent about 10 million soldiers to the war?

3. Which country sent the fewest soldiers to the war?

4. Which country sent the most soldiers?

5. About how many soldiers did Great Britain send to the war?

6. About how many total soldiers did the three Axis Powers send?

7. Based on the graph, which alliance sent more soldiers to the war?

CHAPTER 35

The End of World War II

The Axis Powers had been winning World War II when the United States entered the war. The Battle of Stalingrad in 1943 marked an important change in the war. After this battle, the Allies began to win World War II.

Great Britain, the United States, and the Soviet Union worked hard to create a plan to defeat the Axis Powers in Europe. First, they planned to push the Germans and the Italians from northern Africa. From Africa, the Allies would conquer Italy. Then they would invade France. Their plan worked.

General Dwight Eisenhower was from the United States. He led the Allied soldiers in northern Africa and in Europe. The Allies freed Africa from the Axis nations. Then the Allied soldiers went to Italy. Italy surrendered to the Allies in 1943.

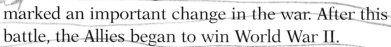

Allied soldiers were welcomed by the French people after the soldiers defeated the Germans at Normandy.

THINK ABOUT AS YOU READ

1. How did the Allies free France?
2. Why did Germany finally surrender?
3. How did the United States force Japan to surrender?

NEW WORDS

♦ D-Day
♦ Holocaust
♦ atomic bomb
♦ isolationism
♦ rebuild

PEOPLE & PLACES

♦ Dwight Eisenhower
♦ Normandy
♦ Philippines
♦ Douglas MacArthur
♦ Harry Truman
♦ Hiroshima
♦ Nagasaki
♦ Anne Frank
♦ Jewish Germans

THE END OF WORLD WAR II IN EUROPE

The Allies worked hard to plan a way to defeat the Axis Powers. To which nation did most of their routes of attack finally lead?

Dwight Eisenhower

The Allies planned to free France from Germany. General Eisenhower led the Allied soldiers in these attacks. On June 6, 1944, the Allies invaded France. This important date is known as **D-Day**. On D-Day, thousands of Allied soldiers sailed from Great Britain across the English Channel. They landed on the beaches of Normandy, an area of northern France.

The Allies surprised the Germans in France on D-Day. But the Germans fought hard against the Allies. Thousands of soldiers died. The Allies fought their way through France. In August the Allies freed the city of Paris from the Germans.

The Germans were losing the war. But they were not ready to surrender. Then the Allies attacked Germany. Allied planes dropped bombs on German cities. Many cities were destroyed. At last, the Germans knew they could not win. Adolf Hitler killed himself. A few days later, on May 7, 1945, Germany surrendered. The war in Europe had ended.

The world soon learned about the terrible things the Nazis had done during the war. Hitler had planned to kill all Jews as he conquered the world.

Jews and other people in the concentration camps were forced to live in terrible conditions.

Prisoners in a concentration camp in Germany

Prisoner (handwritten)

Douglas MacArthur

Douglas MacArthur (handwritten)

million Jews from all over Europe were killed by Nazis during the war. At least five million (handwritten annotation)

About six million Jews from all over Europe were killed by Nazis during the war. At least five million other people were also killed. Most were killed in concentration camps. People in the concentration camps were starved, beaten, and forced to work as slaves. Millions were shot or were killed with poison gas. People who spoke out against Hitler were also sent to the concentration camps. This killing of six million Jews and so many other people is now called the **Holocaust**.

World War II was not over. The war against Japan went on after the war in Europe had ended. The Japanese had captured parts of China. They also had captured islands in the Pacific Ocean, including Guam and the Philippines. The Allies fought hard to free Asia from Japan's control. American soldiers were an important part of these battles.

General Douglas MacArthur of the United States led the Allied soldiers in Asia. MacArthur had promised to help the Philippines become free. He kept his promise. He captured the Philippine capital

American soldiers helped free many Pacific islands from Japanese control.

American soldiers capture the island of Iwo Jima.

Harry S. Truman

in 1945. There were many other battles. Americans and other Allies slowly recaptured islands from the Japanese.

In 1945 the Allies were winning the war against Japan. But Japan would not surrender. The Japanese believed it was better to die than to surrender. Every day more Allied soldiers were killed in the war with the Japanese.

President Roosevelt had died during the war. Harry Truman was the new President of the United States. He decided to use a powerful weapon to force Japan to surrender. This weapon was called the **atomic bomb**. The atomic bomb was much more dangerous than any other weapon ever used.

President Truman warned Japan. He told Japan that the United States would drop an atomic bomb on a Japanese city. He told Japan that it was time to surrender. But Japan refused.

On August 6, 1945, an American plane dropped an atomic bomb on Hiroshima, a Japanese city. Thousands of people were killed. Most of the city was destroyed. But Japan would not surrender. Three days later, Americans dropped an atomic bomb on the Japanese city of Nagasaki. This time, the Japanese surrendered. There was peace in the world again.

World War II caused the deaths of millions of people. Many cities and roads were destroyed. Many Europeans and Asians were starving and homeless.

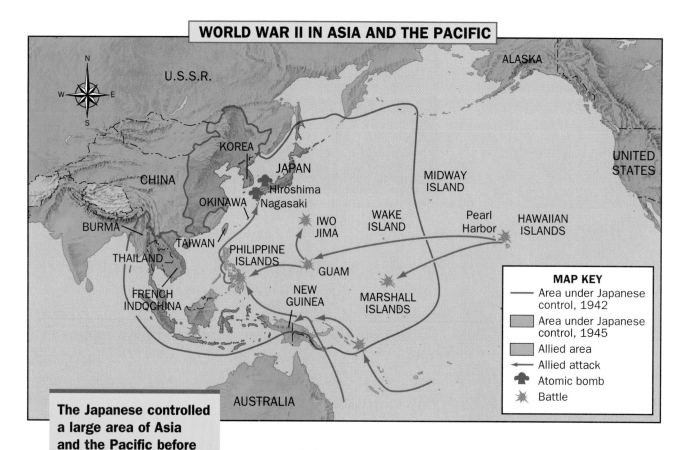

WORLD WAR II IN ASIA AND THE PACIFIC

N
W — E
S

ALASKA

U.S.S.R.

UNITED
STATES

KOREA

JAPAN

MIDWAY
ISLAND

CHINA

Hiroshima
Nagasaki

OKINAWA

BURMA

TAIWAN

THAILAND

PHILIPPINE
ISLANDS

IWO
JIMA

WAKE
ISLAND

Pearl
Harbor

HAWAIIAN
ISLANDS

FRENCH
INDOCHINA

GUAM

NEW
GUINEA

MARSHALL
ISLANDS

AUSTRALIA

MAP KEY
— Area under Japanese control, 1942
▢ Area under Japanese control, 1945
▢ Allied area
← Allied attack
✿ Atomic bomb
✳ Battle

The Japanese controlled a large area of Asia and the Pacific before World War II ended. Was Midway Island under Japanese control?

Powerful nations like Japan and Germany were now weak. Communist nations began in Eastern Europe. After the war, the United States and the Soviet Union were the two strongest world powers. A lot of tension between these two powerful nations would soon lead to a different type of war.

After World War I, Americans did not want to be involved in the problems of other countries. They did not want to fight in another war. This **isolationism** ended when the United States entered World War II. After World War II, the United States did not return to isolationism. Instead, Americans helped their allies become stronger. The United States worked to spread democracy in nations such as Japan and Italy. The United States also helped **rebuild** many nations in Europe.

People around the world decided it was time to work for peace. They did not want another world war. In the next chapter, you will learn how nations worked together for peace.

The sky after an atomic bomb landed on Nagasaki

Anne Frank (1929–1945)

Anne Frank was a Jewish girl who lived during World War II. She and her family hid from the Nazis during the Holocaust. The diary that Anne wrote while in hiding tells what life was like for many Jews during this terrible time.

Anne Frank was born in Frankfurt, Germany, in 1929. Anne and her mother, father, and sister moved to Holland in 1933. They moved when the Nazis began to take away the rights of Jewish Germans.

In 1942 the Nazis took control of Holland. To hide from the Nazis, Anne's family began living in a secret place behind the office of her father's business. Four other Jewish people hid with the Franks. They all had to be very quiet so that they would not be discovered. Sometimes they would have to sit for hours without moving. They could not turn on lights at night. Friends who were not Jewish would sneak food, clothing, and books to the families.

While in hiding, Anne Frank wrote her thoughts in a diary. She described what it was like to live in hiding. She wrote about her hopes for the future.

Two years later the Nazis discovered the secret hiding place. The Franks and the other Jewish people were sent to concentration camps. Anne died in a camp when she was 15 years old.

After World War II ended, people were looking through the ruins of the office building where Anne had hid. There they found Anne's diary. In 1947 her diary was made into a book called *The Diary of a Young Girl*. It was also made into a movie.

Anne's diary is famous throughout the world. Today the place where Anne and her family hid is the Anne Frank Museum. Near the museum is a statue that honors the memory of Anne Frank.

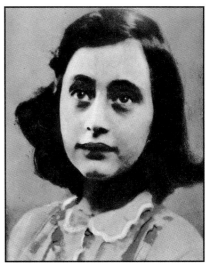

Anne Frank

Building where Anne Frank and her family hid

Using Vocabulary

Finish the Paragraph   Number your paper from 1 to 4. Use the words in dark print to finish the paragraph below. Write on your paper the words you choose.

rebuild   D-Day   atomic bomb   isolationism

Before World War II, Americans did not want to be involved with the problems of other nations. This was called ___1___ . But after Japan attacked Pearl Harbor, the United States entered the war. On June 6, 1944, or ___2___ , American soldiers and Allied soldiers landed in France. They conquered Germany by 1945. To force Japan to surrender, the United States dropped a deadly weapon called the ___3___ on two Japanese cities. After the war, Americans helped ___4___ many European cities and towns that had been destroyed.

Read and Remember

Finish Up   Choose words in dark print to best complete the sentences. Write on your paper the words you choose.

**Anne Frank   concentration   Hitler
Eisenhower   world powers**

1. _____ led the Allied soldiers to free France from Germany.

2. _____ planned to kill all Jews as he conquered the world.

3. Millions of Jews and other people were killed in _____ camps during the Holocaust.

 4. _____ wrote a diary about her life during the Holocaust.

5. After World War II, the United States and the Soviet Union were the two strongest _____ .

Think and Apply

Distinguishing Relevant Information   Imagine that you want to tell a friend about World War II in the Pacific. Read each sentence below. Decide which sentences are relevant to what you will say. Write the relevant sentences on your paper. There are four relevant sentences.

1. The Allies went to Africa to fight Germany and Italy.

2. The Japanese captured many islands in the Pacific Ocean.

3. On D-Day the Allies began their fight to free France.

4. General Douglas MacArthur led the Allied soldiers to free the Philippines.

5. American planes dropped atomic bombs on Hiroshima and Nagasaki.

6. World War II ended when Japan surrendered.

Skill Builder

Reading a Time Line   The time line below shows some of the events of World War II. Study the time line. Then write on your paper the answer to each question.

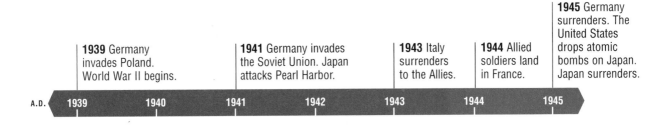

1. When did World War II begin?

2. When did Italy surrender to the Allies?

3. Did Germany invade the Soviet Union or Poland first?

4. What happened in 1944?

5. How many years passed between Japan's attack on Pearl Harbor and Japan's surrender?

Reading a Flow Chart   The flow chart on this page shows how **sonar** was sometimes used to destroy submarines in World War II. Sonar is a type of technology that can allow ships to locate objects underwater. Ships send **sound waves** that bounce off of an object that is in the path of the waves. Read the flow chart. Then write on your paper the words that best complete the sentences.

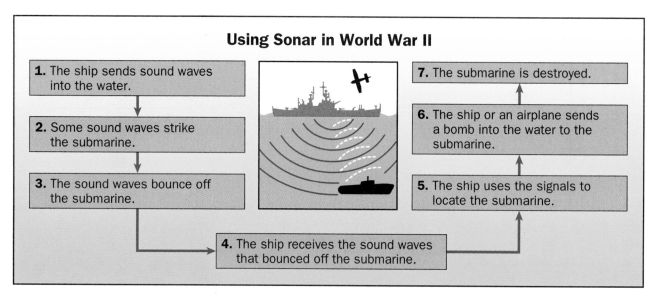

Using Sonar in World War II

1. The ship sends sound waves into the water.

2. Some sound waves strike the submarine.

3. The sound waves bounce off the submarine.

4. The ship receives the sound waves that bounced off the submarine.

5. The ship uses the signals to locate the submarine.

6. The ship or an airplane sends a bomb into the water to the submarine.

7. The submarine is destroyed.

1. In the first step, the _____ sends sound waves into the water.

submarine   airplane   ship

2. In Step 3, the _____ bounce off the submarine.

sound waves   bombs   fish

3. The ship receives the sound waves in _____.

Step 2   Step 4   Step 6

4. After the ship locates the submarine, it _____.

sends a bomb into the water   sends more sound waves   flees

5. In the final step, the submarine _____.

bombs the ship   goes to the top of the water   is destroyed

Journal Writing

Write a paragraph about the Allies' plan to defeat the Axis Powers in Europe.

CHAPTER 36

The United Nations

THINK ABOUT AS YOU READ

1. Why was the United Nations formed?
2. What are the parts of the United Nations?
3. How has the United Nations helped keep peace?

NEW WORDS

♦ organization
♦ United Nations
♦ General Assembly
♦ delegates
♦ secretary-general
♦ Security Council
♦ permanent
♦ resolutions
♦ vetoes
♦ Persian Gulf War

PEOPLE & PLACES

♦ New York City
♦ Iraq
♦ Kuwait
♦ Jean-Bertrand Aristide
♦ Somalia
♦ Bosnia and Herzegovina

After World War I, many nations worked together for world peace. They were part of the **organization** called the League of Nations. But the League of Nations was weak. It could not prevent World War II from starting. During World War II, the Allies decided to start a new organization that would work for peace. This organization is called the **United Nations**.

Why did the League of Nations fail? One reason was that it did not have its own army. It was also weak because important world powers were not members. The United States was not a member. The Soviet Union, Germany, Italy, and Japan all left the League before World War II. Without strong members and an army, the League could not stop wars between nations. The League of Nations finally ended in 1946.

The United Nations was formed in 1945. This meeting in 1995 marked fifty years that the UN has worked for world peace.

The United Nations building in New York City

The UN flag

The UN Security Council

The United Nations, or UN, was formed in 1945. It began with 51 members. Today 185 nations are members of the UN. The UN headquarters are in New York City in the United States.

The UN sometimes sends soldiers to other nations to work for peace. It also gives food and medicine to millions of people in needy nations. The UN teaches people new ways to grow more food. Teachers from the UN help needy people learn to read and write.

The United Nations has many parts. One part is the **General Assembly**. Every member nation of the UN sends **delegates** to the General Assembly. Each member nation has one vote. The General Assembly meets every year. The leader of the United Nations is called the **secretary-general**. Every five years the General Assembly chooses a new secretary-general.

The **Security Council** is the most powerful part of the UN. The Security Council has 15 member nations. There are five **permanent** members. The United States, Great Britain, France, Russia, and China are the five permanent members. Ten other members are chosen by the General Assembly. They work on the Security Council for two years.

The members of the Security Council vote on actions that the United Nations can take to keep peace. They also vote on other **resolutions** that tell what they think of the actions of some nations. All five permanent members of the Security Council must agree on the resolution. If a permanent member **vetoes** a resolution, the resolution is not passed. The General Assembly can also vote on resolutions. Two thirds of the General Assembly must agree in order for the resolution to pass.

The Security Council can send UN soldiers to a land where there is fighting. These soldiers come from many nations. They try to stop nations from fighting. They do not fight to win a war. They try to win peace.

The UN sent soldiers to Bosnia and Herzegovina to try to help end the civil war there.

UN soldier during the Persian Gulf War

The UN hoped to bring peace and food to the people of Somalia.

In 1990 the oil-rich nation Iraq attacked its neighbor Kuwait. Iraq wanted Kuwait's oil wells. The UN demanded that Iraq leave Kuwait. The United States and many other UN nations sent soldiers to help Kuwait become free. In 1991 a short war was fought. It was called the **Persian Gulf War**. Iraq lost the war, and Kuwait was freed. Many people were glad that the UN was able to help. It had stopped one country from taking over another country.

The UN also helped Haiti. The people of Haiti had elected Jean-Bertrand Aristide as president. But in 1991 the military leader of Haiti used force to take control of Haiti away from Aristide. In 1994 the UN voted to send soldiers to Haiti. Within months, Aristide was again the leader of Haiti.

Many times the UN has not been able to stop wars in countries. In 1992 the UN sent a peace-keeping force to try to end a civil war in the African country of Somalia. The UN also hoped to feed the starving people in the country. The UN saved many people, but it was not able to end the civil war.

In 1992 a civil war began in the European nation of Bosnia and Herzegovina. The UN sent soldiers there to work for peace. But the fighting continued. In November 1995, the United States worked with the Bosnian groups to create a peace treaty. There is still serious tension in this nation, but the UN continues its peace-keeping efforts.

Using Vocabulary

Find the Meaning   Write on your paper the word or words that best complete each sentence.

1. The **United Nations** is an organization of nations that works for _____.

   world trade   world peace   world banks

2. **Delegates** in the United Nations are people who _____ member nations.

   represent   trust   are at war with

3. The **secretary-general** is the leader of the _____.

   League of Nations   country of Somalia   United Nations

4. A **permanent** member of the Security Council is a member _____.

   for two years   for five years   every year

Read and Remember

Find the Answer   Find the sentences that tell something true about the United Nations. Write the sentences on your paper. You should find five sentences.

1. The United Nations was formed in 1945.

2. Every member nation of the UN is part of the General Assembly.

3. The Security Council can never send soldiers to nations where there is fighting.

4. The UN helped put President Aristide back in power in Haiti.

5. The UN teaches people new ways to grow more food.

6. The UN has always been able to stop wars in different parts of the world.

7. A vote against a resolution is called an organization.

8. The UN is working for peace in Bosnia and Herzegovina.

Journal Writing

Write a short letter to the United States delegate to the United Nations. Ask the delegate to work to solve a world problem. Tell the delegate why you believe the problem is important.

Skill Builder

Reading a Diagram   Study the diagram below of the headquarters of the United Nations. Then write on your paper a sentence to answer each question.

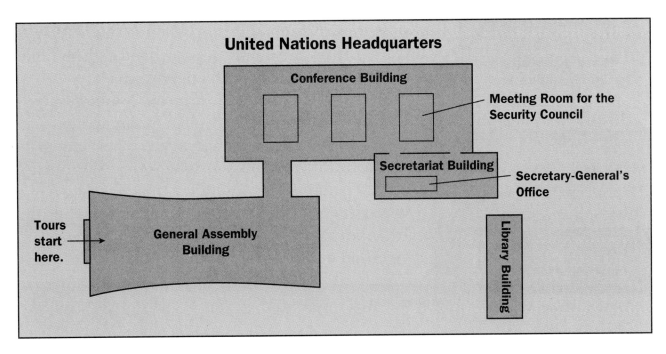

1. What four buildings of the United Nations headquarters are shown in the diagram?

2. In what building does the Security Council meet?

3. To what building would you go to get a tour of the United Nations headquarters?

4. In what building is the secretary-general's office?

5. Which two buildings are attached to the Conference Building?

6. Which building is not shown to be attached to any other building at the UN headquarters?

CHAPTER 37

The Cold War

THINK ABOUT AS YOU READ

1. What was the Cold War?
2. How did the Cold War lead to a nuclear arms race?
3. Why was the Korean War fought?

NEW WORDS

♦ conflict
♦ Cold War
♦ resist
♦ Marshall Plan
♦ North Atlantic Treaty Organization
♦ Warsaw Pact
♦ nuclear arms race
♦ missiles
♦ space race
♦ satellite
♦ Korean War
♦ nuclear war

PEOPLE & PLACES

♦ Korea
♦ Berlin
♦ Cuba
♦ John F. Kennedy

When World War II ended, many nations that had fought in the war were very weak. But the United States and the Soviet Union were stronger than they had been before the war. These two nations had fought for the Allies. But after the war, a **conflict** began between the two nations. This conflict was called the **Cold War** because there was usually not any fighting. The Cold War was mostly fought with angry words.

The Cold War was a war between Communists and non-Communists. The United States and its allies wanted to spread democracy to other nations. The Soviet Union and its Communist allies wanted to spread communism. There was much tension between the two sides. The Communists and the non-Communists did not trust one another. People were afraid that a third world war might occur.

The Soviet Union built the Berlin Wall to keep East Germans from escaping into West Berlin.

The Marshall Plan helped rebuild the nations of Western Europe.

MAP KEY
☐ NATO members in 1955
▨ Warsaw Pact members in 1955

Nations of NATO and the Warsaw Pact in 1955

The Soviet Union wanted to have a strong control over Eastern Europe. After World War II ended, the Soviet Union forced many Eastern European nations to have Communist governments. Some of these nations were Czechoslovakia, Poland, Hungary, and part of Germany. Winston Churchill said that an "Iron Curtain" had come down over Eastern Europe. The Soviet Union was the leading power behind the Iron Curtain.

In 1947 the United States said that it would help nations **resist** the spread of communism. One way it did this was with the **Marshall Plan** in 1948. This plan allowed the United States to send money to help rebuild Western Europe. The Marshall Plan helped nations in Western Europe become stronger. Communism did not spread to Western Europe.

In 1949 the United States, Canada, and many Western European nations started a new military organization. This was the **North Atlantic Treaty Organization,** or NATO. The NATO nations agreed to help protect one another from the Soviet Union and other Communist nations. Soldiers from member nations work for NATO. Today there are 16 nations that belong to NATO.

In 1955 the Soviet Union and other Eastern European nations signed a treaty called the **Warsaw Pact**. Like NATO, the Warsaw Pact nations agreed to help one another if any of them was attacked.

The Cold War led to many changes. One change was new technology. During World War II, the United States was the only country that built an atomic bomb. By 1949 the Soviets had their own atomic bomb. This was the beginning of the **nuclear arms race**. The United States and the Soviet Union began testing other types of nuclear weapons. They also began to build powerful new weapons called **missiles**.

The Cold War also led to the **space race**. In 1957 the Soviet Union sent its first **satellite** into space.

The Cold War led to a space race between the Soviet Union and the United States. In 1969 Americans walked on the moon.

North Korea and South Korea

UN soldier in Korea

Satellites are machines that travel around Earth. Soon after that, the United States began its own space program. In 1961 the Soviets sent a man into space. In 1969 the United States sent the first people to the moon. Both nations continued to spend a lot of money on their space programs.

The Cold War led to a real war in Korea, a country in eastern Asia. After World War II, the Soviet Union had soldiers in northern Korea. The United States had soldiers in southern Korea. When all the soldiers left, Korea was divided into two parts. North Korea became a Communist state. In 1950 the Communists invaded South Korea. They wanted to make Korea one Communist nation.

The United States did not want South Korea to be a Communist nation. The United States and the United Nations sent soldiers to fight in the **Korean War**. For three years they helped the South Koreans fight the North Koreans. The Communists were forced back into North Korea. At last the fighting ended. North Korea and South Korea are two separate nations today.

Cuba

John F. Kennedy

American missiles being tested

The Cold War also took place in Germany. After World War II, Germany was divided into four parts. In 1949 three parts became West Germany. West Germany was a democracy. The fourth part became East Germany. East Germany had a Communist government controlled by the Soviet Union. The capital city of Berlin was also divided. There was much more freedom in West Berlin. The standard of living there was much higher than in East Berlin. Many people from East Germany tried to escape to West Berlin.

In 1961 the Soviets built a wall between East Berlin and West Berlin. They built the wall in order to stop East Germans from escaping into West Berlin. The United States wanted the Soviets to tear down the Berlin Wall. But the wall was not removed for many years.

The Cold War also spread to Cuba. Cuba is an island near Florida. It became a Communist nation in 1961. In 1962 the Soviet Union sent missiles to Cuba. Many people thought these missiles might be used to destroy American cities. John F. Kennedy was the President of the United States. He demanded that the Soviets remove the missiles. People were afraid that a **nuclear war** might occur. After a few days, the Soviets removed the missiles from Cuba.

The Cold War lasted almost forty years. During that time, the United States and the Soviet Union tried to remove some of the tension between the two nations. One way they did that was by limiting nuclear weapons during the 1970s and 1980s.

There are still Communist nations in the world today. But people in Eastern Europe did not like communism. After many years, communism in Eastern Europe became weaker. By the year 1991 communism in Eastern Europe and the Soviet Union had ended. This brought an end to the Cold War. You will learn about these changes in Chapter 44.

Using Vocabulary

Finish Up   Choose the word or words in dark print to best complete each sentence. Write on your paper the word or words you choose.

resist	satellite	nuclear war	nuclear arms
Cold War	NATO	Marshall Plan	Warsaw Pact

1. The conflict between Communist nations and non-Communist nations was called the _____ .

2. To _____ means to keep from giving in to something.

3. The _____ allowed the United States to send money to help rebuild Western Europe.

4. The organization that worked to protect member nations from the Soviet Union and other Communist nations is called _____ .

5. The _____ was a treaty between the Communist nations of Eastern Europe.

6. A _____ is a war that uses such weapons as the atomic bomb.

7. A _____ is a machine that travels around Earth.

8. The _____ race was a struggle between the United States and the Soviet Union to increase their supplies of powerful weapons.

Read and Remember

Finish the Sentence   Write on your paper the word or words that best complete each sentence.

1. At the end of World War II, the United States and the Soviet Union were _____ than other nations.

   stronger   weaker   slower

2. The United States created the Marshall Plan to help European nations _____ the spread of communism.

   enjoy   encourage   resist

3. The Soviet Union forced Czechoslovakia and _____ to have Communist governments.

China   Poland   West Germany

4. The United States sent people to the moon because of the _____.

nuclear arms race   space race   Korean War

5. In 1950 Communists invaded _____.

Cuba   North Korea   South Korea

6. Cuba became a _____ in 1961.

Communist nation   democracy   republic

Think and Apply

Understanding Different Points of View   People in the Soviet Union and the United States had different points of view during the Cold War. Read each sentence below. Write **Soviet** on your paper for each sentence that might show the point of view of a Soviet during the Cold War. Write **American** on your paper for each sentence that might show the point of view of an American during the Cold War.

1. Germany, Italy, and Japan should be democracies.

2. Eastern European countries should have Communist governments.

3. East Germans should not go to West Berlin.

4. The Berlin Wall should be removed.

5. Korea should be one Communist nation.

6. The United Nations should send soldiers to South Korea to fight the North Koreans.

7. It is important to stop the spread of communism and to help nations become democracies.

8. Cuba should have powerful missiles.

Journal Writing

The Cold War lasted almost forty years. During that time there were many different conflicts. Write a paragraph that tells how the Cold War started. Include in your paragraph two examples of Cold War conflicts.

Riddle Puzzle

Number your paper from 1 to 7. Choose words in dark print to best complete the sentences. Write the correct answers on your paper.

atomic bomb   **United States**   **island**   **removed**
Communist   **technology**   **nuclear**

1. During the Korean War, North Korea tried to make all of Korea a _____ nation.

2. The _____ and Canada are members of NATO.

3. The Berlin Wall was not _____ for many years.

4. The Cold War led to many changes, including new _____.

5. During World War II, the United States was the only nation that built an _____.

6. In 1962 the Soviet Union sent missiles to the _____ of Cuba.

7. An atomic bomb is a _____ weapon.

Now look at your answers. Circle the first letter of each answer you wrote on your paper. The letters you circle should spell a word. The word answers the riddle below.

RIDDLE: What is usually made of fabric but in Eastern Europe was made of iron?

Write on your paper the answer to the riddle.

China Becomes a Communist Nation

THINK ABOUT AS YOU READ

1. How did China become a Communist nation?

2. Why did China have civil wars?

3. What is China like today?

NEW WORDS

♦ warlords
♦ better relations
♦ protesters
♦ Cultural Revolution
♦ recover

PEOPLE & PLACES

♦ Nationalists
♦ Sun Yat-sen
♦ Chiang Kai-shek
♦ Mao Zedong
♦ Taiwan
♦ People's Republic of China
♦ Deng Xiaoping
♦ Jiang Zemin
♦ Red Guards

China was an empire for more than 2,000 years. However, during the 1800s China's trade and some of its land were controlled by imperialist nations. Many Chinese wanted China to become an industrial nation. They did not want China to be controlled by emperors or other nations. Nationalism became very important.

A group of people called Nationalists wanted to change the government of China. A man named Sun Yat-sen was the leader of the Nationalists. In 1911 he helped China become a republic. China no longer had an emperor.

Sun Yat-sen became the president of the new republic. He hoped that all of China would become a democracy. But the new government was weak. Different **warlords** ruled small parts of China. A civil war began between the Nationalists and China's warlords.

China today is still a strong Communist nation.

Sun Yat-sen

Chiang Kai-shek

Communist soldiers marching through a Chinese city in 1949

When World War I began, the Chinese joined the Allies against the Central Powers. But after the war, China's civil war continued. Sun Yat-sen asked the Soviet Union to help the Nationalists fight. The Soviet Union agreed to help teach the Nationalist army how to fight. Some Chinese people liked the Communist ideas of the Soviet Union. They started a Communist party. The Communists worked with the Nationalists to fight the warlords.

Sun Yat-sen died during the civil war in China. A man named Chiang Kai-shek became the new leader of the Nationalists. The Nationalists and the Communists continued the fight against the warlords. But Chiang Kai-shek did not trust the Communists. He thought that the Soviet Union wanted the Communists to rule China after the warlords were defeated. Chiang started a battle against the Communists. Most of the Communists were killed. The rest of the Communists hid from the Nationalists.

By 1928 China was united and ruled by the Nationalists. Chiang Kai-shek promised democracy and new rights for the Chinese. But Chiang did not give people all the freedom he had promised. Life did not improve for the millions of poor peasants. Many peasants decided to become Communists. One of these peasants was Mao Zedong. Mao started a Communist army.

Mao led the Communists in another civil war in 1930. This time the Nationalists pushed the Communists into the northwest part of China.

In 1937 Japan attacked China. Japan knew that the Chinese were fighting a civil war. The Japanese decided that it was a good time to attack China. The Chinese Communists and the Chinese Nationalists fought together against the Japanese. The Japanese conquered much of China. But the Chinese did not stop fighting. When Japan lost World War II, all of China became free of Japanese control.

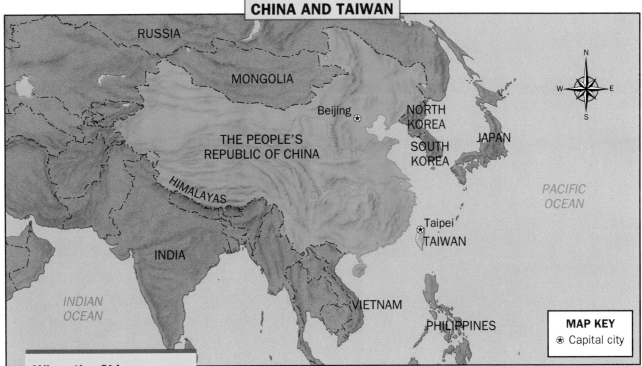

CHINA AND TAIWAN

RUSSIA

MONGOLIA

Beijing ✦

THE PEOPLE'S REPUBLIC OF CHINA

NORTH KOREA

SOUTH KOREA

JAPAN

HIMALAYAS

Huang He

Chang Jiang

INDIA

Taipei ✦
TAIWAN

PACIFIC OCEAN

INDIAN OCEAN

VIETNAM

PHILIPPINES

MAP KEY
✦ Capital city

When the Chinese Communists defeated the Nationalists in 1949, the Nationalists fled to the island of Taiwan. What is the capital of Taiwan?

Mao Zedong

After World War II, the Nationalists and the Communists in China fought again. In 1949 the Communists won. Chiang Kai-shek and the Nationalists escaped to an island near China. This island is called Taiwan.

Since 1949 Communists have ruled China. They changed its name to the People's Republic of China. More than one billion people live in China under the Communist government. The Nationalists rule Taiwan. Taiwan is not a Communist nation.

Mao Zedong ruled the People's Republic of China until he died in 1976. He was a dictator. Everyone had to obey Mao. There was no freedom. People who spoke out against Mao were sent to jail or killed. All businesses were owned by the government. But Mao also helped China become a world power. The Chinese had a strong army. They learned how to build atomic bombs.

For many years, the United States and China were enemies. This was a result of the Cold War. The United States did not want China to be a Communist nation. Since 1972 there have been **better relations**

In 1989 many Chinese gathered in cities and spoke out against communism. Many of these protesters were killed by soldiers.

Deng Xiaoping

Woman in Beijing

between the nations. American Presidents have visited China. The two nations trade with each other. Many Americans have businesses in China.

A few years after Mao died, a man named Deng Xiaoping became the leader of China's government. He helped China become a stronger nation. Deng increased China's trade with other countries. He also helped the growth of business in China. He allowed Chinese people to own some farms and businesses. Many Chinese earned more money.

Many Chinese wanted Deng to bring democracy to China. In 1989 Chinese university students tried to win more freedom. They became **protesters**. They marched in the streets of Beijing and other cities. The students carried signs that said that China needed freedom and democracy.

Deng Xiaoping did not want China to become a democracy. He sent the Chinese army to fight the protesters. Thousands of protesters were killed by the army. The protests ended. There was even less freedom in China after the protests ended.

Since 1911 China has changed from a nation ruled by emperors to a Communist nation. China is a world power today. Jiang Zemin is now China's leader. More people own businesses. Most Chinese have enough food and can read and write. But there is not much freedom in China today. Many people still hope that China will become a democracy.

Mao Zedong (1893–1976)

Mao Zedong led the fight to make China a strong Communist nation. He was one of the most powerful leaders in China's history.

Mao was born to a poor family in China in 1893. He became interested in communism while he was working in Beijing. Mao led peasants to form the Chinese Communist party in 1921. In 1949 the Communists defeated the Nationalists. Mao became the leader of the People's Republic of China.

Mao Zedong

Mao was a dictator. He controlled every part of the daily lives of the Chinese. He had pictures of himself put on posters all over China. The Chinese had to study Mao's ideas. The government took control of farms and businesses. Most people worked on collective farms. People were paid very low wages.

Some Chinese leaders tried to help China become a more modern nation. But Mao said that these changes went against the ideas of communism. In 1966 Mao began the **Cultural Revolution** to make communism in China stronger. He sent soldiers called the Red Guards all over China. The Red Guards closed schools and colleges. Scientists, factory owners, doctors, and other people were sent to work on farms. Many people were killed or arrested. The revolution led to years of hard times in China. Factories closed. Farmers grew less food.

Mao realized that China was in trouble. He made efforts to help China **recover**. Schools opened again. People went back to work. But it was hard to bring back order to China.

Mao died in 1976. He left behind a China that was struggling with many problems. But Mao died believing in communism. Even today his writings are studied by people in other nations.

Red Guards during the Cultural Revolution

Using Vocabulary

Match Up   Finish the sentences in Group A with words from Group B. Write on your paper the letter of each correct answer.

Group A

1. Chinese _____ were people who ruled small parts of China.

2. People who speak out against an issue or a government are _____ .

3. One example of _____ between the United States and China is an increase of trade.

4. The _____ was a time in which the Red Guards closed schools and sent people to work on farms.

5. To _____ means to get better.

Group B

a. protesters

b. warlords

c. Cultural Revolution

d. recover

e. better relations

Read and Remember

Write the Answer   Write on your paper one or more sentences to answer each question.

1. Why did Chiang Kai-shek order the Nationalists to fight the Communists?

2. Why did Japan think 1937 was a good time to attack China?

3. What new name did the Communists give China?

4. In what ways did Deng Xiaoping help China become a stronger nation?

Journal Writing

Mao Zedong was one of China's most powerful leaders. He ruled as a dictator. Write a few sentences that tell some of the ways Mao was a dictator.

Think and Apply

Sequencing Events   Number your paper from 1 to 5. Write the sentences to show the correct order.

China and the United States began to trade with each other after 1972.

Chiang Kai-shek started a battle against the Communists in China.

Sun Yat-sen became the leader of the Nationalists.

Mao Zedong led the Communists to gain control of China in 1949.

Deng Xiaoping sent the army to fight protesters in Beijing.

Skill Builder

Reading a Chart   Read the chart below. Then write on your paper the answer to each question.

LEADERS OF CHINA

Leader	When did he become leader?	Communist or Nationalist?	What did he do?
Sun Yat-sen	1911	Nationalist	Helped China become a republic.
Chiang Kai-shek	1926	Nationalist	Defeated the warlords in China. Became president of Taiwan in 1949.
Mao Zedong	1949	Communist	Helped China become a Communist nation. Started a cultural revolution.
Deng Xiaoping	1980	Communist	Helped the growth of business in China.

1. Which two leaders were Nationalists?

2. When did Mao become China's leader?

3. Who became president of Taiwan in 1949?

4. Who helped China become a republic?

5. What did Deng Xiaoping do for China?

6. Which leader defeated the warlords in China?

The Vietnam War

THINK ABOUT AS YOU READ

1. **Why did wars begin in Southeast Asia?**
2. **Why did the United States fight in the Vietnam War?**
3. **How have the United States and Vietnam improved relations?**

NEW WORDS

◆ **Vietnam War**
◆ **troops**
◆ **civilians**
◆ **protested**
◆ **cease-fire**
◆ **damage**
◆ **refugees**
◆ **boat people**

PEOPLE & PLACES

◆ **Southeast Asia**
◆ **Vietnam**
◆ **North Vietnam**
◆ **South Vietnam**
◆ **Viet Cong**
◆ **Ho Chi Minh**
◆ **Australia**
◆ **New Zealand**
◆ **Thailand**
◆ **Cambodia**
◆ **Laos**

You have read how in the 1950s the Korean War brought fighting to the Cold War. It turned the Cold War into a hot war. In 1957 fighting began that turned the Cold War into a hot war again. This was the **Vietnam War**. The Vietnam War took place in Southeast Asia.

Southeast Asia separates the Indian Ocean and the Pacific Ocean. Part of Southeast Asia is a large peninsula that is south of China. The rest of the region is made up of thousands of islands. There are forests, rivers, fertile soil, and a lot of rain. Southeast Asia is rich in natural resources.

Vietnam is a country in Southeast Asia. It was a French colony for many years. Vietnam won its independence from France in 1954. Then Vietnam was divided into two countries called North Vietnam and South Vietnam. A Communist government was

Battles of the Vietnam War often were fought in the jungle.

North Vietnamese soldiers helped the Viet Cong fight against the South Vietnamese government.

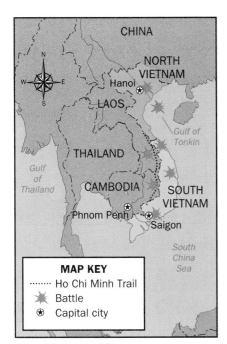
The Vietnam War

Ho Chi Minh

set up in North Vietnam. South Vietnam was a non-Communist republic.

Many Communists lived in South Vietnam. They were called the Viet Cong. The Viet Cong wanted South Vietnam to be a Communist nation. In 1957 the Viet Cong began to fight against the South Vietnamese government.

North Vietnam wanted South Vietnam to have a Communist government, too. A man named Ho Chi Minh was the president of North Vietnam. He sent soldiers and weapons to help the Viet Cong. The Soviet Union and China also helped the Viet Cong.

The United States wanted to stop the spread of communism in Southeast Asia. So it helped the government of South Vietnam. At first, the United States just sent money and weapons to South Vietnam. Then it began to send soldiers to help teach the South Vietnamese how to fight. Other countries also helped South Vietnam. These countries were Australia, New Zealand, South Korea, Thailand, and the Philippines.

By 1965 the fighting had spread to two countries that shared Vietnam's western border. These two

American soldiers walking in a rice field in South Vietnam

Many helicopters were used during the Vietnam War.

Americans protesting against the Vietnam War

countries were Cambodia and Laos. Then the United States became more involved in the war. American planes dropped bombs on North Vietnam. The United States also sent thousands of American **troops** to help South Vietnam. By 1969 there were over 500,000 soldiers from the United States that were involved in the Vietnam War.

For a long time, neither side was winning the war. The United States had a lot of modern technology and weapons. But the Viet Cong and the North Vietnamese knew the land of Vietnam. They fought well in the jungles and mountains of Vietnam. The Viet Cong also attacked many villages in South Vietnam. Millions of soldiers and **civilians** died during the Vietnam War. Civilians are people that are not in the military.

Many Americans did not think that the United States should fight in Vietnam. They said that too many Americans were dying in the war. They believed that too much money was being spent on the war. These Americans **protested** against the Vietnam War. In many cities large numbers of people marched to show that they were against the war. Some people burned American flags.

In 1973 the United States, South Vietnam, North Vietnam, and the Viet Cong signed a **cease-fire** agreement. This means that they agreed to stop fighting. American troops came home.

Fighting began again soon after the American troops left. By 1975 North Vietnam and the Viet Cong had defeated South Vietnam. In 1976 North Vietnam and South Vietnam became one nation called Vietnam. Vietnam became a Communist nation. Laos and Cambodia also became Communist nations. The Communist governments took over businesses and farms. Many people were executed by the Communists.

More than 2 million people from Vietnam were killed during the war. Much of North Vietnam was

Many refugees traveled by boat to reach safe countries. These boat people are arriving in Hong Kong near China.

American soldiers captured during the Vietnam War

People in Vietnam

destroyed. Large parts of Laos and Cambodia were also destroyed. Most of the fighting had taken place in South Vietnam. So South Vietnam had the most **damage** to its villages, cities, and roads.

About half of South Vietnam's population became **refugees**. Refugees are people who leave their country in order to escape danger. By the early 1980s, millions of refugees had left Vietnam, Cambodia, and Laos. Some refugees lived in camps near Thailand's border with Laos and Cambodia. Other people became **boat people**. These refugees escaped from their countries in boats. They hoped to reach safe countries or to be rescued. Many of the boat people moved to other parts of Asia. The largest number of boat people came to the United States.

Many people in the United States and in Vietnam still feel angry about the Vietnam War. But the nations are looking to the future. In recent years the United States and Vietnam have worked to improve relations. The government of Vietnam has helped to find and return the bodies of American soldiers who were killed in Vietnam. In 1995 the United States agreed to trade with Vietnam. These better relations give people hope that peace will continue.

Using Vocabulary

Finish the Paragraph   Number your paper from 1 to 4. Use the words in dark print to finish the paragraph. Write on your paper the words you choose.

refugees   boat people   cease-fire   damage

There was much fighting during the Vietnam War. South Vietnam received the most __1__ , because more roads, buildings, and farms were destroyed there than in North Vietnam. The United States, South Vietnam, and North Vietnam agreed to stop fighting when they signed a __2__ agreement. But North Vietnam later gained control of South Vietnam. More than half of South Vietnam's population became __3__ because they wanted to escape danger in their country. Some of these people became __4__ who tried to reach safe countries by traveling on water.

Read and Remember

Choose the Answer   Write the correct answers on your paper.

1. Who started a war against the South Vietnamese government in 1957?
   the Soviets   the Viet Cong   South Koreans

2. Why did the United States help South Vietnam in the war?
   to increase trade   to gain land   to stop the spread of communism

3. Where else did fighting occur during the Vietnam War?
   Canada and Mexico   Cambodia and Laos   France and China

4. What kind of government was set up in Vietnam after the war?
   Communist government   democracy   monarchy

5. What did many Americans do to protest the Vietnam War?
   became soldiers   held marches   sent money to South Vietnam

Skill Builder

Reading a Resource Map   Southeast Asia has many natural resources. It has many forests and fish. The resource map below shows where some other natural resources are found in Southeast Asia. Study the map and the map key. Then write on your paper the answer to each question.

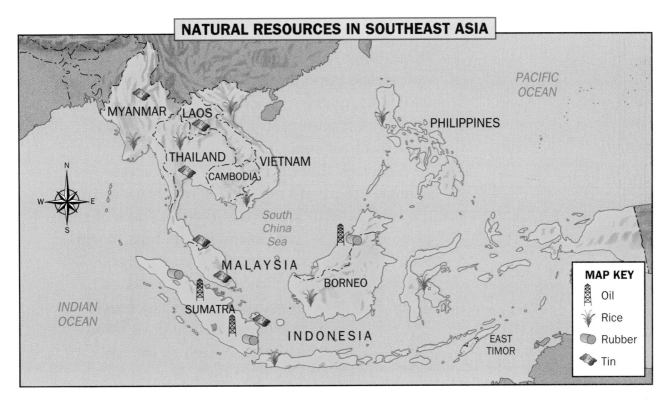

NATURAL RESOURCES IN SOUTHEAST ASIA

1. What resources are shown on the map?

2. What symbol is used to show rubber?

3. Does the map show that Laos has tin?

4. What is one resource of Vietnam?

5. Does the map show that the Philippines has oil?

6. Which two countries have both tin and rice?

7. What two resources does the island of Sumatra have?

8. Which resource can be found in more places in Southeast Asia than any other resource?

Unit 8   The World Today

The world today is very different from the world before World War II and the Cold War. Most nations today are independent. Many nations are industrial. Developing nations are trying to increase their industries. Populations are growing. In some countries, people are working for more rights and more freedom. Trade has become very important for most nations.

Although there have been many good changes, there are also problems. Nations in the world today are trying to solve some of the same problems that people had before World War II. Many people are poor and hungry. Many people do not know how to read and write. In some countries, there is not much freedom. Some nations do not have enough money to help their people. Some nations have civil wars. Pollution is increasing.

In some ways, the nations of today have not changed. Millions of people follow old traditions. In some nations of the world, religion is as important today as it was long ago. In developing nations, many farmers still grow food the same way farmers did hundreds of years ago.

How have nations changed since World War II and the Cold War? How have they

stayed the same? Who are some of the important leaders of today? As you read Unit 8, think about the ways that nations of the world today are alike and different. Think about the important problems that many nations are working to solve.

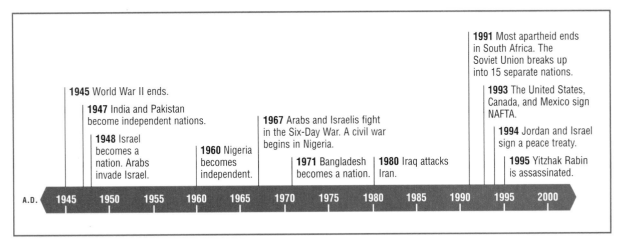

1945 World War II ends.

1947 India and Pakistan become independent nations.

1948 Israel becomes a nation. Arabs invade Israel.

1960 Nigeria becomes independent.

1967 Arabs and Israelis fight in the Six-Day War. A civil war begins in Nigeria.

1971 Bangladesh becomes a nation.

1980 Iraq attacks Iran.

1991 Most apartheid ends in South Africa. The Soviet Union breaks up into 15 separate nations.

1993 The United States, Canada, and Mexico sign NAFTA.

1994 Jordan and Israel sign a peace treaty.

1995 Yitzhak Rabin is assassinated.

A.D. 1945 1950 1955 1960 1965 1970 1975 1980 1985 1990 1995 2000

Asia Today

Asia is the world's largest continent. More than half of the world's population is in Asia. The Himalayas, the world's tallest 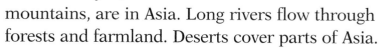 mountains, are in Asia. Long rivers flow through forests and farmland. Deserts cover parts of Asia.

There have been many wars in Asia. You have read how wars were fought in China, Korea, and nations of Southeast Asia. Wars have made it hard for these nations to solve their problems.

Many nations in Asia are **developing nations**. In developing nations, most people earn very little money. The standard of living is low. Hunger and **poverty** are usually large problems. Most people are farmers who work the same way farmers worked long ago. It is hard for them to grow enough food for the people. **Illiteracy** is another problem. Illiteracy

THINK ABOUT AS YOU READ

1. **What are some of the problems that developing nations in Asia have?**
2. **How did Gandhi help India?**
3. **In what ways is Japan an industrial nation?**

NEW WORDS

♦ **developing nations**
♦ **poverty**
♦ **illiteracy**
♦ **developed nations**
♦ **export**
♦ **Green Revolution**
♦ **assassinated**
♦ **trading partners**
♦ **traditions**

PEOPLE & PLACES

♦ **Singapore**
♦ **Mohandas Gandhi**
♦ **Bangladesh**

Many Asian cities, such as Hong Kong City, are very large, modern, and crowded.

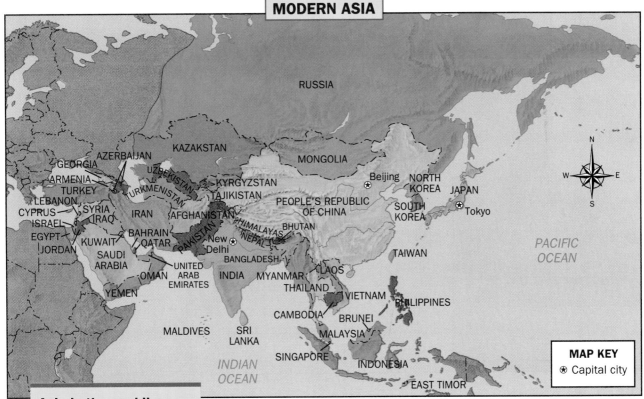

Asia is the world's largest continent. Are nations of the Middle East part of Asia?

means people cannot read or write. Many developing nations are trying to build new factories.

Other nations in Asia have become modern industrial nations. These nations are **developed nations**. Japan, South Korea, Singapore, and Taiwan are developed nations. These nations **export** factory products to many nations. The standard of living is high in these nations.

Religion is very important in many Asian nations. Hinduism, Buddhism, Christianity, and Islam are the main religions in Asia. At times, conflicts about the religions have caused wars.

India is a large developing nation in southern Asia. India has more than 936 million people. It is very crowded. There are not enough schools and teachers. Less than half of India's people know how to read. It is hard to grow enough food for all of the people. But farmers in India are using new ways to grow more food. Some of these methods come from the **Green Revolution**. The Green Revolution is a

Worker in a computer factory in Taiwan

Mohandas Gandhi helped bring peace and freedom to India.

Poverty in India

A new hotel being built in New Delhi, India's capital

way of farming that uses more irrigation, more energy, and better seeds to grow more crops.

In 1858 India became part of the British empire. Many Indians did not want their country to be ruled by the British. One man, Mohandas Gandhi, helped India become an independent nation again. He said that people should find peaceful ways to end British rule. He told Indians to stop obeying British laws and to stop buying British goods. During the 1920s and 1930s, Gandhi led many peaceful protests against British rule. Millions of Indians took part in the protests. Finally in 1947 India became an independent nation. India became a democracy.

Millions of Muslims lived in India. The Hindus and the Muslims often fought one another about religion. Gandhi tried to end the fighting between the Hindus and the Muslims of India. He helped people to think about how the fighting was hurting India. The leaders of the two religious groups agreed to end the fighting. But in 1948 Mohandas Gandhi was **assassinated** by a Hindu who was angry about the religious problems in India. Since then, Indians have continued to have many riots about religion.

Today India is the world's largest democracy. India is working to become a developed nation. The government is helping farmers use modern methods

Floods in Bangladesh have left millions of people without homes.

to grow food. New factories make cars, clothing, and other products. Each year more schools are built.

In 1947 some of India's Muslims started a new Muslim nation called Pakistan. People in the northeast and northwest parts of India became citizens of Pakistan. The two parts of Pakistan were separated by India. In 1971 the people of eastern Pakistan started their own nation called Bangladesh. Today, Bangladesh and Pakistan are poor, developing nations. Like India, they must solve many problems, including hunger and illiteracy. In 1988 Bangladesh had one of the worst floods in its history. More than 2,000 people were killed. More than 25 million people were left without homes.

Like India, Japan is a very crowded Asian nation. Japan is also a democracy. But unlike India, Japan is a rich, developed nation.

Japan has few natural resources. It does not have much farmland. Only a small part of Japan's people are farmers. They use modern tools and machines on their small farms. They grow a lot of the food Japan needs. The Japanese eat a lot of fish from the sea. Japan must buy some food from other nations.

Most of Japan was destroyed during World War II. After the war, the United States helped Japan rebuild and become a rich democracy. The Japanese built

Modern rice farming in Japan

Supermarket in Japan

Dance and clothing are two traditions in many nations. These two dancers are helping tradition stay important in Indonesia.

Japanese family eating at home

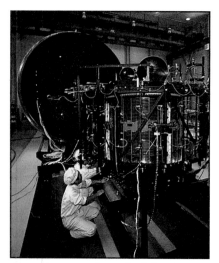
Japanese workers helping to build a satellite

thousands of new factories. Today, the Japanese buy raw materials from other nations. They use these raw materials to make cars, televisions, radios, and cameras. Japan sells these products to many nations.

The United States is one of Japan's main **trading partners**. This means that the nations buy products from each other. In recent years, there have been trade problems between the two nations. The United States thinks that Japan should buy many more American products than it already does. Japan thinks it buys enough products from the United States.

China is still a Communist nation. But its leaders are working to make China a nation with modern farms, factories, and technology. More people own businesses. China trades with the United States and other countries. Nations are building factories in China. China is becoming a modern nation. But people in China still do not have many freedoms.

Today many people in Asia's industrial nations enjoy western activities like movies, baseball, and music. But **traditions** are still important in Asia. Asians still enjoy religions, music, clothing, stories, and dances from long ago. However, people in Asia are looking to the future. They are trying to find ways to make their lives better.

Using Vocabulary

Find the Meaning Write on your paper the word or words that best complete each sentence.

1. **Poverty** means having very little _____ .

    money   time   power

2. **Traditions** are ways of life that people have _____ .

    forgotten   followed for many years   changed

3. A leader who has been **assassinated** has been _____ .

    elected   punished   killed

4. Countries that have a problem with **illiteracy** have many people who do not know how to _____ .

    read or write   grow crops   find jobs

5. Nations that are **trading partners** _____ from one another.

    collect taxes   buy goods   refuse to buy products

Read and Remember

Finish Up Choose a word in dark print to best complete each sentence. Write on your paper the word you choose.

Pakistan   farming   developing   Bangladesh   Asia

1. More than half of the world's population is in _____ .

2. Most people in _____ nations do not make as much money as do people in industrial nations.

3. India's Muslims started the nation called _____ in 1947.

4. Only a small part of the land of Japan is used for _____ .

5. Terrible floods in _____ in 1988 left millions of people without homes.

Think and Apply

Compare and Contrast   Read each sentence below. Decide whether the sentence tells about India, Japan, or both countries. Write **I** on your paper for each sentence that tells about India. Write **J** on your paper for each sentence that tells about Japan. Write **IJ** on your paper for each sentence that tells about both India and Japan.

1. This is a modern industrial nation.

2. This nation is very crowded.

3. This country is a democracy.

4. Much of this country was destroyed during World War II.

5. This nation has had many riots between Hindus and Muslims.

6. This nation has had recent trade problems with the United States.

7. This nation was once controlled by Great Britain.

Skill Builder

Reading a Political Map   Look at the political map of Asia on page 287. This map shows how Asia is divided today. Study the map. Then write on your paper the answer to each question.

1. What country shares India's northwest border?

2. In what ocean are the Philippines and Taiwan?

3. What country in Asia is the largest?

4. What island nation is east of South Korea?

5. What two nations are between Russia and China?

6. What is the capital city of India?

7. Of what nation is Beijing the capital city?

8. What nation is north of Kazakstan?

Journal Writing

Mohandas Gandhi was a very important person in India's history. His ideas helped bring many changes to India. Write a few sentences that tell some of the ways that Gandhi worked to help India.

Skill Builder

Reading a Double Bar Graph

This double bar graph shows how the populations of India and Japan changed from 1980 to 1995. Study the graph. Then write on your paper the answer to each question.

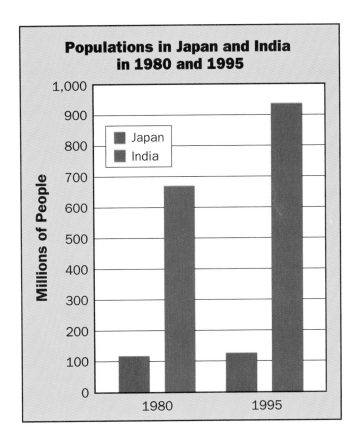

Populations in Japan and India in 1980 and 1995

1. What color are the bars that show the population of Japan?

2. Which nation has more people?

3. About how many people did India have in 1995?

4. Which nation's population only increased a small amount from 1980 to 1995?

5. About how many more people lived in India in 1995 than in 1980?

6. About how many more people lived in India than in Japan in 1995?

7. Which nation's population changed more between 1980 and 1995?

The Middle East Today

THINK ABOUT AS YOU READ

1. How is the Middle East different from other parts of the world?
2. What problems does the Middle East have?
3. Why have so many wars occurred in the Middle East?

NEW WORDS

♦ shah
♦ embassy
♦ hostages
♦ homeland
♦ Six-Day War
♦ Palestine Liberation Organization
♦ terrorists
♦ terrorism

PEOPLE & PLACES

♦ Arab
♦ Iran
♦ Ayatollah Khomeini
♦ Saddam Hussein
♦ Palestinians
♦ Jordan
♦ Syria
♦ Yasir Arafat
♦ Yitzhak Rabin
♦ King Hussein I

In many ways the Middle East is like other areas of the world. Nationalism is very important. It helped many nations of the Middle East become independent from European rule. Religion is also very important in the Middle East. Many countries are trying to become industrial nations. But the Middle East is also very different from other areas of the world.

The Middle East is the only region in which most of the nations are Arab nations. Most Arabs are Muslims. There are also millions of Christian Arabs in the region. The Middle East is the only region with a Jewish nation. This is the small nation of Israel.

About two thirds of the world's oil is found in the Middle East. Many industrial nations buy their oil from the Middle East. They need this oil for their factories, cars, and homes.

There are many problems in the Middle East today. In some nations, poverty and illiteracy are

People from many cultures shop in a market in Jerusalem.

THE MIDDLE EAST

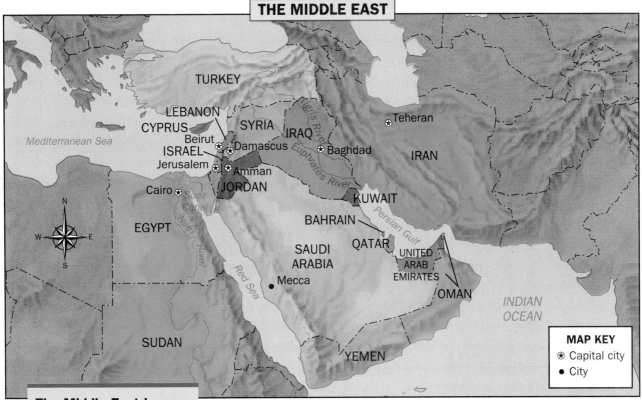

The Middle East has many Arab nations. In which nation is the city of Mecca located?

Ayatollah Khomeini

problems. Most nations do not have enough water. They cannot grow all the food they need. Many nations have little industry. They do not make many products to sell to other nations. There are not enough doctors. A large problem is war. Wars have occurred all over the Middle East. Many of the wars have been about religion or the control of oil fields.

In the late 1970s, Muslims in Iran forced the **shah,** or king, of Iran to leave the country. The Ayatollah Khomeini, a Muslim religious leader, became the nation's leader. A new government was started that was based on the laws of Islam. Everyone in Iran had to follow the laws of Islam. People in Iran were not allowed to use ideas, clothing, music, or businesses that were from European nations or the United States.

The shah of Iran had fled to the United States. People in Iran were angry that the United States protected the shah. In 1979 a group of people in Iran attacked the United States **embassy**. They forced the

People from Iraq set hundreds of Kuwait's oil wells on fire during the Persian Gulf War. It was very difficult to stop the fires.

Angry Muslims in Iran burning an American flag

Saddam Hussein

Americans in the embassy to become **hostages**. Iran refused to release the hostages unless the shah was returned to Iran for a trial. The shah died in 1980. Finally in 1981, the Americans were set free.

In 1980 the Arab nation of Iraq attacked Iran. Iraq was led by President Saddam Hussein. About one million people were killed or injured in the war. Finally in 1989 the United Nations helped the two nations agree to a cease-fire.

Iraq needed money after the war with Iran. In 1990 Iraq invaded Kuwait in order to control Kuwait's oil fields. The UN told Iraq to leave Kuwait, but Iraq refused. The United States and other UN countries from Europe and the Middle East sent troops to help free Kuwait. Iraq and the UN signed a cease-fire agreement to end the Persian Gulf War. But since then, Saddam Hussein has broken some of the promises he made in the cease-fire agreement.

Since 1948 four wars have occurred between Arab nations and Israel. Israel was once part of the land of Palestine. Jews had lived there for thousands of years. After World War II, many Jews wanted Palestine to be their **homeland**. In 1947 the UN divided Palestine into two parts. One part would be ruled

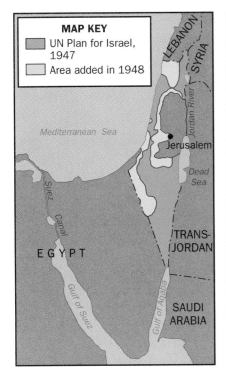

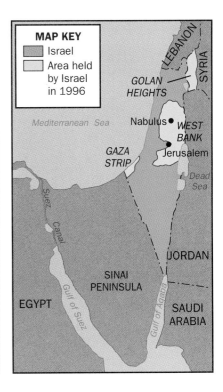

Israel held other lands after different wars with Arab nations. Compare the first two maps above. Which area of Egypt did Israel hold in 1967?

Israelis fighting in Jerusalem during the Six-Day War

by Arabs who lived there. These Arabs were called Palestinians. The other part would be ruled by Jews. In 1948 the Jewish part became the state of Israel.

Many Arabs did not like the UN plan. They did not want any part of Palestine to be a Jewish nation. In 1948 five Arab countries invaded Israel. The UN helped end the fighting. But Israel controlled more of Palestine than it had before the war of 1948. Many Palestinians fled from Israel. About 700,000 Palestinian refugees went to live in other Arab lands.

There was another war in 1956. This war was between Israel and Egypt. Again the UN helped end the fighting. Israel remained free.

In 1967 the Arabs and the Israelis fought again. After six days the Arabs surrendered. During the **Six-Day War,** Israel captured lands that had been ruled by Egypt, Jordan, and Syria. Israel still controls some of these lands.

In 1973 there was a fourth war against Israel. The war was started by Egypt and Syria. Israel fought back with weapons from other countries. This time the Arabs used their oil as a weapon. They stopped

Thousands of Palestinians live in refugee camps. Many of these refugee camps have become small towns.

selling oil to all the countries that were helping Israel. After that, only the United States and Holland would help Israel. The war in 1973 lasted three weeks. Israel won the war. Israel remained a free nation.

In 1979 Egypt became the first Arab nation to sign a peace treaty with Israel. The United States helped the two nations write the peace treaty. In 1982 Israel returned to Egypt land that had been captured in 1967. Egypt and Israel have kept their promises to live in peace.

For more than forty years, many Palestinians have lived in refugee camps in Arab nations. The United Nations pays for food, medicine, and schools for the camps. The refugees cannot return to Israel. Most refugees have not been allowed to become citizens of other Arab lands.

The **Palestine Liberation Organization** (PLO) was formed in 1964. The goal of the PLO is to have a Palestine nation again. Yasir Arafat is the leader of the PLO. For years the PLO said there should not be a Jewish nation in the Middle East. Many PLO members and other Arabs have become **terrorists**. They have bombed buses, planes, schools, and stores. Terrorists have killed Israelis and other people who have helped Israel. These Palestinians believe that **terrorism** will help them win their own nation.

Yasir Arafat

President Bill Clinton of the United States helped the leaders of Israel and of the PLO reach a peace agreement in 1993.

Yitzhak Rabin

King Hussein I

In 1988 Yasir Arafat said that the PLO would accept Israel as a nation. In 1991 the Israelis and the Palestinians started peace talks. In 1992 the Israelis elected Yitzhak Rabin as prime minister of Israel. Rabin worked to make peace between Israel and its Arab neighbors. In 1993 Israel and the PLO signed a peace agreement. Israel agreed to return some land to the Palestinians. Rabin and Arafat received the Nobel Peace Prize for their work toward peace.

In 1994 Jordan became the second Arab nation to sign a peace treaty with Israel. The United States helped King Hussein I of Jordan and Rabin of Israel write the treaty. Jordan and Israel have agreed to work together to solve problems.

In 1995 Yitzhak Rabin and Yasir Arafat signed another peace agreement. That same year Rabin was assassinated by an Israeli. The man who killed Rabin said that he was protesting the peace agreements between the Arabs and the Israelis.

The Middle East is still troubled by war and terrorism. But nations are trying to find ways to make peace. Perhaps one day lasting peace will come to the people of the Middle East. Then they can work together to solve the problems of the Middle East.

Using Vocabulary

Finish Up   Choose the word in dark print to best complete each sentence. Write on your paper the word you choose.

PLO	embassy	terrorism
homeland	hostage	shah

1. The _____ was the king of Iran.

2. In 1947 the United Nations said that part of Palestine should be a Jewish _____ , or country.

3. Attacks on people, planes, and schools are examples of _____ .

4. A _____ is a person who is being held prisoner.

5. An _____ is the headquarters of a representative from another nation.

6. Another name for the Palestine Liberation Organization is the _____ .

Read and Remember

Finish the Paragraph   Number your paper from 1 to 8. Use the words in dark print to finish the paragraph below. Write on your paper the words you choose.

Jordan	Iraq	Six-Day War	Arab
war	oil	Yasir Arafat	Muslims

The Middle East is a region that has many __1__ nations. The Middle East is very rich in __2__ . One of the Middle East's biggest problems is __3__ . In 1979 __4__ in Iran forced the shah to leave the country. __5__ invaded Kuwait in 1990. There have been four wars in Israel. One was the __6__ in 1967. Since then, the nation has signed peace treaties with Egypt and __7__ . The prime minister of Israel also worked with __8__ for peace between Israel and the PLO.

Think and Apply

Exclusions   One word or phrase in each group does not belong. Find that word or phrase and write it on your paper. Then write on your paper a sentence that tells how the other words are alike.

1. poverty
illiteracy
not enough water
oil

2. laws of Islam
leader was Khomeini
hostages from embassy
Palestinian refugees

3. leader was Saddam Hussein
ally of the United States
attacked Iran in 1980
started the Persian Gulf War

4. prime minister of Israel
signed treaty with Arafat
member of the PLO
assassinated in 1995

Skill Builder

Reading a Circle Graph   This circle graph shows how the world oil supply was divided among regions of the world in 1994. Study the circle graph. Then write on your paper the correct answers to the questions below.

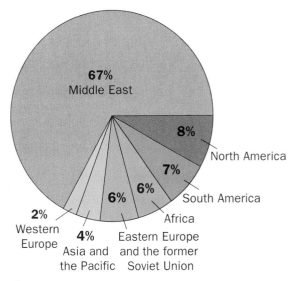

World Oil in 1994

1. Which region had the largest amount of oil?

Western Europe   Middle East   Africa

2. Which region had the same amount of oil as Eastern Europe and the former Soviet Union had?

Africa   North America   Asia and the Pacific

3. What was the total percent of the world oil in the Americas?

8%   15%   73%

Africa Today

Africa is the world's second largest continent. There are 53 nations in Africa today. Africa has **rain forests,** mountains, and

grasslands. The Sahara is the world's largest desert. The Nile River is the world's longest river.

Africa is very rich in natural resources. South Africa has most of the world's gold. It also has a lot of the world's diamonds. Nigeria is rich in oil. The Democratic Republic of Congo is rich in copper and diamonds. Many nations buy natural resources from Africa.

Africa has more than 800 **ethnic groups**. Each group has a different language and culture. Some African nations have hundreds of ethnic groups. It is often hard for the groups to get along. Problems between the ethnic groups have caused civil wars.

Some of the world's earliest civilizations began in Africa. During the 1400s, Europeans began to explore

People in Eritrea celebrated the African nation's independence in 1992.

THINK ABOUT AS YOU READ

1. What are some of the problems in Africa today?
2. Where have some civil wars occurred in Africa?
3. How is Africa working to solve its problems?

NEW WORDS

♦ rain forests
♦ grasslands
♦ ethnic groups
♦ droughts
♦ starvation
♦ mass killings
♦ apartheid
♦ tribal chief
♦ African National Congress

PEOPLE & PLACES

♦ Nigeria
♦ Zaire
♦ Rwanda
♦ Hutu
♦ Tutsi
♦ Coloreds
♦ Nelson Mandela

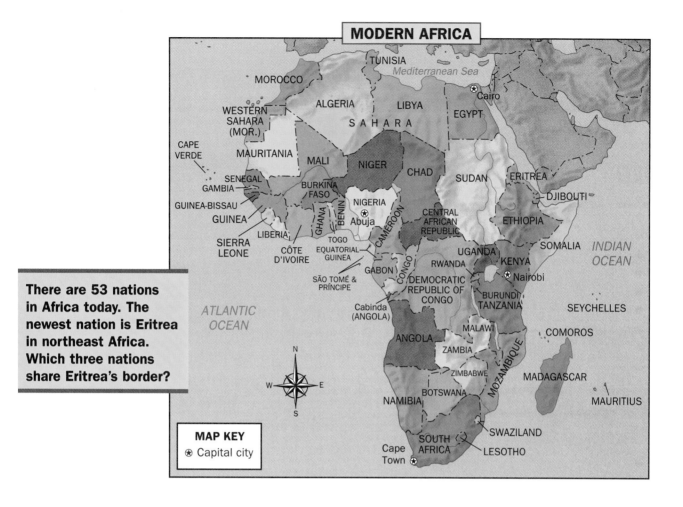

MODERN AFRICA

TUNISIA
Mediterranean Sea
MOROCCO
ALGERIA
LIBYA
EGYPT
WESTERN SAHARA (MOR.)
S A H A R A
Cairo
CAPE VERDE
MAURITANIA
MALI
NIGER
CHAD
SUDAN
ERITREA
SENEGAL
GAMBIA
BURKINA FASO
NIGERIA
DJIBOUTI
GUINEA-BISSAU
GUINEA
GHANA
BENIN
Abuja
CAMEROON
CENTRAL AFRICAN REPUBLIC
ETHIOPIA
SIERRA LEONE
LIBERIA
TOGO
CÔTE D'IVOIRE
EQUATORIAL GUINEA
GABON
CONGO
UGANDA
RWANDA
KENYA
SOMALIA
INDIAN OCEAN
SÃO TOMÉ & PRÍNCIPE
DEMOCRATIC REPUBLIC OF CONGO
Nairobi
BURUNDI
TANZANIA
SEYCHELLES
ATLANTIC OCEAN
Cabinda (ANGOLA)
MALAWI
COMOROS
ANGOLA
ZAMBIA
MOZAMBIQUE
MADAGASCAR
ZIMBABWE
NAMIBIA
BOTSWANA
MAURITIUS
N W E S
SWAZILAND
Cape Town
SOUTH AFRICA
LESOTHO

MAP KEY
⊛ Capital city

There are 53 nations in Africa today. The newest nation is Eritrea in northeast Africa. Which three nations share Eritrea's border?

Women in a village in the African country of Kenya

Africa. They forced many Africans to work as slaves in Europe and in colonies. Most of the slave trade ended by the early 1800s. After the Industrial Revolution began, Europe wanted raw materials from Africa. Soon most of Africa was ruled by imperialist nations. After World War II, nationalism became important to Africans. From 1950 to 1980, 47 colonies in Africa gained independence.

Many nations of Africa are developing nations. Poverty, hunger, and illiteracy are big problems. The biggest problem is that Africa's population is growing very fast. The nations do not have enough food or schools for the people.

Most people in Africa live in small villages. Most are farmers who work the same way that farmers worked long ago. The soil is often poor. The farmers are not able to grow enough food for everyone.

As the city of Cairo, Egypt, grows, new buildings are sometimes built around ancient statues.

People watching lions in Africa

Oil workers in Nigeria

Droughts have made problems worse for many nations. During a drought there is very little rain for many months. There is not enough water to grow food. During the 1980s and 1990s, there have been terrible droughts in many parts of Africa. Millions of people have died because of droughts. Most of these people starved to death.

Nigeria is a developing nation in western Africa. It gained independence from Great Britain in 1960. Nigeria has the largest population in Africa. More than 100 million people live there.

In the 1970s Nigeria earned a lot of money by selling oil to industrial nations. In the 1980s the price of oil went down. Nigeria could not earn enough money by selling oil. The nation learned that it needs to sell many different kinds of products to other nations.

Nigeria has more than 250 ethnic groups. In 1967 a civil war between ethnic groups began in Nigeria. It ended in 1970. More than two million people died in the war. Since then the people of Nigeria have worked to rebuild their nation.

In 1991 a civil war also broke out in Somalia. The civil war and a drought caused the **starvation** of more than 270,000 Somalians. In 1992 the United Nations sent troops to Somalia to try to bring peace and food to the nation. Many people were saved

More than four million refugees fled Rwanda to escape the mass killings in 1994.

Doctor examining children in Africa

Worker in a South African mine

from starvation, but the UN failed to bring peace to Somalia. The civil war continued. UN troops left Somalia in 1995.

The African country of Rwanda has had civil wars between two main ethnic groups, the Hutu and the Tutsi. In 1994 some of the Hutu tried to kill all of the Tutsi in Rwanda by **mass killings**. More than 750,000 people were killed during the civil war. About four million refugees fled from Rwanda to nearby African countries. But fighting has also occurred in the refugee camps. The UN is trying to help bring food and peace to the camps.

South Africa is the most developed nation in Africa today. It is an industrial nation that is rich in resources. The nation has good soil. Farmers grow most of the food that the nation needs.

Around 1650 many Dutch people moved to South Africa. In 1820 people from Great Britain began to move to South Africa. South Africa was part of the British empire for many years. In 1931 South Africa became an independent nation.

Beginning in the late 1940s, South Africa passed laws called **apartheid**. These laws divided people into four groups. White people belonged to the smallest group. Coloreds belonged to the second

Discrimination in South Africa

The city of Nairobi in Kenya

Children in school in Sierra
Leone, Africa

group. Coloreds are people that come from mixed Black, White, and Asian families. Asians were the third group. Black Africans were the fourth and largest group.

The purpose of apartheid was to keep the four groups of people apart. The laws gave Whites full power to rule the nation. Blacks were not allowed to vote. Members of each group were not allowed to marry members of other groups. Blacks and Whites could not use the same hotels, beaches, schools, or hospitals. Blacks were forced to live in the poorest parts of South Africa. They worked at difficult jobs for low wages.

South African Blacks and some South African Whites worked hard to end apartheid. They became protesters. One Black protest leader, Nelson Mandela, was kept in prison for 27 years. He was finally freed in 1990.

People around the world were also angry about the apartheid laws. The UN told South Africa to change its laws. Some nations stopped trading with South Africa. Finally in 1991, South Africa ended most of its apartheid laws. In 1993 South Africans agreed to a new constitution. Blacks were given the right to vote. The country is becoming a democracy. In 1994 Nelson Mandela was elected president of South Africa. Many other Blacks were elected to Parliament. South Africa is trying to find ways for all groups of people to take part in the government.

Nations in Africa are trying to find ways to work together to solve their problems. Africans are using their natural resources to improve their lives. More children are going to school. Nations are trying to become more modern. New factories are being built. Farmers are learning ways to grow more food. Workers from the United Nations are also helping African countries. Perhaps one day there will be less poverty, hunger, and civil war in Africa. Perhaps one day there will be more peace and unity.

PEOPLE IN HISTORY

Nelson Mandela (1918–   )

Nelson Mandela was born in South Africa in 1918. His father was a **tribal chief** of an ethnic group in South Africa. Nelson Mandela was trained to be a tribal chief. But he chose to go to college to become a lawyer.

In 1944 Mandela joined the **African National Congress** (ANC). The ANC was the largest Black group against the South African government. During the 1950s Mandela became famous for leading protests against the South African government. His role in these protests finally led to his arrest in 1956. Mandela was found not guilty and was released.

In 1960 the South African government said it was against the law to belong to the ANC. This did not stop Mandela. He led more protests against the South African government. In 1962 Mandela was arrested again. This time he was found guilty. He was sent to prison for life.

Many people began to think of Mandela as a symbol of the protest against apartheid. People in South Africa and around the world called for his release. More protests were held in South Africa. Finally in 1989, the president of South Africa met with Mandela. Mandela agreed to help work for peace in South Africa. The South African government agreed to allow people to be members of the ANC. Mandela was released from prison in 1990.

Nelson Mandela worked with the South African government to write a new constitution. In 1994 Blacks and Whites voted in the nation's first free election. Mandela was elected president of South Africa. He was the nation's first Black president. Nelson Mandela helped South Africa end apartheid and move toward democracy.

Nelson Mandela

Nelson Mandela voting for the first time in South Africa

Using Vocabulary

Analogies   Use the words in dark print to best complete the sentences. Write the correct answers on your paper.

rain forest   **drought**   **grasslands**
apartheid   **starvation**

1. Forests are to woods as meadows are to _____ .

2. Tall is to short as flood is to _____ .

3. Bacteria are to diseases as scarce food is to _____ .

4. Caste system is to India as _____ is to South Africa.

5. Dry is to wet as desert is to _____ .

Read and Remember

Write the Answer   Write one or more sentences on your paper to answer each question.

1. How many colonies in Africa gained their independence between 1950 and 1980?

2. What are four problems found in Africa today?

3. What happens during a drought?

4. What are three African nations in which civil wars have occurred?

5. What did the Hutu try to do in Rwanda in 1994?

6. What was the purpose of apartheid in South Africa?

Journal Writing

Nelson Mandela was a symbol of the protest against apartheid in South Africa. Write a paragraph that tells what Mandela did to bring change to South Africa.

Skill Builder

Reading a Population Map

This population map shows about how many people per square mile live in Africa. Study the population map and the map key. Then write the correct answers on your paper.

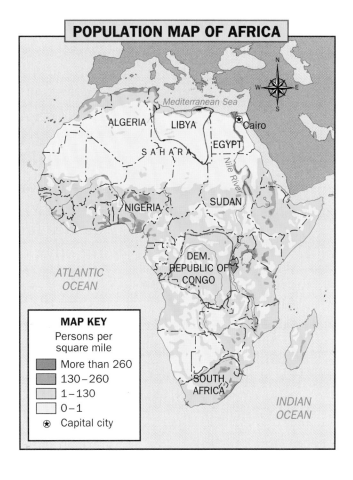

POPULATION MAP OF AFRICA

MAP KEY
Persons per square mile
- More than 260
- 130–260
- 1–130
- 0–1
- ✷ Capital city

1. How many people per square mile does most of the nation of South Africa have?

   0–1   1–130   more than 260

2. Which of these countries has the fewest people per square mile?
   Libya   Democratic Republic of Congo   South Africa

3. Which of these three nations has the most people per square mile?
   Nigeria   Algeria   Sudan

4. What part of Egypt has the highest population?
   along the border of Libya   along the border of Sudan
   along the Nile River

5. Where do most people in Africa live?
   south of the Sahara   in Cairo   in the Sahara

CHAPTER 43

The Americas Today

North America and South America are often called the Americas. The Americas sometimes are divided into two regions based on culture. The United States and Canada are one **cultural** region. Latin America is the other cultural region. All of the countries to the south of the United States are part of Latin America.

Latin American countries have many types of land. The Andes Mountains and the mountains of the Sierra Madre cover thousands of miles. There are large rain forests, deserts, grasslands, and beaches.

Latin America also has many natural resources, such as metals and trees. Mexico is rich in oil and silver. Venezuela is also rich in oil. Brazil is rich in iron and gold. Chile is rich in copper.

Most of the people of Latin America speak Spanish. Portuguese is the language of Brazil. Some people speak American Indian languages. Most people are Roman Catholics.

THINK ABOUT AS YOU READ

1. What are the two cultural regions in the Americas?
2. What are some of the problems in Latin America?
3. In what ways are Canada and the United States alike?

NEW WORDS

♦ cultural
♦ gap
♦ inflation
♦ debt
♦ repay
♦ extinct
♦ North American Free Trade Agreement
♦ illegal drugs

PEOPLE & PLACES

♦ Sierra Madre
♦ Portuguese
♦ Fidel Castro
♦ Rocky Mountains
♦ Great Plains
♦ Great Lakes

The beautiful Andes Mountains are some of the tallest mountains in the world.

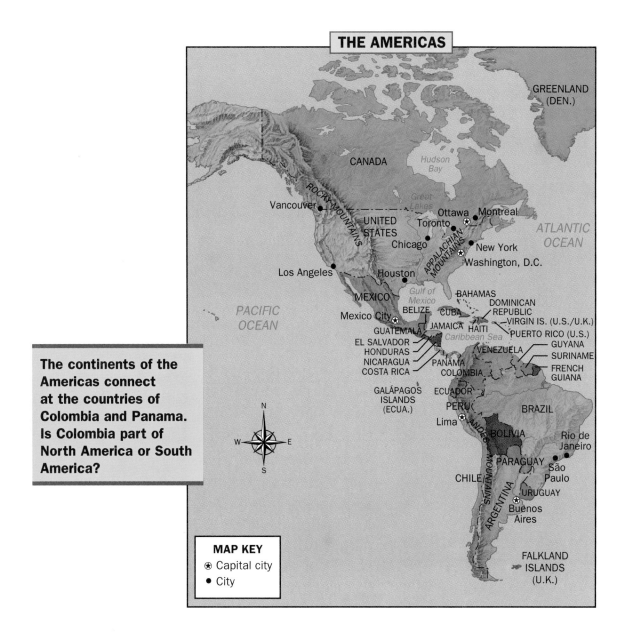

THE AMERICAS

GREENLAND (DEN.)

CANADA

Hudson Bay

Great Lakes

ROCKY MOUNTAINS

Vancouver

UNITED STATES

Ottawa · Montreal
Toronto

Chicago

APPALACHIAN MOUNTAINS

New York
Washington, D.C.

ATLANTIC OCEAN

Los Angeles

Houston

Gulf of Mexico

PACIFIC OCEAN

MEXICO

Mexico City

BAHAMAS

BELIZE CUBA
GUATEMALA JAMAICA HAITI
EL SALVADOR
HONDURAS
NICARAGUA PANAMA
COSTA RICA COLOMBIA

DOMINICAN REPUBLIC
VIRGIN IS. (U.S./U.K.)
PUERTO RICO (U.S.)
Caribbean Sea
VENEZUELA GUYANA
SURINAME
FRENCH GUIANA

GALÁPAGOS ISLANDS (ECUA.)

ECUADOR

PERU

Lima

BRAZIL

ANDES MOUNTAINS

BOLIVIA

Rio de Janeiro

PARAGUAY

São Paulo

CHILE

ARGENTINA

URUGUAY

Buenos Aires

FALKLAND ISLANDS (U.K.)

MAP KEY
✪ Capital city
● City

The continents of the Americas connect at the countries of Colombia and Panama. Is Colombia part of North America or South America?

People walking on a beach in Puerto Rico

In Latin America today, there is a very big **gap** between the rich and the poor. Most people are very poor. Not many people are part of the middle class. Rich people are part of a small, powerful group. They own most of the land and the factories. They have the most power in the government. Latin American nations are trying to end this gap. Some governments are giving land to the poor. In some nations the middle class is growing larger.

Brazil is the largest nation in Latin America. It is becoming a developed nation. For many years, Brazil earned most of its money by exporting coffee. Today,

The government of Brazil is in the capital city Brasília. The city is known for its many modern buildings.

Ships carrying goods from Brazil

Brazil exports more cars and steel than any other Latin American nation exports. Industry is helping Brazil become a richer nation. But many parts of Brazil still have poverty.

Inflation is a problem in Brazil. Inflation means that everything becomes more and more expensive. During a period of inflation, milk that costs $1.00 in April might cost $3.00 by June. Many people lose their jobs during a period of inflation. Inflation is also a problem in Mexico, Argentina, and many smaller nations in Latin America.

Debt is one of Brazil's largest problems. Brazil borrowed billions of dollars from the United States, Japan, and other nations. The Portuguese used the money to build roads, schools, and factories. Brazil must **repay,** or pay back, this money. Brazil now uses most of its money to repay its debt.

Brazil has the world's largest rain forest. Much of the rain forest is destroyed each year. Trees are cut down and cleared away. The land is then used for farming or for roads. Many important resources in rain forests are lost when the trees are destroyed. Some plants and animals have become **extinct**.

Mexico is a democracy. Like Brazil, Mexico is becoming a developed nation. Mexican factories

Poverty in Brazil

People have been destroying the rain forests in Brazil in order to create new farmland.

Air pollution in Mexico City

A border crossing between Mexico and the United States

export cars, steel, and clothing to other nations. Mexico also exports oil, coffee, and sugar.

Mexico is working to solve many problems. Its cities have terrible pollution from cars and factories. Poverty is another problem. Like Brazil, Mexico also has inflation and a very large debt.

In the 1970s Mexico earned a lot of money by selling oil to other nations. In the 1980s the price of oil went down. Mexico was forced to sell its oil for less money. It had to borrow billions of dollars. Now Mexico must repay its debt. Many people have lost their jobs. Many Mexicans have become poorer. Some of these Mexicans have tried to move to the United States.

The government of Mexico is working hard to make Mexico a better place to live. It has built many schools in all parts of Mexico. Today, most Mexicans know how to read and write. The government has given farmland to many poor people. The middle class is growing larger.

Cuba is a Communist nation. For many years Cuba has worked to spread communism to other Latin American countries. Fidel Castro is the leader of Cuba. He is a dictator. He has been in power since 1959. Since then, hundreds of thousands of Cuban

Fidel Castro

A Cuban immigrant in the United States

The White House, home of the President of the United States

immigrants have moved to the United States. These people did not want to live in a Communist country. They did not like the way Castro ruled Cuba.

Many nations in Latin America are struggling with revolutions and unfair governments. Some nations have been ruled by many different dictators. But people are working to bring peace to Latin America. Many people are working to give everyone in Latin America a good life. New industries are being started. The nations of Latin America are exporting more products. Cities are growing larger. Many schools are built each year.

Like many Latin American nations, the United States and Canada have many types of land. The Rocky Mountains, the Great Plains, and the Great Lakes are found in both nations. Both countries are rich in natural resources. They have fertile soil, forests, coal, iron ore, and oil.

The United States and Canada are alike in many ways. They are both world powers and democracies. They are industrial nations with high standards of living. The United States and Canada also have some of the same problems. Some of their natural resources, such as trees and fish, are being used up. Pollution from factories and cars is another problem.

The United States, Canada, and Mexico are major trading partners. In 1993 the three nations passed the **North American Free Trade Agreement** (NAFTA). NAFTA will help trade among the three countries increase.

The United States is one of the world's strongest nations. It creates new technology and medicines. It works hard to help many nations end hunger, civil war, and poverty. It helps many nations fight the spread of communism and the rise of dictators. It also works for stronger world trade. People from many different nations have moved to the United States. The United States has been called "a nation of immigrants."

More than 150,000 people gathered in Montreal, Quebec, about whether Quebec should leave the nation of Canada.

Fireworks above the Statue of Liberty in New York City

Rodeo in Alberta, Canada

The United States is working to end problems with Latin America. One way it does this is through trade. It is also trying to end the movement of **illegal drugs** from some Latin American countries into the United States. Illegal drugs are dangerous drugs that are against the law to sell and to use in a nation.

Canada is the second largest country in the world. It was once part of the British empire. The two main languages in Canada are English and French. Like the United States, Canada works to bring peace and to end problems in other nations.

Many Canadians who speak French live in the area of Quebec. Many of the people in Quebec feel that Quebec should be its own nation. But in 1995 the people of Quebec voted to remain part of the nation of Canada.

The nations of the Americas help one another in many ways. They are increasing trade with one another and are working to end poverty and pollution. Each year the nations of the Americas are finding more ways to work together.

Using Vocabulary

Finish the Paragraph   Number your paper from 1 to 5. Use the words in dark print to finish the paragraph below. Write on your paper the words you choose.

gap   repay   inflation   debt   extinct

There are many problems in Latin America today. Pollution is a problem. There is a large __1__, or amount of differences, between the rich and the poor. Many goods in Latin America are becoming more expensive. This is called __2__. Some Latin American countries borrowed millions of dollars that they must __3__, or pay back. When a nation owes money, the nation has a __4__. Whole groups of animals and plants in the rain forests of Brazil are dying, or becoming __5__.

Read and Remember

Choose the Answer   Write the correct answers on your paper.

1. How are the Americas often divided into regions?

based on population   based on culture   based on natural resources

2. Which nation exports more cars and steel than any other Latin American nation exports?

Brazil   Mexico   Cuba

3. Which is the smallest class of people in Latin America?

the rich   the middle class   the poor

4. Which three nations signed NAFTA?

Brazil, Argentina, and Canada   Mexico, the United States, and Canada

Cuba, Canada, and Great Britain

Finish the Sentence Write on your paper the word or words that best complete each sentence.

1. Portuguese is the language of _____ .

  Mexico   Cuba   Brazil

2. Mexico had to borrow money after the price of _____ went down in the 1980s.

  oil   farmland   diamonds

3. Fidel Castro became the leader of _____ in 1959.

  Argentina   Chile   Cuba

4. Mexico has terrible pollution from _____ .

  cars and factories   rain forests   debt

5. One problem between the United States and some Latin American nations is _____ .

  hunger   illegal drugs   standard of living

Think and Apply

Distinguishing Relevant Information Imagine that you want to tell a friend about the ways that the United States and Canada are alike. Read each sentence below. Decide which sentences are relevant to what you will say. Write the relevant sentences on your paper. There are four relevant sentences.

1. Both nations are industrial nations and democracies.

2. The Rocky Mountains and the Great Plains can be found in both nations.

3. Trees, fish, and other natural resources are being used up.

4. The people of Quebec voted to remain part of Canada.

5. There is a large gap between the rich and the poor.

6. The nations work to spread peace and to prevent the rise of dictators in other nations.

7. Many Cuban immigrants have moved to the United States.

Skill Builder

Reading a Double Line Graph   This double line graph shows how the populations of the Americas have changed over time. On this graph, North America includes the United States and Canada. Latin America includes Mexico. Study the graph. Then write on your paper the answer to each question.

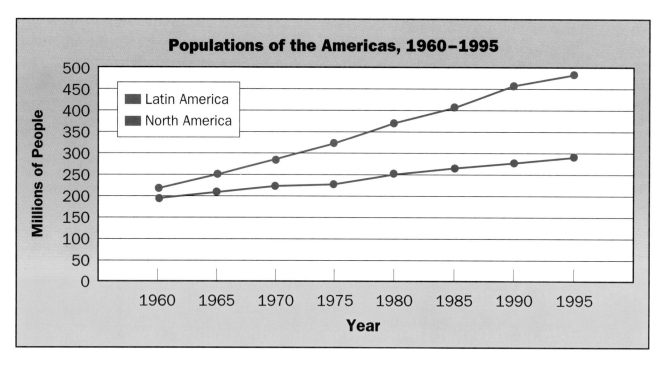

1. What color is used to show the population of North America?

2. About how many people were living in North America in 1980?

3. Which region had about 450 million people in 1990?

4. About how many more people were living in Latin America in 1995 than in 1965?

5. About how many more people were living in Latin America than in North America in 1995?

6. In what year were the populations of Latin America and North America about the same?

7. Which region's population increased the most?

Europe Today

Europe is a continent with many nations, languages, and cultures. Its land has many hills, mountains, peninsulas, and plains. There are many canals, ports, and harbors that help Europeans trade with nations around the world. Some nations of Europe are rich in natural resources, such as iron, coal, and oil. Today most of Europe has many kinds of industries. Factories produce cars, chemicals, steel, and other items.

After World War II, Europe became divided into two regions—Eastern Europe and Western Europe. During the Cold War, the people in the Communist countries of Eastern Europe had a lower standard of living than did the people of Western Europe. Many goods were scarce. Most people were not able to own cars or washing machines.

THINK ABOUT AS YOU READ

1. **Why did communism grow weaker in Eastern Europe?**
2. **How did communism end in nations such as Poland and the Soviet Union?**
3. **How does the EU work to help the nations of Europe?**

NEW WORDS

◆ **Solidarity**
◆ **freedom of the press**
◆ **Channel Tunnel**
◆ **European Union**
◆ **Common Market**
◆ **shipyards**
◆ **trade unions**
◆ **candidates**

PEOPLE & PLACES

◆ **Polish**
◆ **Lech Walesa**
◆ **Mikhail Gorbachev**
◆ **Yugoslavia**
◆ **Gdansk**

Many people enjoy visiting the beautiful city of Prague, the capital of the Czech Republic.

Europe is a continent with many peninsulas. Which of these three countries is on a peninsula: Ireland, Romania, or Italy?

Mikhail Gorbachev

The people in Eastern Europe and in the Soviet Union grew tired of communism. People wanted more freedom and a better standard of living. During the 1980s the governments of Eastern Europe and the Soviet Union began to change. These changes gave people more freedom. People began to demand the end of communism.

Poland was the first nation in Eastern Europe in which communism grew weaker. In 1980 Polish workers started a labor union called **Solidarity**. Solidarity worked to create a non-Communist government. In 1989 Poland had its first free election since the Cold War began. Lech Walesa, the leader of Solidarity, became the president of Poland.

Communism grew weaker in the Soviet Union soon after Mikhail Gorbachev became the nation's leader in 1985. He allowed people to have freedom of speech and **freedom of the press**. There was also more religious freedom. People began to own farms, factories, and businesses.

Thousands of people gathered to watch the Berlin Wall being torn down by the East Germans in 1989.

By 1991 communism in the Soviet Union had grown very weak. The nation began to fall apart. It was divided into 15 republics. Russia was the largest of these republics. Russia and other republics held free elections. Communism ended. The once strong Soviet Union was no longer a nation.

Throughout Eastern Europe, people voted in free elections for new leaders. Communism in Eastern Europe ended. This brought an end to the Cold War.

Modern factory in Germany

The people of East Germany and West Germany had wanted the two nations to become united again. In 1989 many people gathered to watch as the Berlin Wall was torn down. East Berlin and West Berlin became one city again. In 1990 East Germany and West Germany united. Today Germany is a non-Communist nation.

In 1991 and 1992, changes also occurred in the Communist nation of Yugoslavia. During this time, Yugoslavia was divided into six different republics. Four republics declared their independence. One of these nations was Bosnia and Herzegovina.

In the year 1992, a civil war began in Bosnia and Herzegovina. The war began because three ethnic groups fought to win control of the new country.

Many buildings were destroyed during Bosnia's civil war. This man is taking bricks from a library in order to rebuild his home.

Train going into the Channel Tunnel

A market in Spain

Much of Bosnia was destroyed. The UN and NATO sent troops to the nation to help stop the fighting there. In 1995 the United States helped the leaders of the ethnic groups agree to a peace plan. But there is still tension between the groups.

The nations of Europe are working to improve relations with one another. One way that Great Britain and France did this was to make it easier to travel between the two nations. They built a tunnel for trains under the English Channel. The **Channel Tunnel** opened in 1994.

Fifteen nations of Western Europe are members of the **European Union** (EU). This organization makes it easier for member nations to sell goods and services to one another. The EU makes it easier for people of one nation to work in another EU nation. The EU helps to lower the prices of many goods and services in Europe. The EU was called the European **Common Market** when it first began. Many nations in Eastern Europe hope to one day join the EU.

The European Union is working to make Europe a more united continent. The EU plans to have one money system for all member nations. As European nations work for better business and trade, they will also be working for peace.

Lech Walesa (1943–   )

Poland became a Communist nation in 1945. By the 1980s communism was growing weaker in Poland. Workers were going on strike. Their leader was Lech Walesa. He became a symbol of freedom in Eastern Europe. Walesa and the workers helped end communism in Poland.

Lech Walesa

Lech Walesa was born in Poland during World War II. In 1967 he began working in the **shipyards** in Poland's port city Gdansk. He joined the strikes for workers' rights. In 1980 Walesa became the leader of Solidarity. Solidarity was a non-Communist organization of **trade unions**. The members of Solidarity held protests and went on strike. They wanted lower food prices and better wages.

In 1981 the Communist government arrested Walesa and some other members of Solidarity. In 1982 government leaders said that it was against the law for people to be members of Solidarity. Walesa was released from prison in 1982. In 1983 Walesa received the Nobel Peace Prize for using peaceful ways to gain workers' rights.

In 1989 Poland's government allowed people to join Solidarity. Changes were made in Poland's government. Non-Communists were allowed to be **candidates** in elections. Free elections were held. In 1990 Walesa became president of Poland. Poland became a non-Communist nation.

Lech Walesa speaking during a workers' strike in Poland

Poland was one of the first Eastern European nations to end its Communist government. However, Poland faced new problems. Prices for many goods increased. Many people did not have jobs. Workers went on strike. In 1995 Walesa lost the election for president. But Lech Walesa is respected for working to end communism in Poland.

Using Vocabulary

Find the Meaning   Write on your paper the word or words that best complete each sentence.

1. The **Channel Tunnel** is an underwater railway tunnel between _____ and France.

   Great Britain   Germany   the United States

2. The **European Union** is an organization that makes it easier for member countries to _____ .

   fight communism   hold free elections   sell goods and services

3. The **Common Market** is another term for _____ .

   NAFTA   the UN   the EU

4. **Solidarity** was a non-Communist organization of _____ in Poland.

   candidates   trade unions   government leaders

Read and Remember

Find the Answer   Find the sentences that tell about Europe today. Write on your paper the sentences you find. You should find four sentences.

1. The nations of Europe are working together to improve trade and relations with one another.

2. The Soviet Union spread communism to Eastern Europe.

3. Europe has many natural resources and many different industries.

4. A Communist government owns most farms and businesses.

5. The EU is trying to make Europe a more united continent.

6. It is becoming easier for people in one European nation to work in another European nation.

7. Many battles of World War II took place in Europe.

Finish the Paragraph   Number your paper from 1 to 7. Use the words in dark print to finish the paragraph below. Write on your paper the words you choose.

Poland   **communism**   **Cold War**   **West Germany**
standard   **Berlin Wall**   **republics**

The people of Eastern Europe had a lower ___1___ of living than did the people of Western Europe. During the 1980s the people of Eastern Europe demanded the end of ___2___. In 1989 the people of ___3___ held free elections. In 1989 the ___4___ was torn down. In 1990 East Germany and ___5___ were united as one nation. In 1991 the Soviet Union was divided into 15 separate ___6___. The end of communism brought an end to the ___7___.

Think and Apply

Fact or Opinion   Write **F** on your paper for each fact below. Write **O** for each opinion. You should find four opinions.

1. Many goods were scarce in Eastern Europe.

2. Communism should end in Eastern Europe.

3. Mikhail Gorbachev was the best ruler of the Soviet Union.

4. The European Union plans to have one money system for all member nations.

5. The Common Market is a good way to improve trade between the nations of Europe.

6. The civil war in Bosnia and Herzegovina began in 1992.

 7. Lech Walesa and the organization called Solidarity helped bring an end to communism in Poland.

8. Europe is too crowded.

Unit 9 Looking to the Future

The world continues to change all the time. Nations are learning new ways to work together. They are increasing trade and improving relations. People are living longer. Populations are growing. New inventions are being made. They are quickly changing the way we live. Many inventions make life better. People are finding new ways to travel and to share information.

As we look toward the future, we can see many challenges facing the world. Nations know that they need one another to get the things they do not have. They want to have good relations with other nations. They want to work together to make the world better. Nations are working together to end poverty and hunger and to protect the earth. They are finding ways to keep world peace and to protect freedom. People are working together to solve pollution and health problems.

It is hard to know for sure what the future will be like. However, it is important to solve the problems we have today in order to have a better tomorrow. It is also important to learn from past mistakes, such as the reasons that wars have been fought. If we learn from our mistakes, we can prevent the same problems from happening again.

PACIFIC OCEAN

ATLANTIC OCEAN

PACIFIC OCEAN

INDIAN OCEAN

How can we stop pollution? How can nations be better neighbors? What can we do now to make sure we have a better future? As you read Unit 9, think about how the world is changing. Think about what you can do to build a better world for tomorrow.

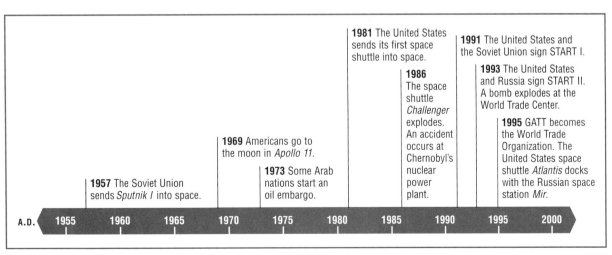

1981 The United States sends its first space shuttle into space.

1986 The space shuttle *Challenger* explodes. An accident occurs at Chernobyl's nuclear power plant.

1991 The United States and the Soviet Union sign START I.

1993 The United States and Russia sign START II. A bomb explodes at the World Trade Center.

1995 GATT becomes the World Trade Organization. The United States space shuttle *Atlantis* docks with the Russian space station *Mir*.

1969 Americans go to the moon in *Apollo 11*.

1973 Some Arab nations start an oil embargo.

1957 The Soviet Union sends *Sputnik I* into space.

A.D. 1955   1960   1965   1970   1975   1980   1985   1990   1995   2000

Technology Brings Change

Technology has changed the world in many ways since World War II. It has changed the ways people travel, work, and share information. It has helped doctors save lives and businesses grow. There is new technology being used every day in industrial nations. Developing nations have less technology than industrial nations have.

Computers have become very important in many nations. Before the 1970s few people had computers in their homes or schools. Industrial nations now have computers everywhere. Computers are used in airplanes and spaceships. They are in banks, offices, schools, stores, and homes. Every year people make computers that can do more things. Computers have become smaller, cheaper, and more useful.

Communication is better than ever before. Communication is how people share information. People **communicate** with one another by talking,

THINK ABOUT AS YOU READ

1. **How has technology changed the ways we live?**
2. **How has technology improved space travel?**
3. **How have computers and satellites helped communication?**

NEW WORDS

- ◆ **communication**
- ◆ **communicate**
- ◆ **cellular phones**
- ◆ **fax machines**
- ◆ **Internet**
- ◆ **electronic mail**
- ◆ **fertilizers**
- ◆ **bullet trains**
- ◆ **astronauts**
- ◆ **space shuttles**
- ◆ **space station**
- ◆ **orbit**
- ◆ **docked**

Computers have become an important part of schools and businesses.

Today farmers are learning ways to grow food using little soil and water.

Person using a cellular phone on a beach in Thailand

Computers are used in many offices.

writing, or touching. People can communicate using telephones, televisions, radios, and computers. Today people can use **cellular phones** to call people from cars or while outdoors. People can also use **fax machines** to send copies of papers and pictures to one another over telephone lines.

Computer owners can also use the **Internet** to share information. The Internet is a large system of computers all over the world that are linked to one another. Messages can be sent very quickly by **electronic mail** from one computer user to another user on the Internet. Electronic mail is sometimes called e-mail. People can also use the Internet to look up information about many subjects.

Technology is part of the agricultural revolution. You have read how new farming machines were invented during the Industrial Revolution. At that time a farmer who worked hard could grow enough food for four people.

Technology has helped farmers grow much more food. Large farm machines can do the work of many farmers. Farmers now use **fertilizers** that help the soil produce more food. Farmers are able to irrigate farms that are far from lakes and rivers. In some

The bullet train in Japan can travel over 150 miles an hour.

Modern wheat farming

places farmers have turned deserts into fertile farm land. Farmers can grow much more food from new kinds of wheat and rice seeds. One farmer today can grow enough food for more than eighty people.

Technology has changed the way we travel. Long ago explorers had to sail for many days in order to cross an ocean. Today a person can fly out of Great Britain after breakfast and eat dinner in New York City. Airplanes have made it easier for people to travel around the world.

On land, trains are an important way to travel. **Bullet trains** in some nations can travel faster than 150 miles per hour. France has trains that travel faster than 185 miles per hour. Modern technology has also made it possible to build underwater tunnels like the Channel Tunnel between Great Britain and France. These tunnels allow trains to travel between lands that are separated by miles of water.

Technology has helped people travel into space. Space travel began in 1957 when the Soviet Union sent the first satellite into space. The first Soviet satellite was called *Sputnik I*. Less than one year later, the United States sent its first satellite into space. The space race became part of the Cold War. Both nations began sending people into space. People who travel in space are called **astronauts**. As time passed, astronauts took longer trips into space.

The United States is a leader in space technology. The space shuttle can travel into space many times.

Communications satellite

In 1969 Americans became the first people to walk on the moon. The Americans went to the moon in a spaceship called *Apollo 11*. It took only four days to fly to the moon.

For many years, spaceships could be used for only one trip into space. The United States began building spaceships that could be used many times. These new spaceships were called **space shuttles**. In 1981 Americans took their first trip in a space shuttle. Since then the United States has built other space shuttles.

Space travel has not always been safe. In 1986 a space shuttle called *Challenger* exploded soon after it went into the sky. All seven people on board the space shuttle were killed. After that, Americans worked to build safer shuttles. In 1988 they began to send shuttles into space again.

In 1986 the Soviets put a new **space station** into **orbit** around Earth. The station is called *Mir*. People can stay in the space station for many months. The station helps us learn more about space and Earth.

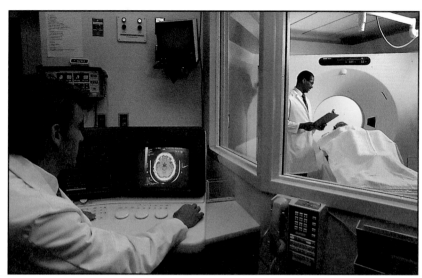
Technology has greatly improved medicine. New machines help doctors save many lives.

A satellite dish receives information from satellites.

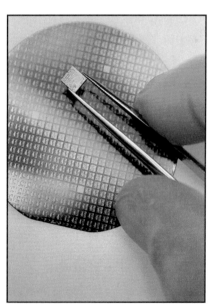
Computers use tiny computer chips to run.

In 1995 and 1996, the United States space shuttle *Atlantis* **docked** with the *Mir* space station. The Russians and the Americans worked together on experiments in space.

Today the United States and Russia are still leaders in space technology. Japan, France, China, Canada, and other nations have their own space programs. Many nations have sent satellites into space. Nations are trying to learn more about Earth and other planets. Several nations are working together to build a new space station.

Space satellites have helped communication. There are hundreds of space satellites in the sky for communication. Weather satellites help us learn when dangerous storms are coming. Some satellites help us make telephone calls to faraway nations. Television satellites help us watch shows from many nations of the world. Satellites can also send news reports from one nation to another as events occur.

Technology has helped nations learn more about one another. It has also helped the growth of trade. Technology has made nations need one another in many ways. Why do nations need one another? How do nations work together to solve problems? You will find the answers in the next chapter.

Using Vocabulary

Finish Up   Choose the word or words in dark print to best complete each sentence. Write on your paper the word or words you choose.

> **orbit**   **communication**   **fertilizers**
>
> **bullet**   **electronic mail**   **Internet**

1. The act of sharing information with other people is called _____ .

2. The _____ is a system of computers that are linked to one another.

3. Computer owners can send messages to other computer owners using a system called _____ .

4. Trains that can travel over a hundred miles an hour are sometimes called _____ trains.

5. To be in _____ is to travel around a planet.

6. Chemicals that help farmers grow more food are called _____ .

Read and Remember

Finish the Sentence   Write on your paper the word or words that best complete the sentence.

1. Developing nations have less _____ than industrial nations.

natural resources   people   technology

2. People can use _____ phones to call people while in a car or outdoors.

orbit   cellular   e-mail

3. Astronauts are people who travel in _____ .

bullet trains   space   fax machines

4. Weather _____ let us know when dangerous storms are coming.

fertilizers   shuttles   satellites

Think and Apply

Exclusions   One word or phrase in each group does not belong. Find that word or phrase and write it on your paper. Then write on your paper a sentence that tells how the other words are alike.

1. *Sputnik I*
   Apollo 11
   Atlantis
   Challenger

2. fertilizers
   new kinds of seeds
   satellite
   large farm machines

3. satellites
   e-mail
   space station
   space shuttles

4. cellular phones
   Internet
   astronaut
   fax machines

Sequencing Events   Number your paper from 1 to 5. Write the sentences to show the correct order.

The United States space shuttle *Atlantis* docked with the *Mir* space station in 1995 and 1996.

Space travel began during the Cold War when the Soviet Union sent its first satellite into space.

In 1969 American astronauts reached the moon after traveling in a spaceship for four days.

The seven people on board the *Challenger* died when the space shuttle exploded in 1986.

United States astronauts traveled in the first space shuttle, a spaceship that could be used many times.

Journal Writing

Technology has changed the world in many ways. Write a paragraph that tells three ways that technology has helped people. Give examples from the chapter.

Nations Depend on One Another

Nations work together for many reasons. Together they trade, work for world peace, and solve problems such as hunger and pollution. **Interdependence** brings nations closer together. Interdependence means that nations need one another for many things. It also means that the problems of one nation can hurt other nations.

Scarcity makes nations need one another. Scarcity means that many people and businesses do not have enough of the products or raw materials that they need. There is a scarcity of oil and coal in many nations. There is a scarcity of food and technology in many developing nations. Nations need one another to get the things they do not have.

Nations became **interdependent** long ago when they began trading with one another. The ancient Romans got silk and foods from far-off lands. About the year 1500, Europeans conquered many lands in

Nations depend on one another for trade. This large tanker is carrying oil from one nation to another.

Ships carry goods all over the world. These goods are being shipped from Bombay, India's largest port.

order to gain colonies. They wanted silks, spices, gold, and silver from their colonies. After the Industrial Revolution, nations got raw materials such as cotton and coal from their colonies.

Trade is very important in the modern world. Trade helps nations get the goods and the raw materials they need. Japan has become one of the world's richest nations because of trade. Japan has few natural resources. It buys raw materials from other nations. Japan uses these raw materials to make factory products. Every year, Japan exports goods that earn billions of dollars.

In 1947 many countries worked together to set up the **General Agreement on Tariffs and Trade** (GATT). This organization helped increase trade between member countries by lowering **tariffs**. Tariffs are special taxes on traded goods. Tariffs make goods more expensive. In 1995 GATT became the **World Trade Organization** (WTO).

As you read in Chapter 43, the United States, Canada, and Mexico agreed to NAFTA. This trade agreement was created to help trade between the three nations. NAFTA helps trade by lowering or removing tariffs. NAFTA also makes it easier for the

Worker in a car factory in Mexico

President Clinton of the United States signed NAFTA in 1993.

Oil wells are used to get oil from beneath land and oceans.

Electric power lines

people in each nation to own businesses or to work in the other two nations.

All industrial nations need energy for their offices, factories, homes, and cars. Light, heat, and electricity are three kinds of energy. Most nations use oil, coal, and **natural gas** to make energy. In many places most energy is made from oil. **Gasoline** is made from oil. Most cars and trucks use oil and gasoline. Oil is used to make electricity. There is a scarcity of oil in many industrial nations. They must **import** oil from the nations of the Middle East, Africa, and Latin America.

During the Arab-Israeli war of 1973, it was hard for many nations to get the oil they needed. This is because the Arabs started an **oil embargo**. They stopped selling oil to the United States and to some other nations. The oil embargo made it hard for people to buy gasoline for cars. Electricity became more expensive. Many people wanted to find new ways to make energy without using oil.

Some countries began to make electricity in **nuclear power plants**. These plants used nuclear energy instead of oil to make electricity. There are many nuclear power plants in Europe and the United

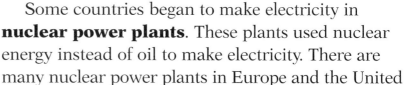

Nuclear power plants provide a way to make electricity without using coal, oil, or natural gas.

Nuclear power plant in Chernobyl

Traffic is one cause of air pollution.

States. A nuclear power plant can be very dangerous if there is an accident in the plant.

In 1986 a terrible accident happened at a nuclear power plant in the Soviet Union. The plant was located in the city of Chernobyl. Today Chernobyl is part of the nation Ukraine. The accident at the plant sent a lot of **radioactive wastes** into the air. Winds blew these radioactive wastes over other nations in northern Europe. Many people died right after the accident. Many animals died from the radioactive wastes. Doctors believe that many people who live near Chernobyl will continue to get cancer from the spread of radioactive wastes.

Each year industrial nations have more cars and factories. These cars and factories cause air pollution and water pollution. Pollution makes air and water unsafe. Sometimes air pollution in one nation becomes part of the rain. Then the rain becomes **acid rain**. Acid rain sometimes falls on other nations. These nations might be far from where the pollution first began. Acid rain kills plants and animals. Acid rain is damaging rivers, lakes, and forests in Europe and in North America.

The world's rain forests are being destroyed. These rain forests have many natural resources. You have

Many buildings and statues become damaged from air pollution. Here a man cleans a damaged statue in Venice.

Trees damaged by acid rain

Tree frogs and many other animals live in rain forests.

read about the rain forests in Brazil. Rain forests can also be found in Asia, Africa, and other parts of Latin America. People chop down the trees in rain forests to use the land for farms and cities. Some people export wood and other resources from these forests. About half of the world's rain forests have been destroyed.

What happens when trees are destroyed by people or by acid rain? Trees help clean Earth's air. Without trees, air and water become more polluted. Trees hold fertile soil to the earth. Without trees, fertile soil is washed away. Thousands of plants and animals live only in rain forests. When rain forests are destroyed, the plants and animals are also destroyed. The rain forests are important to all the people of the world. Nations must work together to save these forests.

There is great interdependence between nations today. Nations are working together to solve trade and energy problems. They are learning ways to protect Earth's land, air, and water. Nations are working together to make the world better.

Using Vocabulary

Match Up   Finish the sentences in Group A with words from Group B.
Write on your paper the letter of each correct answer.

Group A

1. When nations need one another for many things, it is called _____.

2. There is a _____ of food when a nation does not have enough food to feed its people.

3. Special taxes that make traded goods more expensive are _____.

4. When rain has been affected by air pollution, it is called _____ rain.

Group B

a. tariffs

b. acid

c. interdependence

d. scarcity

Read and Remember

Finish the Paragraph   Number your paper from 1 to 5. Use the words in dark print to finish the paragraph below. Write on your paper the words you choose.

animals   nuclear power   interdependent
radioactive   rain forests

Nations are __1__, because the problems of one nation can hurt other

nations in the world. In 1986 a terrible accident happened at a __2__ plant in

the Soviet Union. The accident sent lots of __3__ wastes into the air. The wind

blew this pollution over other nations in northern Europe. In Asia, Africa, and

Latin America, __4__ are being destroyed. When these places are destroyed, the

plants and __5__ that live there are also destroyed.

Finish Up Choose the word or words in dark print to best complete each sentence. Write on your paper the word or words you choose.

cancer   GATT   gasoline   nuclear power
import   trees   scarcity

1. _____ was an organization that helped increase trade by lowering tariffs.

2. Oil is used to make electricity and _____ .

3. Some nations use _____ plants to make electricity without using oil.

4. Doctors believe that people who live near the city of Chernobyl will continue to get _____ .

5. Without _____ , air and water become more polluted.

6. Nations must _____ goods from other nations.

7. There is a _____ of oil in many industrial nations.

Think and Apply

Categories Read the words in each group. Decide how they are alike. Choose the best title for each group from the words in dark print. Write the title on your paper.

Pollution   Oil Embargo
Kinds of Energy   Used to Make Energy

1. light
   electricity
   heat

3. wastes in the water
   wastes in the air
   acid rain

2. electricity became expensive
   Arab-Israeli war
   gasoline was hard to buy

4. oil
   coal
   natural gas

Journal Writing

Write a paragraph that tells at least three ways rain forests are important.

Working for Tomorrow

As years pass, the world changes in many ways. Today, people of all nations have many new problems to solve. We must work for tomorrow by solving today's problems.

Nuclear weapons are a problem that nations must solve. The United States dropped the first atomic bombs on Japan during World War II. For many years, the United States and the Soviet Union had a nuclear arms race. China, France, Great Britain, and India also have made atomic bombs. Some of today's bombs are much more powerful than those used in World War II.

Many people are afraid that there might be a nuclear war some day. If one nation uses its nuclear weapons, then other nations might fight back and use their own nuclear weapons. Atomic bombs

The United States and Russia are destroying many of the airplanes that are used to carry nuclear weapons.

might destroy much of the earth. One powerful atomic bomb could kill millions of people. For this reason, some nations are trying to make sure that nuclear weapons are never used again.

George Bush and Boris Yeltsin signing START II

In 1991 President George Bush of the United States and President Mikhail Gorbachev of the Soviet Union signed a treaty called **START I**. Both nations promised to destroy many dangerous weapons and to make fewer nuclear weapons. That same year the Soviet Union divided into 15 republics. President George Bush worked on another treaty with Russia's president, Boris Yeltsin. In 1993 Bush and Yeltsin signed a treaty called **START II**. In this treaty both nations agreed to destroy even more nuclear weapons.

You have learned that industrial nations use coal, oil, and natural gas to make energy. Many people believe that one day the earth's supplies of coal, oil, and natural gas will be used up. The nations of the world now have two big energy problems. One problem is to find different ways to make energy. The other problem is to learn how to **conserve,** or save, energy for tomorrow.

People can now use wind to create electricity.

Scientists are finding new ways to make energy. Some people are using energy from the sun. This is called **solar energy**. Solar energy can heat homes. It can heat water for homes and factories. Water power from many rivers is used to make electricity. Wind can also be used to make electricity. Many nations use nuclear energy to make electricity.

People in industrial nations are learning ways to conserve energy. People save energy by using less electricity. They turn off lights that are not being used. They use less heat in the winter. They wash clothes in cold water. People try to use their cars less often. They save energy by riding on buses and trains instead of driving their cars.

Pollution has become a serious problem in every industrial nation. Air pollution from cars and

A terrorist bomb destroyed an airplane over Scotland in 1988. All 147 people on board were killed.

People cleaning up a major oil spill in Alaska in 1989

Nations are starting to make cars that run on electricity.

factories has become a big problem in cities such as Mexico City and Los Angeles. It is not healthy to breathe the air in those cities. Water pollution has killed fish and plants in many lakes in the United States and in other nations. **Oil spills** from ships have caused serious water pollution in many oceans and seas. Acid rain is damaging forests and lakes in Canada and in Europe. There are problems like these in many nations of the world.

Some nations are trying to protect Earth's land, air, and water. These nations have laws that prevent factories from dumping garbage into oceans, lakes, and rivers. Other laws force factories to send less pollution into the air. Cars are being built that send fewer **fumes** into the air. Some cars use electricity instead of oil. Nations are also working on ways to prevent oil spills from ships. Oil spills in oceans can kill many fish, birds, and other animals.

Terrorism is a problem for many countries today. In 1988 a terrorist bomb caused a large American airplane to explode over Scotland. All 147 people on the plane were killed. In 1993 a terrorist bomb exploded at the World Trade Center in New York

By helping solve the problem of pollution, people are working for a better tomorrow.

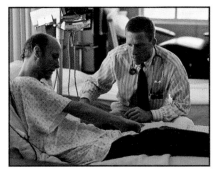

Doctor examining a person who has AIDS

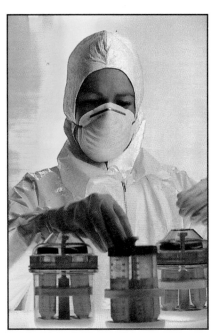

People are working to find a cure for AIDS.

City. Terrorism has occurred in many nations, including France, Great Britain, Israel, and Japan. Many governments are working together to try to end terrorism.

Today the world faces a new problem—the disease called **AIDS**. This disease is caused by a **virus** called **HIV**. AIDS kills more and more people each year. There is no cure for AIDS at this time. Doctors in many nations are studying the disease in order to find a cure. The **World Health Organization** is also working to find a cure for AIDS. The World Health Organization is a part of the United Nations.

In many nations today, people enjoy freedom. They enjoy equal rights with all the people of their nations. But in many parts of the world, people are not free. In some nations, such as China and Iraq, people are killed for speaking against their government. The leaders of free nations are working for freedom all over the world.

In the years ahead, people will continue to work for a better tomorrow. You will also have a chance to work for a better future. You will vote for future government leaders. You might work with scientists and leaders to solve many important world problems. In those ways, you will be writing the next chapter in *World History and You.*

Aung San Suu Kyi (1945–   )

Aung San Suu Kyi is the leader of the fight for democracy in Myanmar. Myanmar is a developing nation in Southeast Asia. Before 1989 Myanmar was called Burma. It has a military government. The people of Myanmar have few rights and little freedom. Since 1988 Aung San has been working to bring democracy to Myanmar. In 1991 she won the Nobel Peace Prize for her peaceful efforts to change Myanmar's government.

Aung San Suu Kyi was born in Rangoon, Burma, in 1945. Her father, Thakin Aung San, led the nation's fight for independence from Great Britain. Burma won its independence in 1948. Since 1962 the nation has had a military government. In 1988 Aung San Suu Kyi helped form the National League for Democracy (NLD), the main group against the military government. In 1989 Aung San was put under **house arrest** for her role in the NLD. She was not put in prison, but she also was not allowed to leave her home.

In 1990 the government allowed NLD candidates to be in an election for Myanmar's parliament. Aung San's group won most of the votes. But the government would not allow the new parliament to meet. Some representatives were sent to prison.

Aung San was held under house arrest for six years. During that time she wrote a book called *Freedom from Fear and Other Writings*. In 1995 Aung San was released by the government. Since her release, she has given many speeches to encourage democracy and human rights in Myanmar. The government has arrested hundreds of people who support Aung San. But Aung San Suu Kyi continues the struggle for change in Myanmar.

Aung San Suu Kyi

Aung San giving a speech from her home

Using Vocabulary

Find the Meaning Write on your paper the word or words that best complete each sentence.

1. **START I** was a treaty signed by the United States and the Soviet Union to destroy many _____ .

   dangerous weapons   rain forests   cities

2. To **conserve** is to _____ .

   buy   save   use up

3. **Solar** energy is energy that comes from _____ .

   oil   wind   the sun

4. **AIDS** is a terrible _____ that has killed many people.

   bomb   oil spill   disease

5. A person who is under **house arrest** is not allowed to _____ .

   stay home   leave home   watch television

Read and Remember

Find the Answer Find the sentences below that tell something true about the ways nations and people are working for a better tomorrow. Write on your paper the sentences you find. You should find five sentences.

1. Some nations are making fewer nuclear weapons.

2. Scientists are finding ways to use the wind and the sun to make energy.

3. People use their cars more often.

4. Nations build more factories that cause air pollution and acid rain.

5. Some nations have laws to protect the air and water.

6. The leaders of free nations work for freedom all over the world.

7. Doctors are working to find a cure for AIDS.

Glossary

absolute rule   page 148
Absolute rule means complete power.

abusing   page 111
A person who is abusing someone is using that person wrongly or is hurting that person.

accused   page 53
An accused person has been charged or blamed for something.

acid rain   page 338
Acid rain forms when pollution in the air becomes part of the rain.

adapted   page 127
A person has adapted to an area if he or she has adjusted to the climate and resources.

adobe   page 128
Adobe is a mixture of desert clay and straw that is used to make buildings.

African National Congress   page 307
The African National Congress is a group that works for the rights of South African Blacks.

agricultural revolution   page 6
The agricultural revolution was a change in the way people got their food.

AIDS   page 345
AIDS is a disease in which the body cannot fight germs. AIDS kills more people each year.

Allah   page 76
Allah is Islam's name for God.

alliances   page 217
Alliances are agreements between nations to work together in order to do something.

allied nations   page 158
Allied nations are nations that are united in order to do something.

allies   page 158
Allies are nations that unite in order to do something.

alphabet   page 22
An alphabet is the letters used to write a language.

American Revolution   page 142
The American Revolution was the war for freedom that the 13 American colonies fought.

apartheid   page 305
Apartheid was a system of laws that kept groups of people apart in South Africa.

aqueducts   page 54
Aqueducts are bridges or pipes that are used to carry water.

archaeologists   page 4
Archaeologists are people who find and study the bones and tools of people from long ago.

arrested   page 230
A person who has been arrested has been held by police.

assassinated   page 288
A person who has been assassinated has been killed for a particular reason.

astronauts   page 330
People who travel in space are astronauts.

atomic bomb   page 253
An atomic bomb is a very powerful weapon.

Axis Powers   page 239
The Axis Powers were a group of nations that fought the Allies during World War II.

bacteria   page 187
Bacteria are tiny living things. Some bacteria cause diseases.

balance of power   page 164
A balance of power means that nations have about the same strength.

barbarians   page 63
Barbarians were groups of people who invaded the Roman Empire.

Bastille   page 149
The Bastille was a prison in Paris. It was captured during the French Revolution.

Battle of Britain   page 245
The Battle of Britain was a German attack on Great Britain during World War II.

Battle of Stalingrad   page 246
The Battle of Stalingrad was a fight during World War II between Germans and Soviets.

battles   page 94
Battles are fights between people or groups of people.

better relations   page 273
Nations that have better relations have found ways to get along with one another.

Bible   page 25
The Bible is a book of the laws, beliefs, and history of Judaism and Christianity.

bill of rights   page 100
A bill of rights is a list of freedoms and rights of the people of a country.

boat people   page 281
Boat people were refugees who left Southeast Asia by boat during the Vietnam War.

bombed   page 245
A person has bombed something if he or she has caused a bomb to explode.

bombs   page 245
Bombs are weapons that destroy things when they are made to explode.

borders   page 163
Borders are lines that separate countries or other areas.

broken the law   page 100
A person who has broken the law has done something that the law says not to do.

Buddhism   page 31
Buddhism is a religion that was started in India about 500 B.C. by a man called the Buddha.

bullet trains   page 330
Bullet trains are trains that can travel at speeds greater than 150 miles per hour.

canals   page 186
Canals are water routes that cross land to connect rivers, lakes, and oceans.

candidates   page 323
Candidates are people who hope to be elected to a particular office or position.

caravans   page 124
Caravans are groups of people who travel together.

castes   page 31
Castes are groups that Hindus believe people are born into.

caste system   page 31
The caste system was the Hindu way of grouping people into classes.

castles   page 73
Castles were large buildings that nobles built to protect people on the manor.

cease-fire   page 280
A cease-fire is when nations agree to stop fighting.

cellular phones   page 329
Cellular phones are phones that people can use while in a car or outdoors.

censored   page 156
A person has censored a newspaper or other item if he or she has refused to let certain information be printed.

Central Powers   page 218
The Central Powers were a group of nations that fought the Allies during World War I.

Channel Tunnel   page 322
The Channel Tunnel is a railway tunnel under the English Channel.

china   page 38
China is dishes made of a fine, white clay.

Christianity   page 25
Christianity is a religion that is based on the teachings of Jesus.

citizens   page 45
Citizens are people of a city, state, or country.

city-states   page 18
City-states are towns or cities that rule themselves and the land around them.

civilians   page 280
Civilians are people who are not in an army or a navy.

civilization   page 10
A civilization is a group of people who have a government and a written language.

civil service system   page 39
A civil service system is a system of people who work for the government.

civil war   page 229
During a civil war, people of the same nation fight against one another.

classes   page 18
Classes are groups of people who are alike in some way.

Code Napoléon   page 156
The Code Napoléon was a system of laws made by Napoleon.

Cold War   page 264
The Cold War was a struggle between the United States, the Soviet Union, and other nations about the spread of communism.

collective farms   page 230
Collective farms are farms that are run by groups of people.

colonies   page 44
Colonies are places that are ruled by nations.

colonists   page 140
Colonists are people living in a colony.

Common Market   page 322
The Common Market was the first name of the European Union.

communicate   page 328
To communicate is to share information.

communication   page 328
Communication is how people share information.

communism   page 227
Communism is a system in which most farms and factories are owned by the government.

Communist   page 227
A Communist nation is a nation that uses communism as the system of government.

compass   page 117
A compass is an instrument that shows directions.

concentration camps   page 237
Concentration camps were prisons where captured Jews and other people were sent by Nazis during World War II.

conflict   page 264
A conflict is a war or fight about something.

Congress of Vienna   page 163
The Congress of Vienna was a meeting held in 1814 by European leaders.

conquered   page 18
A nation or an army that has used force to take control of something has conquered it.

conquerors   page 52
Conquerors are people who conquer other people.

conserve   page 343
To conserve is to save or keep for later use.

Constitution   page 144
The Constitution is the laws and the plan of government of the United States.

cotton gin   page 181
A cotton gin is a machine that pulls the seeds from cotton. It was invented in 1793.

cotton mills   page 195
Cotton mills are factories that prepare cotton for making thread and cloth.

Counter-Reformation   page 113
The Counter-Reformation was the Roman Catholic Church's effort to make people want to stay or to become Catholics.

crescent   page 17
A crescent is the thin, curved shape of a moon.

Crusades   page 83
The Crusades were wars that Christians and Turks fought in order to control Palestine.

cultural   page 310
Cultural means having to do with the way of life of a group of people.

Cultural Revolution   page 275
The Cultural Revolution was a time of change in China to make communism stronger.

culture   page 48
Culture is the way of life of a group of people.

czars   page 226
Czars were rulers of Russia from the 1500s to the early 1900s.

damage   page 281
Damage is harm to something.

D-Day   page 251
D-Day was June 6, 1944. On this date, the Allies landed on the beaches of Normandy.

debt   page 312
Debt is money that is owed.

Declaration of Independence   page 142
The Declaration of Independence was a paper that said the American colonies were free.

declared war   page 203
If a nation says that it is going to fight another nation, it has declared war on that nation.

defeat   page 99
To defeat means to win a victory over.

defended   page 157
When the Russians defended themselves against Napoleon, they protected themselves from an attack by Napoleon.

delegates   page 260
Delegates are people who are chosen to represent a group or a nation.

democracy   page 46
A democracy is a kind of government that is run by the people.

developed nations   page 287
Developed nations are nations that have modern industries and technology, as well as high standards of living.

developing nations   page 286
Developing nations are nations with low standards of living, little industry, and a scarcity of many things.

dictator   page 156
A dictator is a ruler who has all of the power.

discrimination   page 210
Discrimination is when people are treated differently for some reason.

diseases   page 85
Diseases are sicknesses.

divorce   page 113
A divorce is a way to end a marriage by law.

docked   page 332
A space shuttle has docked with a space station if it has connected to the station.

droughts   page 304
Droughts are long periods of time in which there is little or no rain.

dynasties   page 35
Dynasties were groups of kings from the same family. Different dynasties ruled China for thousands of years.

earth   page 4
Earth is dirt or soil.

Eastern Orthodox Church   page 68
The Eastern Orthodox Church is the part of the Christian church that developed in eastern Europe after the Fall of Rome.

electronic mail   page 329
Electronic mail is a way that computer users can send messages to other computer users on the Internet.

elements   page 189
Elements are things in nature from which all other materials are made.

embassy   page 295
An embassy is the headquarters of a representative from another country.

empress   page 64
An empress is a female ruler of an empire.

estate   page 148
An estate was a class of people in France before the French Revolution.

ethnic groups   page 302
Ethnic groups are groups of people who have the same language and culture.

European Union   page 322
The European Union (EU) is an organization of nations in Europe that works to improve trade between member nations.

executed   page 94
A person who has been killed because of someone's orders has been executed.

expand   page 209
To expand means to make larger.

exploration   page 117
Exploration is travel to learn about places.

export   page 287
To export means to send products from one country to another country.

extinct   page 312
Animals that are extinct will never exist again. Dinosaurs are extinct.

factories   page 179
Factories are places where goods are made.

Fall of Rome   page 63
The end of the Roman Empire in A.D. 476 is called the Fall of Rome.

fax machines   page 329
Fax machines are machines that people use to send or receive copies of pictures or papers over telephone lines.

fertile soil   page 11
Fertile soil is land that is good for crops. Soil around rivers is often fertile.

fertilizers   page 329
Fertilizers are materials added to soil to help the soil produce more food.

feudalism   page 72
Feudalism was a way of life that helped kings keep their land and people safe.

feudal system   page 72
The feudal system is another term for feudalism.

Five Pillars of Islam   page 77
The Five Pillars of Islam are five duties that Muhammad said Muslims must do.

forgiven   page 112
To be forgiven is to be excused or to not be blamed for something.

Fourteen Points   page 220
The Fourteen Points was a peace plan written by Woodrow Wilson. It was used for the peace treaty after World War I.

freedom of religion   page 134
Freedom of religion is the right to belong to any religious group.

freedom of speech   page 100
Freedom of speech is the right to speak against the government.

freedom of the press   page 320
Freedom of the press is the right to print anything in newspapers and magazines.

French Revolution   page 148
The French Revolution was the war fought by French people to change France's laws and rulers. It lasted from 1789 to 1799.

fumes   page 344
Fumes are gases that are harmful to breathe.

gap   page 311
A gap between the rich and the poor means that there is a large difference in the amount of money and land owned by these groups.

gasoline   page 337
Gasoline is a liquid made from oil. It can be burned to make energy to power cars.

General Agreement on Tariffs and Trade   page 336
GATT was a group of nations that worked to increase trade between member nations by lowering taxes on traded goods.

General Assembly   page 260
The General Assembly is the part of the UN in which each member nation has a vote.

German Confederation   page 204
The German Confederation was a group of 39 German states that were joined together by the Congress of Vienna.

god   page 11
A god is a person or thing that is considered most important and powerful.

Golden Age   page 49
The Golden Age is the greatest time in the history of a place.

goods   page 83
Goods are things that are bought and sold.

grasslands   page 302
Grasslands are lands that are covered mainly with grass and have few trees.

Great Depression   page 236
The Great Depression was a period of time in which business became very slow. The depression lasted from 1929 to World War II.

Green Revolution   page 287
The Green Revolution is a way of farming that uses more irrigation, more energy, and better seeds to grow more crops.

guilty   page 53
To be guilty means to have done something wrong.

Hinduism   page 31
Hinduism is the main religion in India. Hindus believe in many gods.

HIV   page 345
HIV is the virus that causes AIDS.

Holocaust   page 252
The Holocaust was the killing of millions of Jews and other people by the Nazis during World War II.

holy   page 82
Holy means special for religious reasons.

homeland   page 296
A homeland is a country where a person was born or has a home.

honest   page 24
To be honest means to tell the truth.

hostages   page 296
Hostages are people who are held by others until certain demands are met.

house arrest   page 346
House arrest is when police force a person to stay in his or her home.

House of Commons   page 100
The House of Commons is the group in Parliament that is made up of middle-class people.

House of Lords   page 100
The House of Lords is the group in Parliament that is made up of nobles.

Hundred Years' War   page 94
The Hundred Years' War was a war that was fought between England and France from 1337 until 1453.

illegal drugs   page 315
Illegal drugs are drugs that are against the law to sell and to use in a country.

illiteracy   page 286
Illiteracy is when people are not able to read or write.

immigrants   page 194
Immigrants are people who move to other countries.

imperialism   page 208
Imperialism is the idea that one nation should rule colonies or other nations.

imperialist   page 208
A nation that controls colonies or other nations is an imperialist nation.

import   page 337
To import means to bring goods into one country from another country.

independent   page 142
To be independent is to be free from another's control. An independent country rules itself.

indulgences   page 112
Indulgences were papers sold by the Catholic Church that said a person was forgiven for the wrong things he or she had done.

Industrial Revolution   page 178
The Industrial Revolution was a change from making goods by hand to making goods by machine. It began in the 1700s.

industry   page 180
An industry is a kind of business in which many people and machines work together.

inflation   page 312
Inflation is a rise in the prices of goods and services.

innocent   page 53
To be innocent means to have done nothing wrong.

interdependence   page 335
Interdependence means that nations need one another for many things.

interdependent   page 335
Nations are interdependent when they need one another for many things.

Internet   page 329
The Internet is a large system of computers all over the world.

invaded   page 36
People have invaded a place if they have attacked the place in order to rule it.

irrigate page 11
To irrigate means to bring water to dry land.

irrigation page 30
Irrigation is when water is brought to dry land so that the land will grow crops.

Islam page 76
Islam is the religion started by Muhammad. People who believe in Islam are Muslims.

isolation page 93
Isolation is when something is set apart from the rest of a group.

isolationism page 254
Isolationism is when a nation chooses to not become involved in other nations' problems.

Judaism page 23
Judaism is the religion of the Jews. Judaism has one God.

jury page 100
A jury is a group of people who are chosen to decide about something after hearing the facts about it.

kaiser page 205
A kaiser was a German emperor.

knights page 72
Knights were soldiers during the Middle Ages who fought for nobles and kings.

Koran page 77
The Koran is the book of Muhammad's teachings.

Korean War page 266
The Korean War was a war in the 1950s in which North Korea invaded South Korea to make Korea a united Communist nation.

labor unions page 196
Labor unions are groups of workers who work together to solve problems.

League of Nations page 220
The League of Nations was a group of nations that worked for peace after World War I.

"Liberty, Equality, Fraternity" page 150
"Liberty, Equality, Fraternity" was a phrase from the French Revolution. The words meant that people wanted freedom and equal rights.

literature page 104
Literature is writing. Plays, stories, and books are different types of literature.

Magna Carta page 99
The Magna Carta was a paper that said the king of England must obey laws.

manor page 72
A manor was the land a noble ruled.

Marshall Plan page 265
The Marshall Plan was the United States' plan to help Western Europe after World War II.

mass killings page 305
Mass killings are when many people are killed by other people at one time.

merchant page 83
A merchant is a person who buys things and then sells them to make money.

Middle Ages page 71
The Middle Ages were the years from the Fall of Rome in 476 to about 1500.

middle class page 100
The middle class is the group of people between the rich and the poor.

military page 217
Military is anything having to do with the army, navy, soldiers, or weapons of a nation.

missiles page 265
Missiles are rockets. Some missiles carry bombs.

monarchs page 92
Monarchs are kings and queens.

monarchy page 93
A monarchy is a nation ruled by a king or queen.

monks page 32
Monks are men who study a religion and follow special rules.

mosques page 79
Mosques are places where Muslims pray to Allah.

movable type page 107
Movable type is metal letters that can be put in different orders to make words. Movable type can be used to print books.

National Assembly   page 149
The National Assembly was a group of people who made new laws for France during the French Revolution.

nationalism   page 202
Nationalism is feelings of love and pride for one's nation.

nations   page 92
Nations are groups of people who have the same laws and leaders. People in a nation often speak the same language.

natural gas   page 337
Natural gas is a gas that is found in the earth. It can be burned to make power.

naval base   page 247
A naval base is a place near the sea where a navy keeps ships, weapons, and airplanes.

neutral   page 218
A nation that is neutral does not want to fight in a war.

New Testament   page 67
The New Testament is the part of the Bible that tells about Jesus and his teachings.

New World   page 119
People in Europe called the Americas the New World because they had not known about these continents.

95 Theses   page 112
The 95 Theses was Martin Luther's list of statements about the wrong things that the Roman Catholic Church was doing.

nobles   page 72
Nobles were rich people in the feudal system of the Middle Ages.

North American Free Trade Agreement   page 314
NAFTA is a plan to help improve trade between the United States, Mexico, and Canada.

North Atlantic Treaty Organization   page 265
NATO is a military organization of nations that agree to help protect one another from the spread of communism.

nuclear arms race   page 265
During the nuclear arms race, the United States and the Soviet Union increased their supplies of powerful weapons.

nuclear power plants   page 337
Nuclear power plants are places that use nuclear energy to make electricity.

nuclear war   page 267
A nuclear war is a war that is fought with powerful nuclear weapons.

oil embargo   page 337
An oil embargo is when nations that produce oil stop selling it to nations that need it.

oil spills   page 344
Oil spills happen when ships or factories leak oil into bodies of water.

Old Testament   page 25
Early stories about the Jews are in the part of the Bible called the Old Testament.

opium   page 211
Opium is a drug that is made from a plant called the opium poppy.

Opium War   page 211
The Opium War was a war fought between China and Great Britain in 1839 about the opium trade.

orbit   page 331
To be in orbit is to travel around a planet. Satellites orbit around Earth.

order   page 156
Order in a nation means that people obey laws and rules.

organization   page 259
An organization is a group of people or nations that agree to work together.

outcastes   page 31
Outcastes are people who do not belong to any group in the Hindu caste system.

Palestine Liberation Organization
page 298
The Palestine Liberation Organization (PLO) is a group of Arabs whose goal is to have a Palestinian nation again.

Parliament   page 100
Parliament is the group of people who make laws for Great Britain.

patriarch   page 68
The patriarch is the head of the Eastern Orthodox Church.

peace treaty   page 143
A peace treaty is a promise between nations to not fight against one another.

peasants   page 73
Peasants are people who work on farms. In the feudal system, the peasants worked for the nobles.

peninsula   page 44
A peninsula is an area of land that has water on almost all sides.

permanent   page 260
A permanent member of the UN Security Council can never be removed from the council.

Persian Gulf War   page 261
The Persian Gulf War was a war in 1991 fought by UN nations against Iraq in order to free Kuwait.

pharaohs   page 11
Pharaohs were rulers of ancient Egypt.

pilgrimage   page 77
A pilgrimage is a trip to a place that is special for the members of a religion.

plague   page 64
A plague is a very serious sickness that spreads quickly and kills many people.

plantations   page 133
Plantations are large farms where many people work to grow crops for the owner.

poison gas   page 219
Poison gas is something that can kill a person who breathes it. Germans used poison gas to kill enemy soldiers during World War I.

pope   page 68
The pope is the head of the Roman Catholic Church.

population   page 62
Population is the number of people who live in a place.

poverty   page 286
Poverty is a lack of money, food, and clothing.

power loom   page 181
A power loom is a machine that uses water power to weave thread into cloth.

priests   page 18
Priests are religious leaders.

prime minister   page 202
A prime minister is the leader of the government in some countries.

prison   page 99
A prison is a place where people who have broken the law are forced to live.

prophet   page 76
A prophet is a person who believes that God has spoken to him or her. A prophet tells other people what God said.

protested   page 280
To have protested means that a person has marched, given speeches, or done something else in order to show that he or she is against something.

protesters   page 274
Protesters are people who march, give speeches, or do other things in order to show they are against something.

pyramids   page 12
Pyramids were large stone buildings used as tombs for the rulers of ancient Egypt.

Quadruple Alliance   page 163
The Quadruple Alliance was a group of four nations that worked together to stop revolutions in Europe after 1814.

radiation   page 189
Radiation is a type of energy that travels as waves or as very tiny materials. Light, heat, sound, and x-rays are forms of radiation.

radioactive wastes   page 338
Radioactive wastes are dangerous materials that are left over after nuclear energy is produced.

rain forests   page 302
Rain forests are forests with many trees and plants that receive a large amount of rain.

Ramadan   page 77
Ramadan is a special month during which Muslims do not eat or drink during the day.

raw materials   page 132
Raw materials are things that have not been changed from their natural form. Many raw materials are grown or dug from the earth.

reaper   page 182
A reaper is a machine that cuts wheat quickly.

rebirth   page 104
Rebirth means something is born again. The Renaissance was a rebirth of art and learning.

reborn   page 31
To be reborn means to be born again as a new person or another living creature.

rebuild   page 254
To rebuild means to build something again.

recaptured   page 83
To have recaptured something means to have taken control of it again.

recover   page 275
To recover means to get better.

Reformation   page 111
The Reformation was a movement to make changes in the Roman Catholic Church.

refugees   page 281
Refugees are people who leave their country in order to escape danger.

regions   page 127
Regions are large areas of a country or a continent.

religion   page 23
A religion is a belief in a god or gods.

religious   page 105
Religious means having to do with religion.

Renaissance   page 104
The Renaissance was a time when learning and creating became important in Europe. The Renaissance began about 1300 and lasted about 300 years.

repay   page 312
To repay means to pay back money that is owed.

representatives   page 141
Representatives are people chosen to speak or act for others.

republic   page 52
A republic is a nation that is not ruled by a king or queen.

resist   page 265
To resist means to keep from giving into something.

resolutions   page 260
Resolutions are things that are decided upon by people or nations.

respected   page 37
To be respected means to be shown honor and to be treated well by others.

riots   page 64
Riots are large crowds of angry people that fight and make noise.

Roman Catholic Church   page 68
The Roman Catholic Church is the part of the Christian church that developed in western Europe after the Fall of Rome.

royal   page 150
Royal means having to do with kings or queens.

ruling countries   page 132
Ruling countries are countries that rule colonies.

Russian Revolution   page 228
The Russian Revolution was the war fought in 1917 by the Russian people in order to change Russia's government.

sacrifice   page 126
To sacrifice means to offer something to a god in order to please the god. The Aztec sacrificed people by killing them.

satellite   page 265
A satellite is a machine that travels around Earth.

scarce   page 17
Something that is scarce is hard to find or get.

scarcity   page 335
Scarcity is when many people or businesses do not have enough of the products or raw materials that they need.

Scientific Revolution   page 106
The Scientific Revolution was a time in which people made many inventions and discoveries. The Scientific Revolution began during the Renaissance.

secretary-general   page 260
The leader of the United Nations is called the secretary-general.

secret police   page 164
Secret police are people who pretend not to be police so that they can find people who are against the government.

Security Council   page 260
The most powerful part of the United Nations is the Security Council. The council can send soldiers to where there is fighting.

seed drill   page 179
A seed drill is a machine that pushes seeds into soil to help more plants grow.

Senate   page 53
The Senate is a group of elected leaders in a republic.

senators   page 53
Senators are members of the Senate. They are leaders who make laws.

sepoys   page 210
Sepoys were people in India who were paid by Europeans to be soldiers.

serfs   page 226
Serfs were peasants who were not allowed to leave land on which they lived and worked.

shah   page 295
The shah was the ruler of Iran.

shipyards   page 323
Shipyards are places where ships are built or repaired.

silk   page 38
Silk is a soft, shiny cloth that was first made by the Chinese.

Six-Day War   page 297
The Six-Day War was a war fought between the Arabs and the Israelis in 1967.

slaves   page 13
Slaves were people who were owned by other people. They did hard work without pay and could not leave their owners.

smallpox   page 187
Smallpox is a deadly disease that causes a high fever and many bumps on the skin.

solar energy   page 343
Solar energy is energy from the sun.

soldiers   page 36
Soldiers are members of an army who fight for and guard a nation.

Solidarity   page 320
Solidarity is the name of the first labor union in Poland.

space race   page 265
The space race was a struggle in which the United States and the Soviet Union each tried to be the first nation to have new space technology.

space shuttles   page 331
Space shuttles are spaceships that can be used many times.

space station   page 331
A space station is a place in space where people can live and work for a long time.

Spanish-American War   page 211
The Spanish-American War was a war fought in 1898. The United States fought in this war to help Cuba become free from Spain.

spices   page 85
Spices are seeds or other parts of plants that add different tastes to food.

spinning jenny   page 180
A spinning jenny is a simple machine that can make up to eight threads at one time. A person turns the jenny's wheel.

spinning mule   page 181
A spinning mule is a machine that uses water power to spin thread. It can make thread more quickly than a spinning jenny can.

spinning wheels   page 180
Spinning wheels are simple machines that are used for making thread. The wheels can be turned by hand or by using a foot pedal.

Stamp Act   page 141
The Stamp Act was a British law that forced Americans to pay a tax on printed items, such as newspapers.

standard of living   page 188
Standard of living is how well a person is able to buy things that he or she needs or wants.

START I and START II   page 343
START I was a treaty signed in 1991 by the Soviet Union and the United States. START II was a treaty signed in 1993 by Russia and the United States. In both treaties, the nations agreed to destroy many nuclear weapons.

starvation   page 304
Starvation is when a person suffers or dies from a lack of food.

steamboat   page 186
A steamboat is a boat that uses a steam engine in order to move.

steam engine   page 182
A steam engine is an engine that is run by steam power.

steam locomotive   page 185
A steam locomotive is a train car with a steam engine. It pulls other train cars.

Stone Age   page 4
The Stone Age is the time when most people used stone tools. The Stone Age began more than 2,000,000 years ago.

strike   page 196
A strike is when union members stop working until business owners agree to make changes.

submarines   page 219
Submarines are ships that can travel underwater.

Sugar Act   page 141
The Sugar Act was a law that forced Americans to pay taxes to Great Britain on certain goods brought to the 13 colonies.

surrendered   page 220
An army or a nation has surrendered if it has given up in a battle.

tame   page 6
To tame means to make a wild animal gentle and easy to handle.

tariffs   page 336
Tariffs are special taxes on traded goods.

taxes   page 61
Taxes are money that people pay to the government.

technology   page 217
Technology is the inventions that use science to improve the way things are done.

temple   page 14
A temple is a building in which people worship a god or gods.

Ten Commandments   page 24
The Ten Commandments are laws that tell people how to behave. Jews and Christians believe that God gave these laws to Moses.

tension   page 217
Tension is a harmful feeling of pressure that causes nations to not trust one another.

terrorism   page 298
Terrorism is actions against a group of people or a government in order to cause fear and to gain demands.

terrorists   page 298
Terrorists are people who kill other people or destroy things in order to cause fear and to gain demands.

tombs   page 12
Tombs are graves or buildings where the bodies of the dead are placed.

tools   page 4
Tools are objects that help people do work.

trade unions   page 323
Trade unions are organizations of workers who work to improve job conditions.

trading partners   page 290
Trading partners are nations that buy products from one another.

trading posts   page 134
Trading posts were stores where people could exchange food and supplies.

traditions   page 290
Traditions are customs or beliefs that are passed down from parents to their children.

Treaty of Versailles   page 220
The Treaty of Versailles was the World War I peace treaty between the Allies and Germany.

trenches   page 219
Trenches are long ditches from which soldiers sometimes fight during a war.

trial   page 53
A trial is a meeting to decide whether an accused person has broken the law.

tribal chief   page 307
A tribal chief is the leader of a group of people who share a language and culture.

troops   page 280
Troops are groups of soldiers.

unification   page 204
Unification is when states or nations are brought together or joined to become one.

unified   page 204
States or nations have become unified if they have been brought together or joined.

United Nations   page 259
The United Nations (UN) is a group of nations that work together for peace and to solve world problems.

vaccine   page 187
A vaccine is a type of medicine that prevents people from getting a certain disease.

veto   page 53
A veto is a government leader's power to stop a new law from being passed.

vetoes   page 260
A person vetoes a resolution or a law when he or she says no to keep it from being passed.

Vietnam War   page 278
The Vietnam War was a war fought between 1957 and 1975 in Southeast Asia about the spread of communism.

virus   page 345
A virus is a very tiny thing that causes disease.

voyage   page 118
A voyage is a long journey by water or through space.

wages   page 195
Wages are the pay that workers receive.

warlords   page 271
Warlords are leaders who use force to rule an area of a country.

Warsaw Pact   page 265
The Warsaw Pact was a treaty signed in 1955 by the Soviet Union and other Eastern European nations.

weapons   page 14
Weapons are objects that are used to attack or to protect something.

woodblock printing   page 84
Woodblock printing is a way to make books using letters or symbols carved in wood.

working class   page 188
The working class is a large group of people who work with their hands or with machines.

working conditions   page 195
Working conditions describe what a person's job is like. Working conditions include the amount of pay, the number of hours worked each day, and the safety of the work place.

World Health Organization   page 345
The World Health Organization is part of the United Nations. This organization helps nations build better health systems.

World Trade Organization   page 336
The World Trade Organization (WTO) is a group of nations that work together to increase trade between member nations.

World War I   page 216
World War I was a war fought by many nations between 1914 and 1918.

World War II   page 244
World War II was a major war fought between 1939 and 1945. Nations all over the world became involved in the war.

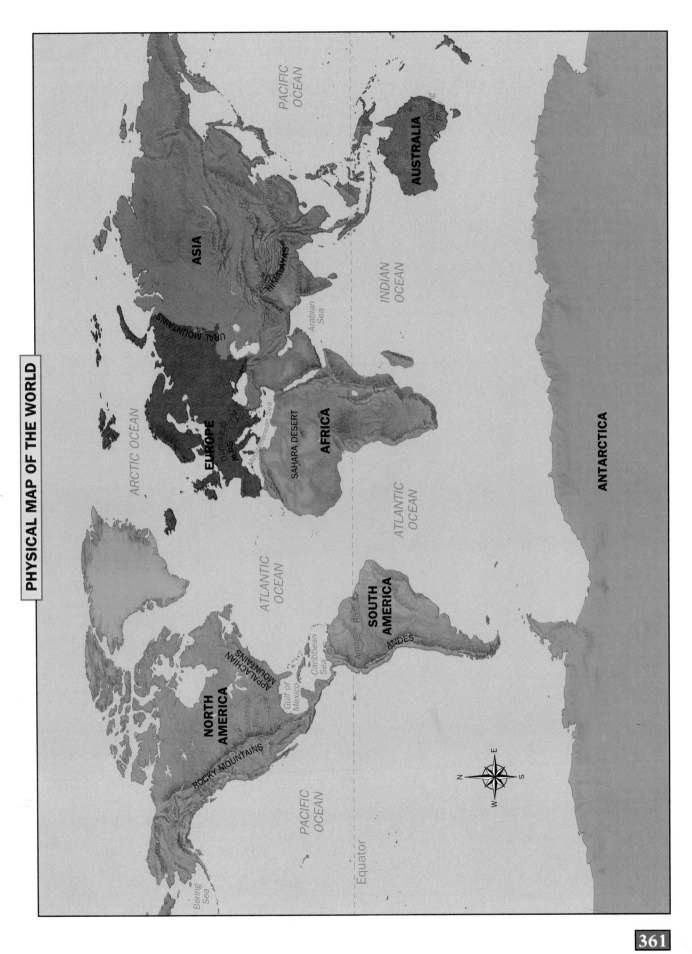

PACIFIC OCEAN

AUSTRALIA

Darling River

ASIA

HIMALAYAS

Yangtze

Ho

Ganges River

URAL MOUNTAINS

INDIAN OCEAN

Arabian Sea

ARCTIC OCEAN

EUROPE

ALPS

Danube River

Mediterranean Sea

River

SAHARA DESERT

AFRICA

ATLANTIC OCEAN

ANTARCTICA

GREENLAND

ATLANTIC OCEAN

APPALACHIAN MOUNTAINS

Caribbean Sea

Gulf of Mexico

Amazon River

SOUTH AMERICA

ANDES

NORTH AMERICA

Mississippi River

ROCKY MOUNTAINS

PACIFIC OCEAN

Bering Sea

Equator

N
E
W
S

POLITICAL MAP OF THE WORLD

GREENLAND
(DEN.)

RUSSIA

ALASKA
(U.S.)

CANADA

UNITED STATES

ATLANTIC
OCEAN

PACIFIC
OCEAN

MIDWAY
ISLANDS
(U.S.)

WAKE
ISLAND
(U.S.)

HAWAII
(U.S.)

MEXICO

Inset, below left

CAPE
VERDE

MARSHALL
ISLANDS

TOKELAU
(N.Z.)

WESTERN
SAMOA

GUATEMALA
EL SALVADOR

VENEZUELA
GUYANA
SURINAME
FRENCH GUIANA
(FR.)

COLOMBIA

Equator

GALÁPAGOS IS.
(ECUA.)

ECUADOR

NAURU

KIRIBATI

PERU

BRAZIL

SOLOMON
ISLANDS

TUVALU

VANUATU

FIJI

TONGA

COOK
IS.
(N.Z.)

FRENCH
POLYNESIA
(FR.)

BOLIVIA

PARAGUAY

NEW
CALEDONIA
(FR.)

NIUE
(N.Z.)

AMERICAN
SAMOA (U.S.)

PACIFIC
OCEAN

CHILE

URUGUAY

ARGENTINA

NEW
ZEALAND

FALKLAND IS.
(U.K.)

Caribbean Inset

SOUTH GEORGIA
(U.K.)

Gulf of Mexico

U.S.

BAHAMAS

ATLANTIC
OCEAN

TURKS &
CAICOS ISLANDS
(U.K.)

MEXICO

CUBA

CAYMAN IS.
(U.K.)

PUERTO
RICO
(U.S.)

VIRGIN ISLANDS
(U.K.)

ANTARCTICA

BELIZE

GUATEMALA

HONDURAS

JAMAICA

DOMINICAN
REPUBLIC

HAITI

ANTIGUA & BARBUDA

GUADELOUPE (FR.)

VIRGIN IS. (U.S.)

DOMINICA

Caribbean Sea

CURAÇAO
(NETH.)

ST. KITTS
& NEVIS

MARTINIQUE (FR.)

EL
SALVADOR

NICARAGUA

ARUBA
(NETH.)

ST. LUCIA

BARBADOS

GRENADA

ST. VINCENT &
THE GRENADINES

Panama
Canal

BONAIRE
(NETH.)

TRINIDAD &
TOBAGO

PACIFIC
OCEAN

COSTA RICA

PANAMA

COLOMBIA

VENEZUELA

GUYANA

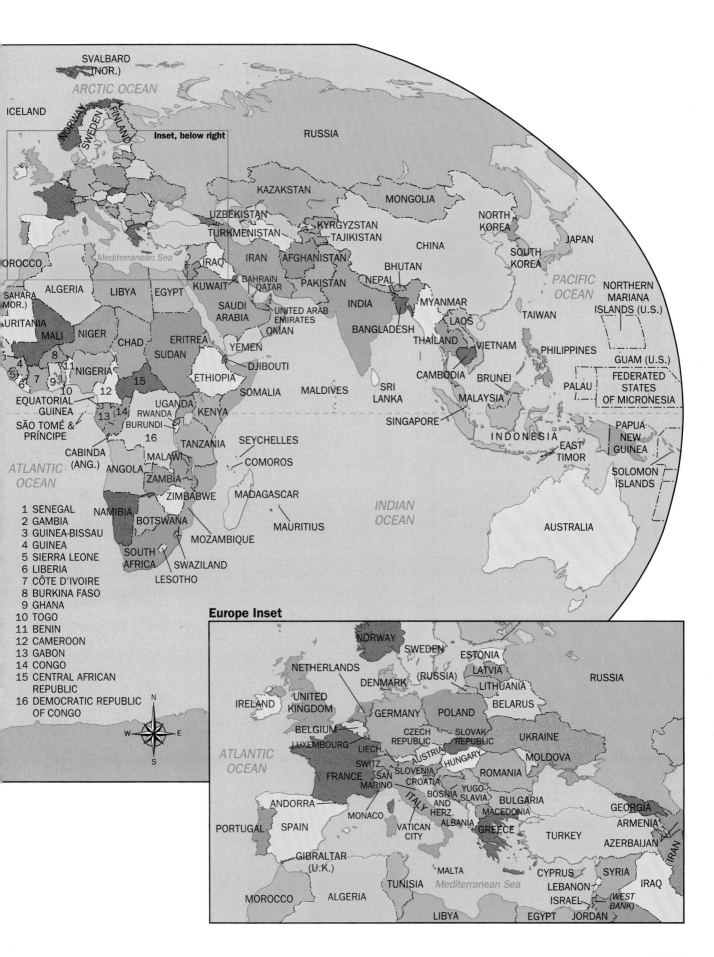

SVALBARD (NOR.)

ARCTIC OCEAN

ICELAND

NORWAY
SWEDEN
FINLAND

Inset, below right

RUSSIA

MOROCCO

Mediterranean Sea

KAZAKSTAN

MONGOLIA

NORTH KOREA

JAPAN

UZBEKISTAN
TURKMENISTAN

KYRGYZSTAN
TAJIKISTAN

CHINA

SOUTH KOREA

PACIFIC OCEAN

NORTHERN MARIANA ISLANDS (U.S.)

SAHARA (MOR.)

ALGERIA

LIBYA

EGYPT

IRAQ

IRAN

AFGHANISTAN

KUWAIT

BAHRAIN
QATAR

PAKISTAN

NEPAL

BHUTAN

MYANMAR

TAIWAN

URITANIA

MALI

NIGER

CHAD

SAUDI ARABIA

UNITED ARAB EMIRATES

OMAN

INDIA

BANGLADESH

LAOS

GUAM (U.S.)

ERITREA

SUDAN

YEMEN

THAILAND

VIETNAM

PHILIPPINES

4
5
6
7
8
9
11
NIGERIA
10
12

EQUATORIAL GUINEA

SÃO TOMÉ & PRÍNCIPE

DJIBOUTI

ETHIOPIA

SOMALIA

MALDIVES

SRI LANKA

CAMBODIA

BRUNEI

MALAYSIA

FEDERATED STATES OF MICRONESIA

PALAU

15

UGANDA
RWANDA
BURUNDI

13 14

KENYA

SINGAPORE

INDONESIA

PAPUA NEW GUINEA

16

TANZANIA

SEYCHELLES

EAST TIMOR

SOLOMON ISLANDS

ATLANTIC OCEAN

CABINDA (ANG.)

MALAWI

ANGOLA

ZAMBIA

COMOROS

MADAGASCAR

INDIAN OCEAN

ZIMBABWE

1 SENEGAL
2 GAMBIA
3 GUINEA-BISSAU
4 GUINEA
5 SIERRA LEONE
6 LIBERIA
7 CÔTE D'IVOIRE
8 BURKINA FASO
9 GHANA
10 TOGO
11 BENIN
12 CAMEROON
13 GABON
14 CONGO
15 CENTRAL AFRICAN REPUBLIC
16 DEMOCRATIC REPUBLIC OF CONGO

NAMIBIA

BOTSWANA

MOZAMBIQUE

MAURITIUS

AUSTRALIA

SOUTH AFRICA

SWAZILAND

LESOTHO

N
W   E
S

Europe Inset

NORWAY
SWEDEN
ESTONIA

NETHERLANDS

DENMARK

(RUSSIA)

LATVIA
LITHUANIA

RUSSIA

IRELAND

UNITED KINGDOM

GERMANY

POLAND

BELARUS

BELGIUM
LUXEMBOURG

LIECH.

CZECH REPUBLIC

SLOVAK REPUBLIC

UKRAINE

AUSTRIA
HUNGARY

MOLDOVA

ATLANTIC OCEAN

SWITZ.

FRANCE

SAN MARINO

SLOVENIA

CROATIA

ROMANIA

ITALY

BOSNIA AND HERZ.

YUGO-SLAVIA

BULGARIA

MACEDONIA

GEORGIA

ANDORRA

MONACO

ALBANIA

ARMENIA

PORTUGAL

SPAIN

VATICAN CITY

GREECE

TURKEY

AZERBAIJAN

IRAN

GIBRALTAR (U.K.)

MALTA

CYPRUS

SYRIA

IRAQ

Mediterranean Sea

LEBANON

MOROCCO

ALGERIA

TUNISIA

ISRAEL

(WEST BANK)

LIBYA

EGYPT

JORDAN

363

Time Line, 3750 B.C. to A.D. 1750

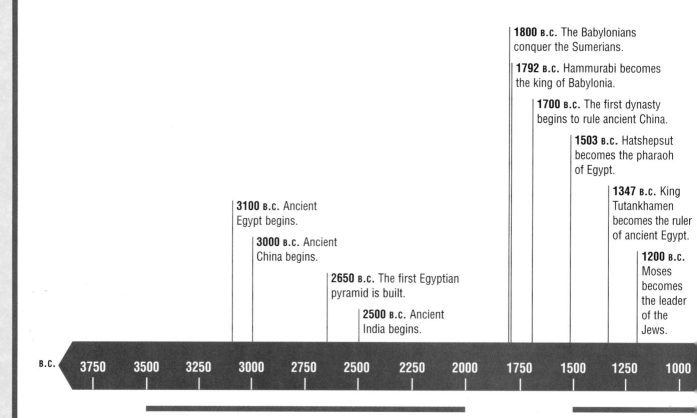

3100 B.C. Ancient Egypt begins.

3000 B.C. Ancient China begins.

2650 B.C. The first Egyptian pyramid is built.

2500 B.C. Ancient India begins.

1800 B.C. The Babylonians conquer the Sumerians.

1792 B.C. Hammurabi becomes the king of Babylonia.

1700 B.C. The first dynasty begins to rule ancient China.

1503 B.C. Hatshepsut becomes the pharaoh of Egypt.

1347 B.C. King Tutankhamen becomes the ruler of ancient Egypt.

1200 B.C. Moses becomes the leader of the Jews.

B.C.   3750   3500   3250   3000   2750   2500   2250   2000   1750   1500   1250   1000

3500 B.C.–2000 B.C. Sumerians live in Mesopotamia.

1500 B.C.–539 B.C. Aryans rule northern India.

753 B.C. Ancient Rome begins.

551 B.C. Confucius is born.

539 B.C. Persians conquer Babylon.

508 B.C. Athens becomes a democracy.

500 B.C. Buddhism begins.

323 B.C. Alexander the Great dies.

221 B.C. People of ancient China begin building the Great Wall.

202 B.C. Han Dynasty begins to rule ancient China.

49 B.C. Julius Caesar becomes the leader of Rome.

0 Jesus is born.

14 Augustus Caesar dies.

180 The Roman Empire's 200 years of peace end.

476 The Roman Empire falls.

527 Justinian and Theodora become rulers of the Byzantine Empire.

622 Muhammad flees to Mecca.

1000 Ghana is a strong empire. Zimbabwe is built.

1071 The Turks capture Jerusalem.

1200 The Aztec and Inca empires begin.

1295 Marco Polo returns to Italy from China.

1307 Mansa Musa becomes the king of Mali.

1453 France wins the Hundred Years' War.

1519 Magellan sails around South America.

1689 The English Bill of Rights is written.

1701 The seed drill is invented.

| 750 | 500 | 250 | 0 | 250 | 500 | 750 | 1000 | 1250 | 1500 | 1750 | A.D. |

27 B.C.–A.D. 476 Roman Empire

539 B.C.–330 B.C. Persians rule a large empire.

A.D. 476–1500 Middle Ages in Europe

1095–1291 Crusades

1200–1700 Growth of democracy in England

1300–1600 Renaissance in Europe

Time Line, A.D. 1750 to 2000

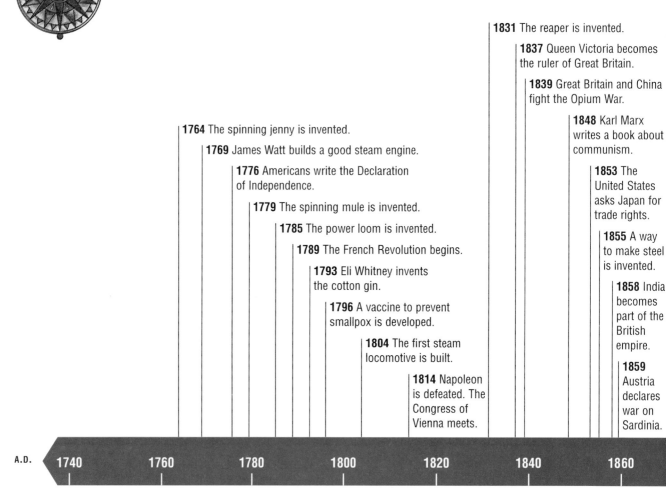

1831 The reaper is invented.

1837 Queen Victoria becomes the ruler of Great Britain.

1839 Great Britain and China fight the Opium War.

1848 Karl Marx writes a book about communism.

1853 The United States asks Japan for trade rights.

1855 A way to make steel is invented.

1858 India becomes part of the British empire.

1859 Austria declares war on Sardinia.

1764 The spinning jenny is invented.

1769 James Watt builds a good steam engine.

1776 Americans write the Declaration of Independence.

1779 The spinning mule is invented.

1785 The power loom is invented.

1789 The French Revolution begins.

1793 Eli Whitney invents the cotton gin.

1796 A vaccine to prevent smallpox is developed.

1804 The first steam locomotive is built.

1814 Napoleon is defeated. The Congress of Vienna meets.

A.D. | 1740 | 1760 | 1780 | 1800 | 1820 | 1840 | 1860

1750–1870 Industrial Revolution

1791–1826
Latin Americans fight for freedom from European rule.

1933 Adolf Hitler becomes the dictator of Germany.

1939 Germany invades Poland.

1941 Japan attacks Pearl Harbor.

1945 World War II ends. The United Nations is formed.

1879 Thomas Edison invents the electric light bulb.

1949 China becomes a Communist nation. NATO is formed.

1894 Nicholas II becomes Russia's czar.

1955 The Warsaw Pact begins.

1898 The Spanish-American war is fought.

1957 The Soviet Union sends *Sputnik I* into space.

1961 The Berlin Wall is built.

1911 Sun Yat-sen helps China become a republic.

1967 Arab nations and Israel fight the Six-Day War.

1969 Americans go to the moon in *Apollo 11.*

1914 World War I begins.

1980 Iraq attacks Iran.

1917 The Russian Revolution occurs.

1991 The Cold War ends. Most apartheid ends in South Africa.

1994 Jordan and Israel sign a treaty.

1920 The League of Nations begins.

1995 GATT becomes the World Trade Organization.

| 1880 | 1900 | 1920 | 1940 | 1960 | 1980 | 2000 |

1870–1914 Growth of Imperialism

1929–about 1940 Great Depression

1939–1945 World War II

1945–1991 Cold War

1957–1975 Vietnam War

Index

French Revolution, 148–151, 152, 156, 157, 159, 163, 164, 165, 168, 172, 230

Gandhi, Mohandas, 288
Garibaldi, Giuseppe, 203
George III, King, 141–142
German Confederation, 204, 205
Germany, 202, 204–205, 209, 212, 236–237, 238, 239, 259, 265, 267, 321
    and World War I, 217–218, 219–220, 221, 222, 235, 236
    and World War II, 244–247, 250, 251, 254, 255
Ghana, 124–125, 129
Gorbachev, Mikhail, 320, 343
Great Britain. *See also* England. 135, 140–144, 158, 163, 193, 194, 195–196, 209–210, 211–212, 217, 218, 219, 239, 244, 245, 247, 250, 251, 260, 288, 304, 305, 315, 322, 330, 342, 345, 346
    and the Industrial Revolution, 179–180, 181, 182, 185, 186–187
Great Depression, 236–237, 238
Great Wall of China, 36
Greece, 42, 44–49, 105, 208
Green Revolution, 287–288
Guam, 211, 252
Gutenberg, Johannes, 107

Haiti, 169, 261
Hammurabi, 18–19
Han Dynasty, 36, 39
Hatshepsut, 11–12, 14
Hawaii, 210, 247
Henry VIII, King, 108, 113
Hidalgo, Father Miguel, 169–170
Hideki Tojo, 238, 247
Himalayas, 29, 286
Hinduism, 31, 32, 287
Hindus, 288
Hiroshima, 253
Hitler, Adolf, 236–237, 239, 244, 245–246, 251, 252
Ho Chi Minh, 279
Holland, 222, 255, 298
Holocaust, 252, 255
Hopi, 128
Huang He (Yellow River), 35
Hundred Years' War, 94

Hungary, 265
Hussein, Saddam, 296
Hussein I, King, 299

Immigrants, 194–195, 314
Imperialism, 208–212, 217, 271, 303
Inca Empire, 127, 134
India, 29–32, 48, 78, 132, 134, 196, 209–210, 287–289, 342
Indulgences, 112, 114
Indus River, 29, 30
Industrial nations. *See also* Developed nations. 212, 271, 287, 290, 294, 304, 305, 314, 328, 337, 338, 343
Industrial Revolution, 178–182, 185–189, 216, 226, 303, 329, 336
    and imperialism, 208, 209, 212
    and the working class, 188, 193–196
Interdependence of nations, 335–339
Internet, 329
Iran, 295–296
Iraq, 261, 296, 345
Iron Curtain, 265
Irrigation, 11, 18, 29–30, 35, 127, 288, 329–330
Isabella, Queen, 95, 119
Islam, 76–79, 129, 287, 295
Israel, 23, 294, 296–299, 337, 345
Italy, 52, 54, 84, 85, 155, 158, 165, 202–204, 235, 236, 238, 239, 244, 247, 250, 254, 259
    in the Renaissance, 104–106

Jacobins, 150–151
Japan, 196, 209, 212, 238, 239, 259, 272, 287, 289–290, 312, 332, 336, 342, 345
    and World War II, 244, 247, 252, 253, 254, 289
Jefferson, Thomas, 142
Jerusalem, 23, 82, 83
Jesuits, 114
Jesus, 67–68, 76
Jews, 22–25, 68, 82, 237–238, 251–252, 255, 294, 296–297, 298
Jiang Zemin, 274
Joan of Arc, 94
John, King, 99–100
Jordan, 297, 299
Judaism, 23, 25